The DevelopMentor Series
Don Box, Editor

Addison-Wesley has joined forces with DevelopMentor, a premiere developer resources company, to produce a series of technical books written by developers for developers. DevelopMentor boasts a prestigious technical staff that includes some of the world's best-known computer science professionals.

*"Works in **The DevelopMentor Series** will be practical and informative sources on the tools and techniques for applying component-based technologies to real-world, large-scale distributed systems."*
   —Don Box

Titles in the Series:

Essential COM
Don Box
0-201-63446-5

Essential XML
Beyond Markup
Don Box, Aaron Skonnard, and John Lam
0-201-70914-7

Programming Windows Security
Keith Brown
0-201-60442-6

Advanced Visual Basic 6
Power Techniques for Everyday Programs
Matthew Curland
0-201-70712-8

Transactional COM+
Building Scalable Applications
Tim Ewald
0-201-61594-0

ASP Internals
Jon Flanders
0-201-61618-1

Essential IDL
Interface Design for COM
Martin Gudgin
0-201-61595-9

Effective Visual Basic
How to Improve Your VB/COM+ Applications
Joe Hummel
0-201-70476-5

Debugging Windows Programs
Strategies, Tools, and Techniques for Visual C++ Programmers
Everett N. McKay and Mike Woodring
0-201-70238-X

Watch for future titles in The DevelopMentor Series.

Effective Visual Basic

How to Improve Your VB/COM+ Applications

Joe Hummel, Ted Pattison, Justin Gehtland,
Doug Turnure, and Brian A. Randell

▲▼▲
Addison-Wesley

Boston • San Francisco • New York • Toronto • Montreal
London • Munich • Paris • Madrid
Capetown • Sydney • Tokyo • Singapore • Mexico City

Many of the designations used by manufacturers and sellers to distinguish their products are claimed as trademarks. Where those designations appear in this book and we were aware of a trademark claim, the designations have been printed in initial capital letters or all capitals.

The authors and publisher have taken care in the preparation of this book, but make no expressed or implied warranty of any kind and assume no responsibility for errors or omissions. No liability is assumed for incidental or consequential damages in connection with or arising out of the use of the information or programs contained herein.

The publisher offers discounts on this book when ordered in quantity for special sales. For more information, please contact:

Pearson Education Corporate Sales Division
One Lake Street
Upper Saddle River, NJ 07458
(800) 382-3419
corpsales@pearsontechgroup.com

Visit us on the Web at www.awl.com/cseng/

Library of Congress Cataloging-in-Publication Data

Effective Visual Basic : how to improve your VB/COM+ applications / Hummel, Joe . . . [et al.].
    p. cm.
 ISBN 0-201-70476-5
  1. Microsoft Visual BASIC. 2. BASIC (Computer program language) 3. COM (Computer architecture) I. Hummel, Joe.

QA76.73.B3 E36 2001
005.2'768—dc21

2001022091

Copyright © 2001 by Addison-Wesley.

All rights reserved. No part of this publication may be reproduced, stored in a retrieval system, or transmitted, in any form or by any means, electronic, mechanical, photocopying, recording, or otherwise, without the prior consent of the publisher. Printed in the United States of America. Published simultaneously in Canada.

ISBN 0-201-70476-5

Text printed on recycled paper.
1 2 3 4 5 6 7 8 9 10—MA—0504030201
First printing, June 2001

To our families and friends . . .

Contents

	Preface		**x**
	Acknowledgments		ix
1	**Shifting from Liberal Arts to Software Engineering**		**1**
	Rule 1-1:	Maximize the Potential of VB's Compile-Time Type Checking	2
	Rule 1-2:	Make Assumptions Explicit via `Debug.Assert`	8
	Rule 1-3:	Consider `#If` When Compile-Time Conditions Differ	14
	Rule 1-4:	Raise Errors to Signal Exceptional Conditions	20
	Rule 1-5:	Trap Locally, Act Globally: Effective Error Handling	26
	Rule 1-6:	Know the Difference Between Type and Class	35
	Rule 1-7	Embrace Good Object-Oriented Design, Not Just VB	41
	Rule 1-8:	Prefer UDTs over Classes for Value Types	49
	Rule 1-9:	Automate Mundane Tasks	53
2	**Designing, Building, and Working with COM-Based Components**		**61**
	Rule 2-1:	Think in Terms of Interfaces	62
	Rule 2-2:	Use Custom Interfaces	64
	Rule 2-3:	Define Custom Interfaces Separately, Preferably Using IDL	73
	Rule 2-4:	Avoid the Limitations of Class-Based Events with Custom Callbacks	83
	Rule 2-5:	Be Deliberate About Maintaining Compatibility	90
	Rule 2-6:	Choose the Right COM Activation Technique	99
	Rule 2-7:	Beware of `Class_Terminate`	111
	Rule 2-8:	Model in Terms of Sessions Instead of Entities	114
	Rule 2-9:	Avoid ActiveX EXEs Except for Simple, Small-Scale Needs	118
3	**MTS, COM+, and VB—The Middle Tier**		**123**
	Rule 3-1:	Understand the Design of MTS and COM+	124
	Rule 3-2:	Don't Use Singletons in MTS or COM+	127
	Rule 3-3:	Know When to Use `New` versus `CreateObject` versus `GetObjectContext.CreateInstance`	129
	Rule 3-4:	Understand the Real Motivation for `SetComplete`	140
	Rule 3-5:	Consider Auto-Abort Style with Transactions	146
	Rule 3-6:	Don't Reinvent the DBMS	150
	Rule 3-7:	Don't Feel Obligated to Configure All Your Components	157

	Rule 3-8:	Avoid Compiling Things into DLLs That You'll Later Regret	159
	Rule 3-9:	Best Practices for Porting MTS Code into COM+	164
	Rule 3-10:	Best Practices for Writing Code That Runs on MTS and COM+	169

4 The Web and VB — 173

	Rule 4-1:	Understand the IIS Architecture	174
	Rule 4-2:	Manage Application State to Maximize Efficiency	184
	Rule 4-3:	Manage Session State to Maximize Scalability	194
	Rule 4-4:	Understand the Differences Between DCOM and HTTP	203
	Rule 4-5:	Write COM Components for Scripting Environments (Like ASP)	209
	Rule 4-6:	Understand How Your COM Objects Interact with ASP	218
	Rule 4-7:	Use XML Instead of Proprietary Data Transfer Formats	227
	Rule 4-8:	Be Deliberate About Presentation versus Business Logic	236
	Rule 4-9:	Use XSLT to Move from Data to Presentation	243

5 Effective Data Access from VB — 257

	Rule 5-1:	Efficiency Basics: Round-Trips, SQL Statements, and Providers	257
	Rule 5-2:	Don't Overencapsulate Data Access	265
	Rule 5-3:	Never Hold Database Connections as Data Members	277
	Rule 5-4:	Deadlock Is Common; Develop Defensively	280
	Rule 5-5:	Use Firehose Cursors Whenever Possible	287
	Rule 5-6:	Make the Right Data Searching Decision (Avoid `SelectSingleNode` Abuse)	293

Index — 299

Preface

Visual Basic (VB) has become the most popular programming language in the United States. It is a large language and a complex product. Yet the ease with which it builds graphical user interfaces, accesses databases, and supports the Component Object Model (COM) is impressive.

This book is written by VB programmers for VB programmers. We assume you have been working with VB for quite some time and, if you're lucky, in a variety of ways: building front ends, reading databases, generating Web pages, programming COM objects. The goal of this book is to summarize a number of effective VB techniques that we have learned—and put into practice—over the years. This book has something for everyone, from general practices and COM-based components to COM+ and distributed applications. The wider your exposure to VB and the Windows Distributed Internet Application Architecture (DNA), the more applicable you'll find the techniques.

We follow the style of other books in the DevelopMentor series, in that each technique stands alone as an independent item ready for application. We try our best to describe each item as concisely as possible, and to let you read the book in any order you like. In a few cases, however, one rule leads quite naturally to another and thus should be read in that order; we'll point these dependencies out to you.

If we've done our job, then reading this book—and taking its ideas to heart—will make you a more effective VB programmer. It will also make you a better practitioner because your skills will improve in other areas as well, such as object-oriented design, MTS, databases, and the Web.

Acknowledgments

We all work for a developer services company called *DevelopMentor*. It's how we met, and how we keep abreast of the technology. It's also a fantastic place to spend one's working hours, and we owe this book (and much more) to our friends and coworkers at DM. If you ever want to see what DevelopMentor is all about, attend one of our Guerilla events—and be sure not to miss out on Thursday night. By the way, it's not just the employees that make DM; it's also the students and their energy. Thank you.

We also thank Gary Clarke for his sustained effort in getting this project off the ground and flying. We owe a great deal, as well, to Kristin Erickson (and her coworkers!) at Addison-Wesley for her tireless work behind the scenes, bringing this book to completion.

The anonymous reviewers did an excellent job, and we thank them for their hard work under a tight schedule. The book is much better as a result.

Finally, we'd like to thank our families for their boundless support and understanding during our late nights of reading, researching, writing, and reinstalling Windows.

Chapter 1

Shifting from Liberal Arts to Software Engineering

1-1   Maximize the potential of VB's compile-time type checking.

1-2   Make assumptions explicit via `Debug.Assert`.

1-3   Consider #If when compile-time conditions differ.

1-4   Raise errors to signal exceptional conditions.

1-5   Trap locally, act globally: effective error handling.

1-6   Know the difference between Type and Class.

1-7   Embrace good object-oriented design, not just VB.

1-8   Prefer UDTs over classes for value types.

1-9   Automate mundane tasks.

Our first set of rules focuses on general-purpose techniques that nearly all programmers will find useful. Although a few may seem obvious (e.g., rules 1-1 and 1-4), it never hurts to revisit the fundamentals to ensure that sound practices are being followed. On the other hand, what is obvious to some is new to others. You may have never worked with *makefiles* (rule 1-9), or felt the benefit of defensive programming via `Assert` (rule 1-2). Finally, it's a brave new world with .NET on the horizon, so you must become comfortable with object-oriented programming (rule1-7) and understand how class-based programming differs from more traditional value-based programming (rules 1-6 and 1-8).

Before we start, a word about naming conventions. We follow the Visual Basic (VB) standard of using one- to three-character prefixes when naming variables, types, classes, and interfaces. This simple technique works surprisingly well, because left-to-right readers naturally discern type information as they read. For example, seeing the variable `iCount` tells you this is an integer count. Here are the prefixes we use throughout the book:

c	A user-defined class
I	A user-defined interface
T	A user-defined type (UDT)
a	Array
b	Boolean
c	Currency
col	A reference to a `Collection` object
db	A reference to an ActiveX Data Object (ADO) database `Connection` object
e	Enumerated type variable
i	Integer
l	Long
r	Reference to an object
rs	A reference to an ADO `Recordset` object
s	String
txt	A reference to a `TextBox` object
u	UDT variable
v	Variant

Note that the prefixes are sometimes joined to reflect a combination of types. For example, `va` denotes a variant array.

Rule 1-1: Maximize the Potential of VB's Compile-time Type Checking

In the real world, no programmer is perfect. Even the best of us introduce errors into our code from time to time. Thus, part of our job as professional developers is to track down errors and eliminate them. This is a critical aspect of delivering reliable software.

For programmers, errors occur at both compile-time and run-time. Although it's best to avoid errors altogether, you should always prefer the compile-time variety because, not only is the error detected sooner, but the compiler highlights the offending line. Run-time errors are usually far more elusive. If you're really lucky, an exception occurs while debugging in VB and a line *near* the error is highlighted. If you're unlucky, a general protection fault (GPF) occurs in production and the application crashes. The question is, could the compiler be used to detect some of these run-time errors at compile-time? Yes.

Unfortunately, VB's default settings, which support the design philosophy of a rapid application development (RAD) tool, hinder its ability to detect errors at compile-time. For example, although traditional languages like C++ and Java perform strict typechecking, VB is far more lenient:

```
Dim i, j As Integer
j = 1000
i = j + "1"     '** reject, add 1, or concatenate "1"?
```

This code is perfectly legal, but what is i after the assignment? In comparison, both C++ and Java would reject this code because they were designed with a cruel-to-be-kind attitude: meaning that compile-time errors are far cheaper and easier to fix than are run-time errors found during testing, or, worse, encountered during production.

As a result, it is our responsibility to know how and when to tell VB to perform more extensive checking at compile-time. In particular, there are three activities a professional developer should always perform when programming in VB:

1. Use the Option Explicit statement at the top of every module.
2. Avoid casual or unintentional use of the Variant data type.
3. Use the Start With Full Compile command when running in the VB Integrated Development Environment (IDE).

Although there's no way to make the current VB compiler perform type checking as strictly as its C++ and Java counterparts do, you can maximize compile-time error detection by performing these basic activities. In addition, the next version of VB will include strict type checking via the `Option Strict` statement. Now, let's discuss each of these activities in more detail.

Activity 1: Use `Option Explicit` at the Top of Every Module

Although the use of the `Option Explicit` statement is optional, it should be the first statement in every module of your VB project. The presence of `Option Explicit` tells the compiler to ensure that every variable is declared before it is used—a requirement in other languages such as C++ and Java. However, requiring variable declarations is optional in VB and is turned off by default.

Let's look at an example of how errors become harder to find when a VB module doesn't include `Option Explicit`. In this case, you are not required to declare a variable before you use it in that module. Thus, instead of writing code like

```
Dim sDatabasePath As String
sDatabasePath = "C:\MyData\MyDB.mdb"
```

you are free to write

```
sDatabasePath = "C:\MyData\MyDB.mdb"
```

VB implicitly declares the variable `sDatabasePath` on the fly as a variant. Although not having to supply variable declarations makes coding faster (RAD), it also opens the door for many types of errors that the compiler could have easily detected. For example, what happens when we call the following subroutine?

```
OpenDatabase sDatabasPath, ...
```

Notice that the variable name has been misspelled in the call. This is an obvious error, yet the code still compiles and runs. The problem is that the misspelled variable name is not seen as a compile-time error. Instead, VB simply assumes there are two variables: the variable `sDatabasePath` (which contains the value you want) and the implicit variable `sDatabasPath` (which is initialized to an empty variant). When you eventually run the application, it will most likely fail somewhere in the implementation of `OpenDatabase`—far from where the actual coding error was introduced. This error would have been easily caught if variable declarations were required.

There are two things you should do to require variable declarations, and consequently to ensure that VB will perform more extensive compile-time checking. The obvious thing is to add an `Option Explicit` statement to the top of every *existing* module that doesn't have one already. The second thing is to ask VB to add `Option Explicit` automatically whenever you create a *new* module in the IDE. This is done by checking the Require Variable Declaration option in the Editor tab of the Tools >> Options menu item. Note that this setting is global, and thus remains on across all VB projects.

For a professional developer, it is simply unacceptable to develop applications and components in VB without the use of `Option Explicit`. If you inherit an existing VB project, one of your first steps must be to check and make sure that every module begins with an `Option Explicit` statement. Note that the VB IDE never adds `Option Explicit` to an existing module; you must always do this by hand. Moreover, after adding `Option Explicit`, note that you may be faced with a series of compile-time errors, and the task of adding lots of `Dim` statements. However, the good news is that this extra work will give you the opportunity to define your variables with an explicit type and scope, and to prevent such easily detectable errors in the future.

Activity 2: Avoid Casual or Unintentional Use of the `Variant` Data Type

This rule implies that you should always assign an explicit data type to your variables, parameters, and function return values. If you don't explicitly give a type, VB automatically assigns `Variant`. For example, consider the following module-level variable declarations:

```
Option Explicit
Private sFirstName As String
Private vLastName
Private vAge, iWeight As Integer
```

In this example, `sFirstName` and `iWeight` have been declared with explicit types. However, both `vLastName` and `vAge` were declared without regard to type, in which case VB declares these variables as variants. If you are coming from a C++ or Java background, take note that `vAge` is not of type `Integer`; in VB, you must individually declare the type of each variable.

Let's take a step back and discuss what a variant really is. A variant is a flexible, self-describing data type. Variants are valuable because they can hold just about any type of data. But, in addition to storing a value, a variant also contains metadata that describes the type of data it's holding. This allows VB to perform automatic type conversions, which can be very useful.

So what's the problem with using variants? Besides the fact that a variant takes up more memory than is strictly necessary, it also prevents the VB compiler from performing basic type checking. For example, if a routine is declared with a variant parameter, VB doesn't care what the caller passes at compile-time. Thus, given the subroutine

```
Public Sub SomeSub(ByVal vParam As Variant)
    .
    .
    .
End Sub
```

you (or another developer) can write, compile, and run the following:

```
SomeSub 23
SomeSub "This is arbitrary string data"
SomeSub #1/1/2002#
```

This is fine, unless `SomeSub` isn't designed to handle these varying types of data, in which case a run-time error will occur. Obviously, if you want to restrict the caller to passing only one type of data—and otherwise trigger an easy-to-fix compile-time error—then declare your parameter of that specific type.

However, even if you avoid variants, you still have to keep on your toes. VB's form of type checking is simply not as strict as that of C++ or Java. For example, consider the following:

```
Dim lNum As Long
lNum = "my string data"
```

Although this code obviously contains an error, the VB compiler will not report it at compile-time. Instead, VB waits until run-time to determine that the assignment will fail as a result of a non-numeric string, and then conveys the error. Note that it's still better to declare `lNum` as a specific type rather than a variant. If a run-time error occurs, you want the error as close to the offending statement as possible. Declaring `lNum` of type `Variant` will trigger an error farther away, because the assignment will now succeed. Thus, "strongly typed" variables are more likely to yield errors that are easier to locate and to fix.

Of course, there are times when it's entirely appropriate to use variants. This is the case when reading fields from a database that potentially contain null values. It may also be the case when designing a class for use in a scripting environment. For example, languages such as VBScript only support `ByRef` parameters when they're declared as variants. In other words, we are not suggesting that variants are evil and should never be used, but we do recommend that their use be a conscious, documented decision. When using a variant, a good rule of thumb is to be explicit: State the type as `Variant`, and code in a type-safe manner. For example, consider the following subroutine, which deletes a customer from a database based on a numeric or string-based value:

```
Public Sub DeleteCustomer(ByVal vCust As Variant)
    Select Case VarType(vCust)
        Case vbLong          '** delete customer based on ID
            .
            .
            .
        Case vbString        '** delete customer based on name
            .
            .
            .
        Case Else            '** illegal parameter type
            Err.Raise ...
    End Select
End Sub
```

Note that the parameter is explicitly declared as `Variant`, and that the subroutine explicitly checks for an acceptable type of data, or a run-time error occurs (see rule 1-4 for a discussion of raising errors at run-time). By the way, although the next version of VB will directly support *overloading* (subroutines with the same name that accept different parameter types), this approach is one way to simulate it safely in VB today.

The key point is that variants diminish VB's ability to perform type checking at compile-time, and thus increases our responsibility to check for errors at run-time.

Activity 3: Prefer `Start With Full Compile` When Running in the VB IDE

The final activity is to use the `Start With Full Compile` (CTRL+F5) command whenever you run your code within the IDE. The usual method is to use `Start` (F5), which by default doesn't compile (or type check!) until run-time. In other words, compile-time checks are not performed on a given routine until the first time it is called. This is particularly dangerous when you consider the fact that unless your testing guarantees 100 percent coverage, a routine may never get called, and thus may never be checked for standard compile-time errors. Running via `Start With Full Compile` overrides this default behavior, executes the expected compile-time checks, and identifies errors that much sooner.

Note that the default—`Compile On Demand`—can be changed so that VB always performs a complete compile-time check of your project before execution. Simply uncheck the Compile On Demand option under the General tab of Tools >> Options. This is a global setting that makes `Start` equivalent to `Start With Full Compile`.

Rule 1-2: Make Assumptions Explicit via `Debug.Assert`

Assumptions are a necessary part of programming. We all make them, and often for good reason: to improve code speed, to reduce memory usage, or to simplify the coding effort. For example, programmers often use VB's `Integer` data type because it's efficient and small (only 16 bits). However, this limits the maximum value to 32,767. Thus, like it or not, assumptions also translate into limitations of our code—limitations that must be remembered as well as passed on to other developers. At best, assumptions find their way into program documentation; at worst, they remain buried in the program code.

The real problem arises when an assumption is not met. All too often, the application simply crashes or generates incorrect results without comment. And it's usually straightforward to locate the exact statement that crashed or output the incorrect result. The more difficult task is identifying the *reason* for the failure, in other words, the underlying assumption and the code that broke it.

Assumptions come in two forms: internal and external. External assumptions are based on circumstances outside the control of the component/application, and thus should be explicitly checked via code. For example, when a user supplies the name of a file to open, you typically want to check that the file exists before trying to open it:

```
<get filename from user>
If <file does not exist> Then
    <inform user of their error>
Else
    <open file and begin processing>
End If
```

Internal assumptions are very different. These presume that the application is coded correctly, and thus *the assumption is always true.* For example, the following code assumes the upper bound of array A is less than 32,767; otherwise, the index variable i overflows:

```
Dim i As Integer
For i = 0 to UBound(A)
    <process A(i)>
Next i
```

Although internal assumptions can also be checked via code, this is typically not done by developers. Why waste computer and human resources checking things that are always true (and if not, that testing will identify and then we'll fix)? The problem is that we all know testing does not guarantee the absence of errors, and the sooner an error is detected the better. This is especially true in large multiperson projects, in which assumptions are often not conveyed. Therefore, a good defensive approach is the following: *Always check an internal assumption before relying on it.* However, this would imply adding lots of `If-Then` statements to your code, thereby slowing it down. But what if you could add such checks without hurting the performance of your final, deployed application? The solution is VB's `Debug.Assert` statement. Mirrored after C's assert macro, this is a mechanism for making assumptions explicit, executable, and removable. For example, let's state our earlier assumption about the array's upper bound:

```
Dim i As Integer
Debug.Assert UBound(A) < 32767
For i = 0 to UBound(A)
    <process A(i)>
Next i
```

When run inside the VB IDE, `Debug.Assert` statements are equivalent to the following:

```
If <condition evaluates to false> Then Stop
```

Thus, if the upper bound of `A` is greater than or equal to 32,767, then execution halts and the debugger is activated with this statement highlighted, informing you that the assumption has not been met. On the other hand, if the upper bound is really less than 32,767, nothing happens and execution continues because the assumption holds. However, the difference between `Debug.Assert` and `If-Then` is that when you compile your component/application, the `Debug.Assert` statements are discarded and do not appear in the executable code. The end result is that *assertions* incur no run-time overhead, yet they simplify the task of identifying and repairing errors because not only do they pinpoint a broken assumption, but they also suggest a fix—fulfill the assumption!

The goal of `Debug.Assert` is to help detect logic and programming errors by verifying assumptions and other requirements during component testing, system integration, and maintenance. They are meant to be retained (and maintained!) in the source code. As a more complete example, consider a VB subroutine that searches for records in a recordset and displays them in a control. In particular, `ListAllSuppliers` searches a recordset of productID/supplier pairs, looking for all suppliers of a particular product. The suppliers are then listed in a list or combo box:

```
Public Sub ListAllSuppliers(rsPairs As ADODB.Recordset, _
                            lProdID As Long, _
                            rGUI As Control)
    Dim vSavedFilter As Variant

    '** save current filter, then filter recordset to this product only
    vSavedFilter = rsPairs.Filter
    rsPairs.Filter = "ProductID = " + CStr(lProdID)

    '** for each product/supplier record, list supplier...
    rGUI.Clear
    Do While Not rsPairs.EOF
        rGUI.AddItem rsPairs.Fields("Supplier").Value
        rsPairs.MoveNext
    Loop

    '** reset recordset back to original filter
    rsPairs.Filter = vSavedFilter
End Sub
```

Although the type of parameter rGUI is Control, the subroutine is written assuming that rGUI refers to an existing ListBox or ComboBox object. Likewise, it is assumed that rsPairs refers to an existing ADO Recordset object. These assumptions can be explicitly stated at the start of the subroutine, as follows:

```
Public Sub ListAllSuppliers(...)
    Debug.Assert rsPairs Is Nothing = False
    Debug.Assert rGUI Is Nothing = False
    Debug.Assert TypeOf rGUI Is ListBox Or _
                 TypeOf rGUI Is ComboBox

    Dim vSavedFilter As Variant
```

Note that VB's type checking will ensure that if rsPairs refers to an object, it is of type ADODB.Recordset. Assertions that precede a body of code are commonly referred to as *preconditions.* Thus, we have specified three preconditions for the execution of `ListAllSuppliers`. Continuing with our subroutine, suppose there is an application-wide assumption that every product has at least one supplier. This implies that after the recordset is filtered, there should remain at least one record in the set:

```
'** save current filter, then filter recordset to this product only
vSavedFilter = rsPairs.Filter
rsPairs.Filter = "ProductID = " + CStr(lProdID)

Debug.Assert rsPairs.BOF = False And _
              rsPairs.EOF = False
```

If both the recordset's `BOF` and `EOF` flags are `False`, then the recordset is non-empty. The previous `Debug.Assert` checks our application-wide assumption. The last step in the subroutine is to populate the list or combo box with the appropriate suppliers, and then reset the original filter:

```
'** for each product/supplier record, list supplier...
rGUI.Clear
Do While Not rsPairs.EOF
    rGUI.AddItem rsPairs.Fields("Supplier").Value
    rsPairs.MoveNext
Loop

'** reset recordset back to original filter
rsPairs.Filter = vSavedFilter
```

Assertions that follow a body of code are known as *postconditions,* and serve to confirm assumptions after execution as well as state any new assumptions that now hold. In the case of `ListAllSuppliers`, we have

```
    Debug.Assert rGUI.ListCount > 0
    Debug.Assert rsPairs.AbsolutePosition = 1 Or _
                  rsPairs.AbsolutePosition = adPosUnknown
End Sub
```

The first assertion is obvious, because we are assuming that every product has at least one supplier. The second conveys the more subtle fact that restoring the original filter has the side effect of resetting the current record pointer back to the first record in the set (or to some unknown position).

How far should one go in using the `Debug.Assert` mechanism? How many assertions are enough? Ultimately this is up to each individual developer; but, in short, the more assertions the better. The trade-off is that assertions are executable statements, and thus represent code that must be debugged and maintained. This will serve to temper one's overuse of assertions. For example, the `ListAllSuppliers` subroutine has a number of other preconditions that could be specified. First, the recordset must be open and contain the fields `ProductID` and `Supplier` in order for the subroutine to execute correctly:

```
Debug.Assert rsPairs.State <> adStateClosed
Debug.Assert Not rsPairs.Fields("ProductID") Is Nothing
Debug.Assert Not rsPairs.Fields("Supplier") Is Nothing
```

Second, it is assumed that the recordset does not contain duplicate productID/supplier pairs; otherwise, the control will display duplicate items. This assumption is more difficult to check, and requires a custom `ItemNotFound` function to search the control before another supplier is added:

```
Debug.Assert ItemNotFound(rGUI, rsPairs("Supplier"))
```

In each case, the programmer must decide whether (1) the assumption warrants explicit specification and (2) whether it is worth the effort of programmatic confirmation.

Finally, keep in mind that `Debug.Assert` is not a technique for trapping errors with the expectation of recovery, nor is it a technique for detecting errors in deployed (i.e., compiled) applications. It is designed for internal assumptions only, and its behavior with respect to the IDE is fixed. However, as you come to rely on assertions more and more, nothing prevents you from defining your own assertion mechanism that works outside the IDE. For example, suppose you want to compile releases of your component/application for testing and thus retain the ability to execute assertions. One solution is to define your own `Assert` subroutine in a standard basic (BAS module)

```
Public Sub Assert(bCondition As Boolean, sMsg As String)
    .
    .
    .
End Sub
```

and then call it much like `Debug.Assert`:

```
Assert rsPairs Is Nothing = False, _
       "ListAllSuppliers: rsPairs Is Nothing!"
```

The trick is to use *conditional compilation* to control whether the assertions are actually executed, and, if so, to control what happens when an assertion fails (e.g., log it). See the next rule for details on exactly how this is done.

Rule 1-3: Consider `#If` When Compile-time Conditions Differ

Often we find ourselves in the position of having to write different versions of our code—in particular, to support different targets: debug versus release, laptop versus desktop, Win98 versus WinNT versus Windows 2000, and so on. These differences can be handled at run-time, typically by checking a global variable set at program start-up:

```
If sWindowsVersion = "Win2000" Then
    <execute Win2k code>
ElseIf sWindowsVersion = "WinNT" Then
    <execute WinNT code>
Else    '** must be Win98
    Debug.Assert sWindowsVersion = "Win98"
    <execute Win98 code>
End if
```

The disadvantage, of course, is that only one of the alternatives is ever executed per run, resulting in code bloat and some degree of performance loss (due to the `if` tests).

These costs can become quite significant. For example, consider a large application with an extensive testing framework. To ensure that the tests are thorough and repeatable, such a framework operates at many levels (from individual blocks to the entire application) and requires the development of a good deal of testing code (*test harnesses*). In fact, for this approach to be viable, the framework must become an integral part of the source code base, yet it must also be removable from the final release to avoid the associated costs. How can this be accomplished?

The solution is to use VB's *conditional compilation mechanism.* In short, conditional compilation gives you control over what code is visible to the compiler, and hence what code eventually becomes part of your application. By simply "flipping a switch" and recompiling, you can include or remove source code during the compilation process. Much like C and C++, VB's mechanism is based on the `#If` statement:

```
#If <condition> Then
   '** include the following code in the application
      .
      .
      .
#End If
```

If `<condition>` evaluates to `True` at compile-time, then the code between `#If Then` and `#End If` is compiled and becomes part of the final application. Otherwise, this code is simply ignored by the compiler. Note that because this process is occurring at compile-time, the condition being evaluated cannot involve traditional variables; they have no value at compile-time! Instead, conditions must be constructed from *conditional compilation arguments,* which represent integer values defined via either (1) the Make tab under Project Properties, (2) a `#Const` statement, or (3) as command-line arguments to VB itself (i.e., VB6.exe).

One of the most common uses of conditional compilation is generating debug builds versus release builds. In this case, before compiling your component/application, you first decide what kind of build you want. Then you set the conditional compilation arguments appropriately, and compile. The result is an executable file that contains either debugging code, or not. As a simple example, suppose we want to log debug information whenever the subroutine `SomeOperation` (part of module `X`) is called. The idea is to surround this logging code with a `#If` statement:[1]

```
Public Sub SomeOperation(...)
    #If Debug_X <> 0 Or Debug_All <> 0 Then
        App.LogEvent ...
    #End If

    .
    .
    .

End Sub
```

If either of the arguments `Debug_X` or `Debug_All` is defined with a nonzero value, then compiling the previous code is equivalent to compiling

```
Public Sub SomeOperation(...)
    App.LogEvent ...

    .
    .
    .

End Sub
```

Otherwise, the `App.LogEvent` statement is discarded by the compiler, and thus does not appear in the resulting executable file. As shown in Figure 1.1, the Make tab of Project Properties is being used to assign projectwide values to these arguments. Note that you are not required to define arguments: An undefined conditional compilation argument has a default value of 0 (i.e. false). Also, avoid the use of `Debug` as an argument name because it conflicts with VB's own `Debug` object.

---

[1] Note that `App.LogEvent` works only when executed outside VB's IDE.

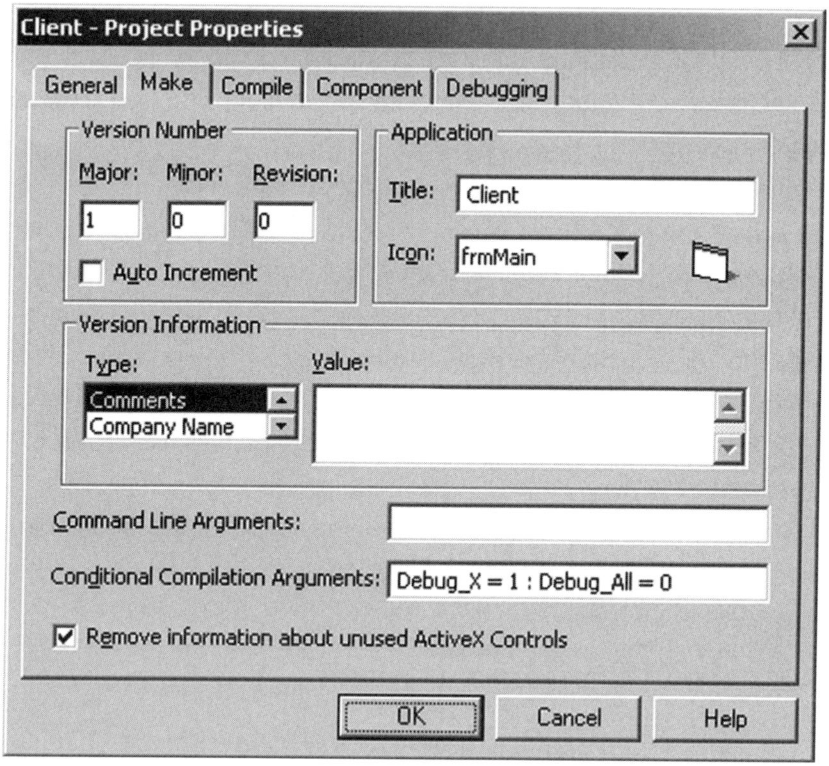

Figure 1.1 Assigning values to conditional compilation arguments

Much like a traditional `If-Then-Else` statement, the `#If` statement can involve complex Boolean conditions and else cases. For example, suppose we need to target a specific version of Windows:

```
#If Windows = 95 Or Windows = 98 Then
    <code for Win95/Win98>
#ElseIf Windows = 4 Then
    <code for WinNT4>
#ElseIf Windows = 2000 Then
    <code for Win2000>
#Else
    '** generate a compiler error to warn developer
    "Undefined target version of Windows!"
#End If
```

The last case generates a compile-time error—a common technique used to identify invalid or undefined arguments. Another good practice is to supply unique version information on each build (see Figure 1.1) for differentiating between the generated executable files.

As a more complete example, consider the use of conditional compilation to define our own form of `Debug.Assert` (see rule 1-2 for a detailed discussion of assertions). Assertions are a useful mechanism for identifying invalid assumptions at run-time, but unfortunately `Debug.Assert` only executes inside the VB IDE. Outside the IDE, `Debug.Assert` has no effect, even if the assumption is found invalid. To change this behavior, we can define our own custom `Assert` subroutine in a BAS module that behaves like `Debug.Assert` when run inside the IDE, yet logs invalid assumptions to the event log (or a file [see help on `App.StartLogging`]) when compiled and run outside. Thus, `Assert` is controlled via conditional compilation, not the presence of the IDE:

```
Public Sub Assert(bCondition As Boolean, sMsg As String)
    #If ASSERT_OUTSIDE_IDE <> 0 Then
        If Not bCondition Then
            App.LogEvent "Assertion failed: " + sMsg
        End If
    #End If

    #If ASSERT_INSIDE_IDE <> 0 Then
        If Not bCondition Then
            Debug.Print "Assertion failed: " + sMsg
            Debug.Assert False
        End If
    #End If
End Sub
```

To make use of this subroutine in your code, simply add the BAS module to your project, define the arguments as appropriate, and call the subroutine:

```
Assert Trim(sParameter) <> "", _
       "SomeSubroutine: string parameter is empty!"
```

Note that `Assert` can be defined to operate inside the IDE, outside the IDE, both, or neither.

Besides the Project Properties dialog, conditional compilation arguments can also be defined via the `#Const` statement. Such statements are typically placed in the Declarations section of a module. For example,

```
Option Explicit
#Const Windows = 2000
```

The argument `Windows` is assigned the value `2000` for this module (and this module only), and this assignment overrides any other value assigned to `Windows` by other means. Another alternative is to define your arguments via the command line when building your component/application outside of VB:[2]

```
C:\VS6\VB6\VB6.exe /make Client.vbp /d Windows=98
```

This is equivalent to defining the arguments in the *Project Properties dialog*. In fact, the arguments defined via the `/d` option completely *replace* all arguments defined via Project Properties. For example, if `Client.vbp` defines X to have the value 1 and Z the value 2, then

```
C:\VS6\VB6\VB6.exe /make Client.vbp /d X=3:Y=4
```

recompiles `Client.vbp` with X assigned the value 3, Y assigned the value 4, and Z assigned the value 0 (undefined).

Keep in mind that testing and maintenance grow more difficult in the presence of conditional compilation because each new conditional argument potentially doubles the number of executable files that must be individually tested and maintained. Thus, in some cases you may want to handle differences at run-time, using traditional `If-Then-Else` statements. A common example is a Win9x client with only a few Win95 versus Win98 coding differences:

```
If <running on Win95> Then
    <make appropriate Win95 API call>
Else    '** assume running on Win98
    Debug.Assert <running on Win98>
    <make appropriate Win98 API call>
End If
```

---

[2] Why would you ever want to do this? See rule 1-9.

Here the cost of maintaining two distinct applications (.EXE files) via conditional compilation would be higher than the cost of a single application with some extra run-time checks and code bloat. Like many things, conditional compilation is a valuable technique that is best used in moderation.

Rule 1-4: Raise Errors to Signal Exceptional Conditions

For developers, exceptional conditions are a part of life: "database not found," "permission denied," "network unavailable," and so on. When a subroutine encounters an exceptional condition, it often needs to report this information back to the caller. One approach is based on *return codes,* where routines are written as integer functions that return either success or an error code. The error codes are typically negative:

```
Public Function SomeOperation(...) As Integer
    SomeOperation = 0    '** assume success by default
        .
        .
        .
    If <exceptional condition> Then    '** return error code
        SomeOperation = -98            '** -98 in this case
        Exit Function
    End If
        .
        .
        .
End Function
```

The advantages are that it's cheap to implement, and the caller knows immediately on return whether the routine has failed (assuming he checks). However, this approach has four disadvantages as well:

1. Existing functions must be rewritten to return values via `ByRef` parameters.

2. Error checks must be repeated at every call site:

    ```
    If SomeOperation1() < 0 Then
        <handle failure>
    End If
    ```

```
         If SomeOperation2() < 0 Then
             <handle failure>
         End If
            .
            .
            .
```

3. Code is more difficult to read because calls are intermixed with error handling.
4. Additional error information (e.g., error messages) must be obtained separately.

The WinAPI is a classic example of a subroutine library based on return codes.

The better approach is to use *exception handling.* In this case, routines either exit normally or *raise* an exception:

```
     Public Sub SomeOperation(...)
            .
            .
            .
         If <exceptional condition> Then   '** raise exception
             Err.Raise -98, "SomeOperation", "error msg"
         End If
            .
            .
            .
     End Sub
```

Instead of returning directly to the caller, raising an exception transfers control to the nearest enabled exception handler—a separate body of code expressly designed to deal with errors (Figure 1.2). This simple mechanism improves code readability, centralizes a caller's error handling, and enables additional information to be passed along with the error code. It works with subroutines or functions, is consistent with the behavior of VB's predefined routines, and, best of all, it supports a programming style based on return codes (see rule 1-5 for a complementary discussion on exception handling).

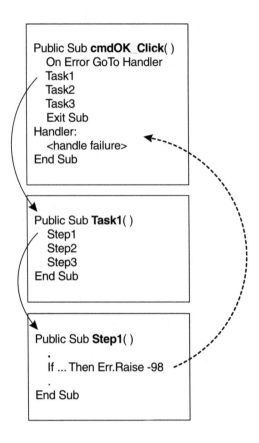

Figure 1.2 An example of exception handling

In VB, exceptions are raised by applying the `Raise` method to the `Err` object. When raising exceptions, the first rule is to provide as much information as possible. The more information you convey, the more likely the exception will be handled properly—or logged and corrected later. VB allows you to convey, at most, five pieces of information:

```
Err.Raise Number, _
          Source, _
          Description, _
          HelpFile, _
          HelpContext
```

This information is used to populate the `Err` object "received" by the exception handler; only the error code (`Number`) is required. These parameters are summarized as follows:

- `Number`: integer exception code
- `Source`: string denoting source of exception (i.e., who raised it)
- `Description`: string message summarizing exceptional condition
- `HelpFile`: string path to a help file with additional information
- `HelpContext`: integer context ID of the help file topic to display

You are free to raise any 32-bit integer as your error number, including VB's predefined error codes. However, if you want to define your own personal set of error codes, do so relative to the predefined constant `vbObjectError`. This is best done using an enumerated type in a BAS or public Class module. For example,

```
Public Enum MyExceptions
    InvalidArg = vbObjectError + 8192    '** large negative number
    FileNotFound                          '** previous value + 1
    .
    .
    .
End Enum
```

`Enum` serves as documentation of your exceptions, improves readability by encouraging the use of named constants, and appears in the type library when building Component Object Model (COM) objects. It is also good practice to start the enumeration at some offset like 8,192 to minimize collision with existing error codes.

The `Source` parameter should identify the exact point in the code where the exception was raised. At the very least, it should specify the module and the routine names, as well as the line number:

```
400 Err.Raise MyExceptions.InvalidArg, _
            "Utility.SomeOperation.400"
```

Line numbers are tedious to do by hand, so use one of the many free tools available for automatic line number generation (for example, see http://www.themandelbrotset.com/html/downloads.html). Note that if you are raising an error in response to an error (as mentioned earlier, see rule 1-5 for a discussion of exception handling techniques), a good strategy is to propagate the source information:

```
400 Err.Raise MyExceptions.InvalidArg, _
            "Utility.SomeOperation.400:" + Err.Source
```

This helps capture the calling sequence that led to the initial exception.

Obviously, the `Description` parameter should be a concise summary of the exceptional condition. The `HelpFile` and `HelpContext` parameters are important if it's possible that the caller may end up displaying the exception to a user. In this case, the help file can list possible corrective actions, or perhaps instructions on submitting a bug report.

Putting it all together, suppose we have a BAS module named Utility. This module is accompanied by a help file Utility.hlp and contains the following subroutine `DoTask`. This subroutine raises an exception if passed an empty string as a parameter:

```
Public Sub DoTask(sName As String)
   100 Dim i As Integer
   200
   300 If Trim(sName) = "" Then
   400     Err.Raise MyExceptions.InvalidArg, _
                "Utility.DoTask.400", _
                "Parameter 'sName' cannot be empty", _
                App.Path + "\Utility.hlp", _
                0   '** table of contents
   500 End If
     .
     .
     .
   End Sub
```

Before raising an error, note that you should make every attempt to clean up explicitly the state of your subroutine. For example, failure to close ADO

`Database` and `Recordset` objects can yield to slower performance (see rule 2-7 in Chapter 2), lost data, and internal errors that overwrite your error information. The solution is simply to call a cleanup routine beforehand:

```
Public Sub DoDBTask(...)
   100  Dim dbConn As ADODB.Connection
   200  Dim rs As ADODB.Recordset
      .
      .
      .
  2000  If <exceptional condition> Then   '** raise an error...
  2100     DBCleanup dbConn, rs           '** but first clean up DB
  2200     Err.Raise ...
  2300  End If
      .
      .
      .
End Sub

Private Sub DBCleanup(ByRef dbConn As ADODB.Connection, _
                      ByRef rs As ADODB.Recordset)
   100  On Error Resume Next    '** ignore any errors this code may cause
   200
   300  If rs.State <> adStateClosed Then rs.Close
   400  Set rs = Nothing
   500
   600  If dbConn.State <> adStateClosed Then dbConn.Close
   700  Set dbConn = Nothing
End Sub
```

Note that `DBCleanup` is a separate routine so that errors, a common occurrence in cleanup code, can be selectively trapped and ignored.

Exceptions have become the standard for signaling errors, not only in VB, but in C++, Java, and COM as well. However, although exceptions do make things easier, there's no free lunch. Good error handling requires a great deal of effort, which is why this discussion continues in the next rule.

Rule 1-5: Trap Locally, Act Globally: Effective Error Handling

As discussed in the previous rule, exceptional conditions are a part of life. When exceptions occur, your best chance of recovery is to *trap locally* within the subroutine or function that triggered the exception. Only in this way do you have access to all the local variables, the option to restart from the exact point of failure, and the knowledge of how best to handle the error. Unfortunately, for optimal results, this implies that *every* subroutine and function must contain exception handling code.

Do people really do this? Yes. (For example, this is the approach taken by Numega's FailSafe product.) The trick to reducing the burden (and increasing the effectiveness) is to trap locally but *act globally*: Centralize your exception handling as much as possible, in particular via a global routine. As shown in Figure 1.3, the idea is to handle any special cases locally, and then fall back on a global `HandleError` function for recovery of general errors:

```
Public Function HandleError(...) As HEResult
    Select Case Err.Number
        Case ...
            <handle this particular error>
            HandleError = ...
        Case ...
            <handle this particular error>
            HandleError = ...
        .
        .
        .
        Case Else    '** at the very least, log error and raise for others to see
            App.LogEvent ...
            HandleError = HEResult.Raise
    End Select
End Function
```

Note the function returns a value indicating how the caller should continue, because only the caller can *resume* execution or perform the proper cleanup. The set of return values is best defined using an enumerated type:

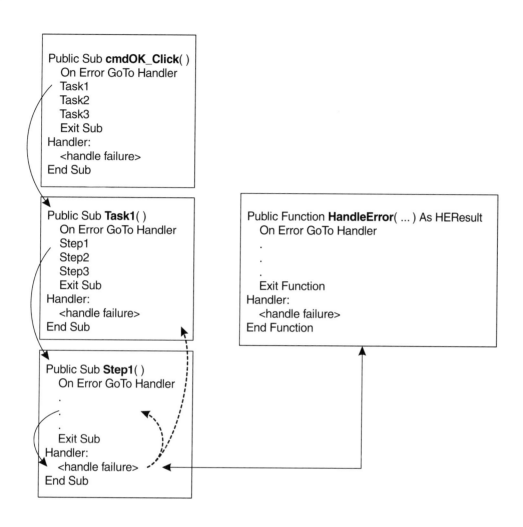

Figure 1.3 Trap locally; act globally

```
Public Enum HEResult
    Retry    = 1   '** retry statement that failed (Resume)
    Continue       '** skip statement(s) that failed (Resume Next/Exit)
    Raise          '** propagate error up call chain (Err.Raise)
End Enum
```

These correspond to some (but not all) of the recovery options available to a local error handler. In particular, observe that *termination* is not one of the recommended return values, because a better approach is to propagate the error up the call stack, giving everyone a chance to recover/clean up. (If you haven't already, read rule 1-4 for a discussion of raising errors.)

In VB you have three strategies for trapping errors locally. The first is to define a handler within the routine that is jumped to if an exception occurs:

```
Public Sub DoTask(...)
    On Error Goto Handler   '** trap exceptions in local handler

    Step1
    Step2
    .
    .
    .
    Exit Sub
Handler:   '** attempt recovery of exceptional condition(s)...
    Select Case Err.Number
        Case ...
            <handle this particular error>
            <Resume [Next/Label] / Exit / Err.Raise>
        Case ...
            <handle this particular error>
            <Resume [Next/Label] / Exit / Err.Raise>
        .
        .
        .
        Case Else
            Dim eAction As HEResult
            eAction = HandleError(...)
            If eAction = HEResult.Retry Then Resume
            If eAction = HEResult.Continue Then Resume Next
            '** otherwise propagate the error up the call chain...
            <perform any cleanup>
            Debug.Assert eAction = HEResult.Raise
            Err.Clear
            Err.Raise ...
    End Select
End Sub
```

The local handler provides the first step of centralized error handling, dealing with any special cases and offloading the remainder to the global error handler. Note that you can fine-tune this strategy with multiple, local error handlers if it becomes difficult to separate the special cases, or write generic cleanup code:

```
Public Sub DoTask(...)
    On Error Goto Handler1
    Step1
    Step2

    On Error Goto Handler2
    Step3
    Step4

       .
       .
       .
End Sub
```

You can also temporarily disable local error trapping if you know you want to raise an error back to the caller (for example, in the case of an invalid parameter):

```
Public Sub DoTask(...)
    On Error Goto Handler

    If <one of the parameters is invalid> Then
        On Error Goto 0    '** disable local trapping (also clears Err object)
        Err.Raise ...      '** raise error, bypassing local handler
    End If

       .
       .
       .
End Sub
```

Obviously, there is a tension between local handling of special cases and centralized handling of more generic ones. The implication is that there is no "right" way to handle errors, but there is a spectrum of choices to balance effectiveness with effort.

A second alternative for local error trapping is to treat every case as a special case, explicitly checking for errors after each operation:

```
Public Sub DoTask(...)
    On Error Resume Next

    Step1
    If Err.Number <> 0 Then    '** handle exceptional condition...
        .
        .
        .
        Err.Clear    '** reset Err object
    End If

    Step2
    If Err.Number <> 0 Then    '** handle exceptional condition...
        .
        .
        .
        Err.Clear    '** reset Err object
    End If

        .
        .
        .

End Sub
```

The advantage of this approach is that we always know exactly which statement failed, and thus how to tailor precisely each error handler. The cost, of course, is a significant increase in programmatic effort, although a global error handler can still be utilized from within the If-Then statements. Note that this style of error handling is required when making application program interface (API) calls, because errors are denoted by function return values (and not raised exceptions). VBScript programmers also take note: This approach is currently your only option for exception handling.

The next version of VB will present a third and final approach for trapping errors locally based on the `Try-Catch` mechanism found in other languages:[3]

```
Public Sub DoTask(...)
    Try         '** to execute the following statements successfully...
        Step1
        Step2
            .
            .
            .
    Catch       '** any exceptions that occur, and attempt recovery...
            .
            .
            .
    Finally     '** always execute this postprocessing/cleanup code
            .
            .
            .
    End Try
End Sub
```

This technique is very similar to the `On Error Goto` style of error handling, in which the `Try` block contains the code to be executed, and the `Catch` block denotes the local error handler. However, there are two important differences: (1) the ability to nest `try-catch` blocks and (2) the guaranteed execution of cleanup code (represented by the `Finally` block) regardless of whether an exception occurs. The latter is a significant advantage because it enables centralized cleanup.

Regardless of which approach you choose for local error trapping (or whether you mix and match from all three), you'll want to incorporate a global `HandleError` function to reduce code duplication. This function also provides a framework for improving the quality of your exception processing, simply by evolving the function over time. Thus, the last issue is to flush out our initial design of `HandleError`.

---

[3] This discussion is based on information from a public beta release of VB.Net.

Recall that this function returns one of three values (defined by `Enum HEResult`), indicating how the caller should continue execution. Because one of these options is to propagate the error up the call chain, we must also have a mechanism for returning the necessary error information to the caller. The simplest solution is to define a set of global variables along with our global function in a BAS module:

```
Public lERR_No As Long
Public sERR_Src As String
Public sERR_Desc As String
Public sERR_HelpFile As String
Public lERR_HelpCtx As Long

Public Function HandleError(sCaller As String, _
                ParamArray vaArgs() As Variant) _
                As HEResult
    .
    .
    .
End Function
```

The first parameter represents the caller, and should be of the format `ModuleName.RoutineName.LineNumber` (because it's used to populate `Err.Source`). The second parameter is a variant array for capturing any additional arguments that are passed for the purposes of error recovery. Note that `UBound(vaArgs)` can be used to determine the number of arguments in the array.

The `sCaller` parameter is critical for identifying the exact point of failure; unfortunately, there is no automatic way of generating it. However, if you take responsibility for numbering each line of your component/application (or better yet, see http://www.themandelbrotset.com/html/downloads.html for a free tool), the undocumented `Erl` function can be used by the *caller* to discover the line number of the local statement that triggered the exception:

```
Public Sub DoTask(...)
   100  On Error Goto Handler
   200
   300    Step1
```

```
    400    Step2
             .
             .
             .
   2900  Exit Sub
Handler:
   3000  Dim eAction As HEResult, sLine As String
   3100  sLine = CStr( Erl() )
   3200  eAction = HandleError("Utility.DoTask." + sLine)
             .
             .
             .
   4700  Debug.Assert eAction = HEResult.Raise
   4800  Err.Clear   '** in case we don't provide complete info to Err.Raise
   4900  Err.Raise lERR_No, sERR_Src, sERR_Desc, _
                   sERR_HelpFile, lERR_HelpCtx
End Sub
```

Note that `Erl` actually returns the last line number (or numeric label) locally encountered before the exception occurred. Thus, you can also use line numbers to delineate blocks of code for special treatment (versus defining multiple, local handlers, as mentioned earlier):

```
Handler:
   3000  If Erl() = 300 Then    '** Step1 failed
            <special handling>
         Else    '** handle other cases using global error handler
            <call HandleError>
         End If
```

`Erl` returns 0 if no line number or numeric label is found.

Given one or more parameters, the first step of `HandleError` is to enable local error trapping for handling exceptions that may occur during the recovery process. However, enabling clears the `Err` object, discarding information about the original error! Hence, we save the error information (in our global variables) and then enable local exception handling:

```
Public Function HandleError(sCaller As String, _
                ParamArray vaArgs() As Variant) _
                As HEResult
```

```
    lERR_No = Err.Number
    sERR_Src = sCaller + ":" + Err.Source
    sERR_Desc = Err.Description
    sERR_HelpFile = Err.HelpFile
    lERR_HelpCtx = Err.HelpContext

    On Error Goto Handler    '** now safe to enable error handling...
```

Once information about the error has been saved, the hard part is deciding what to do in each case:

```
Select Case lERR_No
    Case ...
        <handle this particular error>
        HandleError = ...
    Case ...
        <handle this particular error>
        HandleError = ...
        .
        .
        .
```

At the very least, log the error (note that proper logging may require an initial call to `App.StartLogging`) and suggest the caller raise it up the call chain so everyone has an opportunity to clean up:

```
    Case Else
        Dim sMsg As String
        sMsg = "Error " + CStr(lERR_No) + ": "
        sMsg = sMsg + sERR_Src + "; "
        sMsg = sMsg + sERR_Desc + "."
        App.LogEvent sMsg
        Debug.Print sMsg    '** in case we are running inside the IDE
        HandleError = HEResult.Raise
    End Select
    Exit Function
Handler:
    .
    .
    .
End Function
```

Assuming that every subroutine invokes `HandleError`, note that this approach has a nice side effect of logging the complete call chain that led to the exception.

As you can see, good error handling requires significant effort. The fruits of this effort are rarely appreciated at first, but they become more obvious over time, especially as you evolve `HandleError` from project to project. Note that the techniques discussed here work seamlessly with COM objects because VB maps COM's underlying return code model (based on integer HERESULTs) into standard VB exceptions. However, if you find yourself making API calls (which do not trigger exceptions), you'll need to use a return code-based approach to check for errors (see rule 1-4). Also, consider defining a separate global function for handling errors in this case. This function should work in much the same way as `HandleError`, except look for the error code in the property `Err.LastDllError`, and you must call the WinAPI `FormatMessage` function to obtain the descriptive error message.

Rule 1-6: Know the Difference Between Type and Class

With the introduction of object-oriented programming, programming languages became more complex. This is especially true in the case of C++ and VB, in which object-oriented features were "bolted" onto an existing procedural language. One particularly confusing area is *type* versus *class*.

In most programming languages, data is typed—for efficiency, for safety, and for readability. A type defines a memory layout as well as a set of operations that can be legally performed on data of that type. VB defines a standard set of types: `Boolean`, `Integer`, `String`, and so forth. You can also extend the type system by defining new types (e.g., an employee type called `TEmployee`):

```
Public Type TEmployee    '** TEmployee becomes a new type in VB
    sName As String      '**    name
    iOffice As Integer   '**    office number
End Type
```

A class is similar in that it also defines a new type. What's interesting is that the reverse is not true: A type does not define a class. This implies that a class is somehow more powerful than a type, but how so? First, let's look at types more closely.

Consider VB's `String` type, which denotes a dynamically allocated chunk of memory containing both the string's length and its characters (in Unicode).[4] It also supports a number of operations; for example, concatenation:

```
Dim s1 As String, s2 As String

s1 = "Hello "
s2 = "World!"
s1 = s1 + s2      '** concatenate s1 and s2
```

Like all types in VB, the underlying data is automatically allocated and maintained for you (typically on the stack, or a combination of the stack and the heap, as in the case of strings). Assignment works as traditionally expected; in other words, the data is copied:

```
s2 = s1    '** s2 now contains its own copy of the string "Hello World!"
```

The same holds true for parameter passing: `ByVal` passes a copy, whereas `ByRef` passes a reference to the original variable (so the routine can change the variable's contents if desired). In short, VB's predefined types are easy to use because they are fully integrated into the language. Perhaps the only drawback is that the sets of allowable operations are not well documented. Try locating a complete list of all legal `String` operators, subroutines, and functions available in VB. :-)

Types declared via VB's `Type` statement (known as *UDTs*, or *user-defined types*) are 99 percent equivalent to predefined types. UDTs such as `TEmployee` can be used anywhere a type is required—in variable declarations, parameter declarations, function return types, even within other UDTs. For example, consider the following declarations, which allocate both a single employee variable and an array of 100:

```
Dim uTemp As TEmployee
Dim uaEmployees(1 To 100) As TEmployee
```

---

[4] Actually, it's the length times 2; the number of bytes taken up by the Unicode characters.

Assignment works as expected. The following copies all UDT data as two employees swap positions in the array:

```
uTemp = uaEmployees(i)              '** copy employee i into temp
uaEmployees(i) = uaEmployees(j)     '** now overwrite i with a copy of j
uaEmployees(j) = uTemp              '** finally, overwrite j with copy of i
```

Individual fields are accessed using the dot operator, and operations are written as explicit subroutines and functions. The only significant difference between predefined and user-defined types is that the latter must be passed `ByRef`. This allows the subroutine or function to modify a caller's UDT variable (e.g., when reading an employee's data from a database):

```
Public Sub ReadFromDB(ByRef uEmp As TEmployee, _
                     ByVal rsEmps As ADODB.Recordset)
    uEmp.sName = rsEmps.Fields("Name").Value
    uEmp.iOffice = rsEmps.Fields("Office").Value
End Sub
```

Thus, to read one employee into our variable `uTemp`, we do

```
Dim rsEmps as ADODB.Recordset
   .
   .
   .
ReadFromDB uTemp, rsEmps
```

To read all the employees into our array `uaEmployees`, we pass a different location of the array each time we call `ReadFromDB`:

```
rsEmps.MoveLast : rsEmps.MoveFirst   '** compute RecordCount
Debug.Assert rsEmps.RecordCount <= UBound(uaEmployees)

For i = 1 to rsEmps.RecordCount
    ReadFromDB uaEmployees(i), rsEmps
Next i
```

The danger is that `ByVal` cannot be used to prevent the caller's UDT from changing accidentally.

A class is similar to a UDT because it defines a memory layout as well as a set of legal operations. Classes can also be used anywhere a type is required. However, at this point the similarities end. First, unlike UDTs, both a class's *properties* (data) and its *methods* (operations) are encapsulated in one module, and thus are readily apparent using VB's object browser. For example, here's a class `CEmployee` with the same basic functionality as `TEmployee`:

```
'** class module CEmployee
Option Explicit

Public sName As String
Public iOffice As Integer

Public Sub ReadFromDB(ByVal rsEmps As ADODB.Recordset)
    '** read from DB into MY properties...
    sName = rsEmps.Fields("Name").Value
    iOffice = rsEmps.Fields("Office").Value
End Sub
```

At run-time, when *instances* of this class (i.e., objects) are created in memory, each contains its own set of `sName` and `iOffice` properties, and `ReadFromDB` modifies that set only. Figure 1.4 shows three different instances of `CEmployee`.

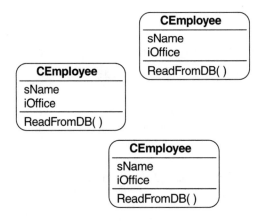

Figure 1.4   Three instances of class `CEmployee`

This leads to the second major difference between class and type: memory allocation. Although data of predefined and user-defined types is automatically managed by VB, the same is not true of class instances. Consider the following declaration:

```
Dim rEmployee As CEmployee
```

Does this statement create an instance of class CEmployee? Absolutely not. Instead, it allocates a much simpler *reference* variable on the stack with an initial value of Nothing (reference to no object). The programmer (you!) is responsible for creating class instances, using the New operator:

```
Set rEmployee = New CEmployee
```

Note that VB requires the use of the Set statement when assigning to a reference variable, emphasizing the fact that objects are different. After execution of New and Set, another instance of CEmployee exists in heap memory, and rEmployee now contains a reference to it (Figure 1.5).

This discussion raises yet another difference between class and type; namely, that the assignment operator copies *references,* not objects. Consider the following:

```
Dim rTemp As CEmployee     '** declare another reference variable
Set rTemp = rEmployee      '** copies reference, not object!
```

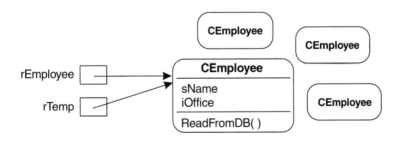

Figure 1.5 Four instances, with one referenced by two different variables

Because only the reference is copied, at this point both `rEmployee` and `rTemp` refer to the same object, as shown in Figure 1.5. Furthermore, as you may suspect, this behavior also applies to parameter passing: `ByRef` and `ByVal` apply to the object reference, not the object itself. As a result, objects are always passed by reference, regardless of the parameter declaration. For example, consider the following call to `ReadFromDB`, where a reference to an `ADO Recordset` object is passed:

```
rEmployee.ReadFromDB rsEmps   '** read name and office into object
```

Even though the parameter is specified as `ByVal`, the `Recordset` object can be modified by the method. What `ByVal` guarantees is that the *variable* being passed, `rsEmps`, cannot be changed to reference another object (nor can it be set to `Nothing`).

So why use classes? They certainly look like more work, and are generally not as efficient in terms of computer resources (see rule 1-8). The reason is that classes are the building blocks of object-oriented design (OOD), which has definite advantages (see rule 1-7). As a quick comparison, consider the case when you have different types of employees: administrative, sales, technical, and so forth. The most efficient usage of memory would result from a unique UDT for each employee type. But to keep track of all the employees, you would then need either a set of different arrays (one per UDT) or a single array of type `Variant`.[5] When it comes time to process the employees, the former requires different code to process each distinct array, whereas the latter requires if-then-else logic to determine the type of employee in each variant:

```
'** write all the employees back to the database...
For i = 1 to UBound(vaEmployees)
   If TypeName(vaEmployees(i)) = "TAdmin" Then
      WriteAdminToDB vaEmployees(i)
   ElseIf TypeName(vaEmployees(i)) = "TSales" Then
      WriteSalesToDB vaEmployees(i)
```

---

[5] Note that only a "global" UDT can be stored in a variant (i.e., a UDT defined within a public class module of a COM server [DLL, EXE, or its type library]).

```
    ElseIf ...
      .
      .
      .
    End If
Next i
```

A better solution is to define a unique class for each type of employee (where the classes are designed to be as similar as possible), create one instance per employee, and store all the references in a `Collection` object. Although this approach uses more memory, it enables the employees to be processed in a much more elegant manner:

```
'** write all the employees back to the database...
For Each rEmployee In colEmployees
    rEmployee.WriteToDB
Next employee
```

The real advantage comes into play when your system evolves to include new employee types: The previous code will continue to work unchanged, whereas the UDT-based code will need to be revisited and modified.

In short, you need to be comfortable with the differences between type and class, and think carefully about when to use one over another. A simple example is moving data across the network: Objects rarely move, whereas UDTs move easily. The next rule (rule 1-7) encourages you to embrace class-based programming fully. Rule 1-8 gives you reasons to pause.

Rule 1-7: Embrace Good Object-Oriented Design, Not Just VB

Even though C++ is an object-oriented language, many C++ programmers treat the language as version 2 of ANSI C. Likewise, even though VB6 is an object-based language, many programmers use objects but don't really embrace an OOD philosophy. This is quite understandable, given the rapid rate of change in our field and the pressures of developing on Internet time. To make matters worse, good OOD takes time and practice as well.

The moral of the story is simple: Now's the time to embrace OOD if you haven't already. In fact, the next version of VB will be fully object oriented. What does this mean to you? When designing systems, you should be thinking in terms of classes and objects. Your classes should employ *encapsulation* and *abstraction,* and should be defined in terms of explicit *interfaces.* You should think hard about when to use *implementation inheritance* because casual overuse can hinder the evolution of your system. Lastly, your classes should be designed with *polymorphism* in mind, and when coding against objects you should look for opportunities to apply this important style of programming.

Let's discuss each of these concepts. *Encapsulation* is the process of packaging data and code together into one entity, a class. Classes typically model real-world entities, whose state and behavior are mapped to properties and methods. For example, a Web-based application may have a customer with a shopping cart that contains items. The obvious design consists of at least three classes, one for the customer, one for the shopping cart, and one for the item. The class `CCustomer` encapsulates the customer's name, his cart, and his ability to purchase items or to log out:

```
'** CCustomer: class
Public sFirstName As String      '** customer's name
Public sLastName As String
Public rCart As CShoppingCart    '** his shopping cart

Public Sub Purchase()    '** buy contents of cart
Public Sub Logout()      '** persist contents of cart
```

The class `CShoppingCart` encapsulates a set of items using a collection, with methods for emptying the cart and calculating the total price:

```
'** CShoppingCart: class
Public colItems As Collection

Public Sub Empty()                              '** empty cart
Public Function TotalPrice() As Currency        '** calculate total
```

With this design, items are added to the shopping cart via the collection's predefined `Add` method, are removed from the cart using the collection's

Remove method, and are iterated using the For-Each statement. Lastly, class CItem encapsulates information about a single item in the cart:

```
'** CItem: class
Public sItemNo   As String     '** unique item number
Public sItemDesc As String     '** item description
Public cPrice    As Currency   '** item price
Public lQuantity As Long       '** quantity in cart
Public bInStock  As Boolean    '** in stock?
```

Note that part of the encapsulation process is to ensure that your objects self-initialize after they are created, and properly clean up before they are destroyed. VB provides special events, Class_Initialize and Class_Terminate, for exactly this purpose, and calls them automatically just after creation/before destruction. For example, in the case of CShoppingCart, the underlying Collection object needs to be instantiated and destroyed. Likewise, in Ccustomer, we need to create and destroy the underlying shopping cart:

```
'** CCustomer
Private Sub Class_Initialize()
    Set rCart = New CShoppingCart
End Sub

Private Sub Class_Terminate()
    Set rCart = Nothing
End Sub
```

What about the customer's name? Because these values differ for each instance of CCustomer, the proper solution is to parameterize Class_Initialize with the customer's first and last name. Unfortunately, this technique is not supported in VB6. Look for it to appear in the next version of VB. Also see rule 2-7 for an interesting discussion of Class_Terminate

Abstraction is the notion of making a class more abstract—fewer details, more powerful methods—in the hope of making it easier to use and/or more useful. For example, consider the class CShoppingCart. It has a method to compute the total price of all items in the cart, even though the user can do this himself by iterating through the `colItems` collection. So why provide it? Because most users will benefit from this functionality:

```
'** CShoppingCart
Public Function TotalPrice() As Currency
   Dim rItem As CItem

   TotalPrice = 0
   For Each rItem In colItems
      TotalPrice = TotalPrice + rItem.cPrice
   Next rItem
End Function

Public Sub Empty()
   Dim l As Long

   For l = colItems.Count To 1 Step -1
      colItems.Remove l
   Next l
End Sub
```

Likewise for the `Empty` method, which is helpful but not strictly necessary.

In conjunction with encapsulation and abstraction, you should also strongly consider the practice of *data hiding* in your designs. In general, classes should hide as much information from the outside world as possible. This strategy not only (1) raises the level of abstraction, but (2) allows internal details to evolve without impacting the users of your class. For example, in `CShoppingCart`, should the outside world really be able to manipulate the `colItems` collection directly? Probably not, because users may inadvertently add or remove items, or insert data of the incorrect type. To hide we use the key word `Private` and provide equivalent functionality via public methods:

```
'** CShoppingCart: class (revised)
Private colItems As Collection      '** inaccessible outside class

Public Sub Add(rItem As CItem)      '** standard collection methods
Public Sub Remove(sItemNo As String)
Public Property Get lCount() As Long
```

```
Public Sub Empty()
Public Function TotalPrice() As Currency
```

Now only these methods have access to `colItems`, thereby preventing uncontrolled use of the collection. Furthermore, this design allows VB's `Collection` class to be used in a type-safe manner, because `Add`'s parameter type restricts the collection to instances of `CItem` (versus any variant-compatible data type). However, there appears to be a serious disadvantage to hiding the collection: Users of our class can no longer iterate through the shopping cart. In other words, the following code written by our users will no longer compile:

```
Dim rCust As CCustomer, rItem As CItem
Set rCust = ...

For Each rItem In rCust.rCart.colItems    '** Error: not found
    <do something with item>
Next rItem
```

The solution is either to provide a custom iteration mechanism or to reveal the underlying collection's *iterator* via the following well-known trick. First, add the following method to the class:

```
'** CShoppingCart
Public Function NewEnum() As IUnknown       '** cart iterator
    Set NewEnum = colItems.[_NewEnum]       '**  = colItems iterator
End Function
```

Second, define the procedure ID of this method to be -4 (Tools >> Procedure Attributes, Advanced). That's it! Users can now iterate through the cart as before, with a slight change:

```
For Each rItem In rCust.rCart
    <do something with item>
Next rItem
```

Note the reference to `colItems` is dropped.

The previous discussion raises a number of interesting questions. First, how far should abstraction be pushed? For example, why not redesign the top-level `CCustomer` class to hide the shopping cart altogether? The result would look something like

```
'** CCustomer: class (revised)
Public sFirstName As String
Public sLastName As String
Private rCart As CShoppingCart    '** now inaccessible outside class

Public Sub AddItem(sItemNo As String, lQuantity As Long)
Public Sub RemoveItem(sItemNo As String)
Public Property Get lNumItems() As Long

Public Sub Purchase()
Public Sub Logout()
```

The answer is that this is a good design because it frees the user from managing the underlying shopping cart. For example, `AddItem` can look up the item number in the database, create a new `CItem` object, and add it to the cart. It also provides more flexibility because, if efficiency demands it, we can eliminate the `CShoppingCart` class altogether and use a private collection instead. In general, the higher the abstraction, the better.

Second, in designing a class, when should a member be a data property versus a method? A rough rule of thumb is that when describing the class, nouns translate into properties and verbs translate into methods. However, when it comes time for implementation, a good strategy is always to use methods, because these give you more flexibility and power. And when combined with VB's *logical property methods,* you get the best of both worlds: the illusion of properties and the benefit of methods. For example, consider the `lCount` property of the redesigned `CShoppingCart` class:

```
'** CShoppingCart
Public Property Get lCount() As Long
    lCount = colItems.Count
End Property
```

This logical property is actually a method that returns the number of items in the underlying collection, yet it is "called" when the user accesses it like a physical property:

```
'** CCustomer
Public Property Get lNumItems() As Long
    lNumItems = rCart.lCount
End Sub
```

Note that by providing only a `Get` method (and not the corresponding `Let`), `lCount` becomes a read-only property and thus users cannot accidentally change it. This approach would be advantageous in class `CItem` as well. Other general advantages include the ability to validate values before a property is updated, and to decouple the types of the public properties from the actual types used internally within the class. The latter allows your implementation to evolve more freely over time.

A third design question concerns *containment* versus *inheritance*: When should one class contain another, versus inherit? For example, `CShoppingCart` contains an instance of the `Collection` class, instead of inheriting from it. Why? If you are programming in VB6, the answer is easy—VB does not support inheritance. :-) But the next version of VB will offer inheritance, so we need a better answer. One rule of thumb is the "is-a" versus the "has-a" rule. If class A is-a special case of class B, then A should inherit from B. On the other hand, if A has-a instance of B, then A should contain B. In the case of `CShoppingCart`, one can easily argue that a shopping cart is-a collection of items, and hence should inherit from `Collection`:[6]

```
'** CShoppingCart: class (revised for VB.Net)
Inherits Collection

Public Sub Empty()
Public Function TotalPrice() As Currency
```

---

[6] This discussion is based on information from a public beta release of VB.Net.

This class definition automatically contains all the properties and method implementations of `Collection` (`Add`, `Remove`, `Count`, and so on). But have we lost type safety? No, as long as we also *override* the inherited `Add` method with our own type-safe version:

```
Overrides Public Sub Add(rItem As CItem)
```

The end result is an equivalent `CShoppingCart` class, with less effort. However, keep in mind that there is a hidden cost associated with implementation inheritance: It increases the coupling between classes, hindering your ability to evolve parent classes over time. This is one of the key motivations for designing your classes based on *interfaces* (see rules 2-1 and 2-2 for a detailed discussion).

Our final question centers on the design of groups of classes: Are there any guidelines to follow? Yes. Perhaps the most important guideline is to define logically related classes as similarly as possible. Not only does this ease the understanding of large class libraries, but it also enables a polymorphic style of programming. *Polymorphism* is the notion that an operation is supported by multiple classes or data types. The advantage is that programmers can then perform this operation across a set of objects without concern for the underlying type. For example, suppose our Web site sells different categories of items (books, music, software, and so on), which translates into a design involving distinct classes (`CBook`, `CMusic`, `CSoftware`, . . .). As long as each class defines a property called `cPrice` (making it polymorphic), it's easy to iterate through a customer's shopping cart and compute the total price:

```
'** CShoppingCart
Public Function TotalPrice() As Currency
    Dim rItem As Object    '**Object handles different types in cart

    TotalPrice = 0
    For Each rItem In colItems
       TotalPrice = TotalPrice + rItem.cPrice
    Next rItem
End Function
```

Even more interesting is the fact that if we extend our Web site in the future to include new item classes, `TotalPrice` continues to work *without modifi-*

cation as long as the new classes also contain a `cPrice` property. Hence a polymorphic style of programming is also more resilient to change.

Are you ready to embrace OOD? Although this discussion is a good start, it represents just the tip of the object-oriented iceberg. Be sure to visit Chapter 2, in particular rules 2-2 and 2-7. The former presents a compelling design alternative to implementation inheritance, which is frequently oversold as the cure-all technique in OOD; the latter goes into more detail concerning the subtleties of class design with `Class_Terminate`.

Rule 1-8: Prefer UDTs over Classes for Value Types

Rule 1-6 highlighted the differences between type and class—i.e., traditional and class-based programming. Rule 1-7 then introduced class design, encouraging you to embrace object-oriented programming. Does this mean you should always use classes to model data? Let's discuss why the correct answer is no.

A *value* type denotes a type that represents data only. Predefined VB types such as `Integer`, `Long`, and `String` are examples of value types. In contrast, a *reference* type defines a type that references an object, and the data lives in the object. For example, suppose you want to store the integer 17 in memory. You could use a value type

```
Dim i As Integer
i = 17
```

or you could design a class that holds an integer

```
'** CInteger: class
Public i As Integer
```

and use a reference type:

```
Dim rInt As CInteger
Set rInt = New CInteger
rInt.i = 17
```

The difference is shown in Figure 1.6. Which is more efficient? Because the former is automatically allocated in memory (using stack-based allocation whenever possible), value types are faster and require less space.

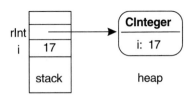

Figure 1.6 Value types versus reference types

Obviously the previous example is an extreme case—using an entire object to store just one integer. However, the same result holds true whether the object stores 1 value or 20: If your goal is simply to store data, value types are always more efficient in terms of computer resources. In this case you would use a UDT—a more complex form of value type.

A UDT is a value type that contains one or more value and reference types. For example, here's a TCustomer UDT similar to the CCustomer class discussed in the previous rule:

```
Public Type TCustomer
    sFirstName As String        '** value type
    sLastName As String         '** value type
    rCart As CShoppingCart      '** reference type
End Type
```

This UDT represents three pieces of data: two values (each a String) and one reference (to an instance of CShoppingCart). The advantage over CCustomer is more efficient memory allocation and access. For example, when the following subroutine is called, the local array declaration automatically allocates space on the stack for 100 TCustomers (technically, note that the string data will be stored on the heap):

```
Public Sub DoTask()
    Dim uaCustomers(1 To 100) As TCustomer    '** value type
        .
        .
        .
End Sub
```

But if the array is declared to use a reference type of `CCustomer`, 100 distinct objects must be created on the heap to hold the data:

```
Public Sub DoTask()
    Dim raCustomers(1 To 100) As CCustomer    '** reference type
    Dim i As Integer

    For i = 1 to 100
        Set raCustomers(i) = New CCustomer
    Next I
    .
    .
    .
End Sub
```

Not only is the heap-based allocation slower (requiring 100 calls to `New`), but each future object access is preceded by a run-time check to ensure that the reference is not `Nothing`.[7] Thus, the following loop to assign each customer a first name also contains 100 hidden reference checks:

```
For i = 1 to 100
        '** If raCustomers(i) Is Nothing Then Err.Raise
        raCustomers(i).sFirstName = ...
    Next i
```

In contrast, because `uaCustomers` is an array of preallocated values, these reference checks are unnecessary.

Another important area in which value and reference types differ is *parameter passing.* The difference is most apparent when the caller and the callee live in separate processes (regardless of whether they are on the same machine). This situation typically occurs when making COM calls from one object to another, and parameter data is being *marshaled* between the objects. In short, values are always copied from one process to the other, enabling efficient access in the callee. However, VB objects are never copied, forcing the callee to access the object across a process or computer boundary—an expensive operation.

---

[7] If this is a COM class, the call to `New` is even more expensive.

For example, suppose a public method of a COM object (residing in another process) is defined using a value type:

```
Public Sub DoAnotherTask(uCust As TCustomer)
    .
    WriteToDatabase uCust.sLastName    '** local access
    .
End Sub
```

When this method executes, it is guaranteed to have a local copy of the caller's UDT data.[8] On the other hand, if the method is defined using a reference type

```
Public Sub DoAnotherTask(rCust As CCustomer)
    .
    WriteToDatabase rCust.sLastName    '** non-local access
    .
End Sub
```

then the method receives a local copy of the *reference,* but the object itself (and its data) remains in the caller's process and thus is costly to access. Note that this holds true for almost any reference type, even those defined within a UDT.[9] For example, recall that `rCart` within `TCustomer` is a reference type. This implies that access to `rCart`'s data in either of the previous subroutines is non-local.

If you are concerned with efficiency, it's clear that you should consider value types whenever you need to store, manipulate, or marshal data. And keep in mind that UDTs and arrays of UDTs are value types, whereas classes are reference types. So when should you use a class? For one, whenever you need to model both state and behavior. More likely, however, you'll use classes when you want to take advantage of OOD and programming—and use *human* resources more efficiently.

---

[8] Marshaling UDTs requires a recent version of DCOM (e.g., SP4 or later on NT), and the UDT must be defined in a public class of a COM server (DLL, EXE, or its type library).

[9] An important exception is `ADO Recordset`, in which case the object is copied.

Rule 1-9: Automate Mundane Tasks

Programming is generally not a mundane task. Far from it. However, it does involve some mundane chores: recompiling applications, reinstalling and reconfiguring COM components, running regression tests, burning CDs, and so forth. DOS and UNIX programmers, raised on command-line tools, are used to automating such tasks with *make* or *batch* files. Windows programmers are much more fortunate because their integrated development environments automate a great many of these activities. This is especially true for VB programmers, because the IDE represents our only compilation tool.

The problem is that many of us fall into the habit of doing things manually when the IDE fails to provide an automated mechanism. This is fine for single-shot activities, but not so good for repetitive ones. In the latter case we are forgetting our history, and the fact that easy alternatives exist. We shall discuss two: `nmake` and Windows Scripting Host (WSH).

When you need to perform recompilation chores, or in general invoke command-line utilities, the use of *makefiles* is your best bet for automation. A makefile is a text file containing macro definitions, dependency lines, and command lines. Think of a makefile as describing how to compile a program: The dependency lines specify relationships between program files, and the command lines give the exact commands for compiling those files. When you need to compile your program, you simply run the makefile through a make tool such as `nmake`:

```
DOS> nmake Client.exe
```

The `nmake` program reads a file called makefile and then issues the necessary set of commands for compilation of `Client.exe`.[10]

What does a makefile look like? Here's a generic example for compiling a VB application `Client.exe`, which consists of a project file (`Client.vbp`) and two program files (`frmMain.frm` and `basUtil.bas`):

---

[10] `nmake` is a command-line tool that is installed as part of Visual Studio.

```
Client.exe: Client.vbp frmMain.frm basUtil.bas
    C:\VS6\VB98\VB6.exe /make Client.vbp

.SUFFIXES: .vbp .frm .cls .bas
```

A dependency line starts in the first column and contains a colon, stating that the *target* file to the left of the colon is dependent on the *source* files to the right. Thus, our target `Client.exe` is dependent on the sources `Client.vbp`, `frmMain.frm`, and `basUtil.bas`. A dependency line may be followed by one or more tab-indented command lines, which define how to build the target. In this case, if `Client.exe` needs to be built, then `nmake` runs VB from the command line to compile the project and produce the .EXE file:

```
C:\VS6\VB98\VB6.exe /make Client.vbp
```

Because every file needs a dependency line (in case it has to be compiled), the remaining dependency line *suffixes* define the standard VB file types. There are no associated command lines, however, because VB files are not separately compiled.

The *key rule* behind `nmake` is the following: Command lines are only executed if the target file doesn't exist or is out of date with respect to its source files. Otherwise the target is considered current, and the command lines are ignored. For example, deleting the target file will trigger recompilation, as will editing a project or program file. Likewise, running `nmake` without changing anything yields the following output:

```
'Client.exe' is up-to-date
```

It's also important to understand that `nmake` applies this rule recursively. If the target X depends on source Y, then `nmake` treats Y as a target and tries to find a dependency line for building it. Once Y is built, then `nmake` returns to the task of building X. Thus, in general, `nmake` identifies dependencies in a depth-first manner, and executes command lines as it works its way back up to the initial target. For example, consider the following more realistic makefile for working with a set of COM components:

```
# define some macros that are easy to change when needed
TARGETS = C1.dll C2.dll
VB = "C:\Visual Studio\vb98\VB6.exe"
ARGS = /d DBUG=1

components: $(TARGETS)

C1.dll: C1.vbp Class1.cls Class2.cls
    $(VB) /make C1.vbp $(ARGS)
    copy C1.dll \\server\public

C2.dll: C2.vbp Class3.cls Class4.cls Class5.cls
    $(VB) /make C2.vbp $(ARGS)
    copy C2.dll \\server\public

.SUFFIXES: .vbp .frm .cls .bas

clean:
    regsvr32 /u /s $(TARGETS)
    del $(TARGETS)
```

The first three lines define macros that can be expanded later in the makefile. In particular, notice the ARGS macro, which is used to define the command-line arguments passed to VB during compilation. The /d argument directs conditional compilation, which is often used to control production versus debug builds (see rule 1-3 for a discussion of conditional compilation in VB). The default (first) target components lead to the compilation of C1.dll and C2.dll in debug mode, as well as copying each file to a public share on the server:

```
DOS> nmake

"C:\Visual Studio\vb98\VB6.exe" /make C1.vbp /d DBUG=1
copy C1.dll \\server\public
"C:\Visual Studio\vb98\VB6.exe" /make C2.vbp /d DBUG=1
copy C2.dll \\server\public
```

To produce a nondebug version, override the ARGS macro from the command line:

```
DOS> nmake /e ARGS=

"C:\Visual Studio\vb98\VB6.exe" /make C1.vbp
copy C1.dll \\server\public
"C:\Visual Studio\vb98\VB6.exe" /make C2.vbp
copy C2.dll \\server\public
```

If desired, the components can be built individually by supplying `nmake` with a specific target (`C1.dll` or `C2.dll`). Finally, the last target is very handy for cleaning up; in this case, for unregistering and then deleting the COM components:

```
DOS> nmake clean

regsvr32 /u /s C1.dll C2.dll
del C1.dll C2.dll
```

If you want to see what commands `nmake` will execute (without actually executing them), include the `/n` option, as in:

```
DOS> nmake clean /n
```

This is particularly helpful if you need to debug a makefile.

Although `nmake` is a very useful tool, it has a significant limitation: It can only interact with other command-line tools. Microsoft also provides a rich collection of "scriptable" objects for interacting with various Windows services—Active Directory, Microsoft Transaction Server (MTS), Component Services, and so forth—services that are not directly accessible to `nmake`. The classic example is the installation and configuration of COM components within the Component Services of Windows 2000. This is often done manually—a tedious and error-prone process (ever forget to set an attribute?). A much better alternative is to automate the procedure using a little VBScript and WSH.

In essence, WSH is an engine for executing code. This code serves the same function as the command lines in a makefile, the difference being that we write these commands in a very familiar language—VB. For example, here's a VBScript equivalent to the earlier makefile for managing two COM components:

```
sVB   = """C:\Visual Studio\vb98\VB6.exe"""
sC1   = " /make C1.vbp"
sC2   = " /make C2.vbp"
sARGS= " /d DBUG=1"

Set rShell = WScript.CreateObject("WScript.Shell")

rShell.Run sVB+sC1+sARGS, 0, True   '** compile C1, hide, wait...
rShell.Run sVB+sC2+sARGS, 0, True   '** compile C2, hide, wait...

Set rFS = WScript.CreateObject( _
              "Scripting.FileSystemObject")

rFS.CopyFile "C1.dll", "\\server\public\C1.dll"
rFS.CopyFile "C2.dll", "\\server\public\C2.dll"
```

To run this code, simply place it in a file called makefile.vbs, and double-click. (This assumes you have WSH installed; if not, see msdn.microsoft.com/scripting.)

Note that scripting and makefiles differ in one important regard: The previous script always compiles the two VB projects, whereas nmake only compiles if a target is missing or is out of date.

Obviously, with the full power of VBScript (and numerous objects) at your fingertips, the sky's the limit. For example, the script can first ask whether it should build a debug or a production version (waiting, at most, 30 seconds for an answer), and then can set up things appropriately:

```
iAnswer = shell.Popup("Build debug version?", 30, _
                      WScript.ScriptName, vbOKCancel)
If iAnswer = vbOK Then    '** build debug version
    sARGS= " /d DBUG=1"
Else   '** build production version since canceled or didn't answer...
    sARGS= ""
End If
```

Alternatively, you could require that such information be supplied to the script in the form of arguments. Here's a generic script that compiles any VB project:

```
Set rScriptArgs = WScript.Arguments
If rScriptArgs.Count <> 1 Then
   WScript.Echo "Usage: ..."
   WScript.Quit(1)
End If

sProj = """" + rScriptArgs(0) + """"
sVB   = """C:\Visual Studio\vb98\VB6.exe"""

Set rShell = WScript.CreateObject("WScript.Shell")
rShell.Run sVB + " /make " + sProj, 0, True
```

Arguments can be specified via drag-and-drop, or by running your script from Windows (using wscript) or a command window (via cscript). Note that extra string delimiters are necessary around the argument to handle properly the filenames containing spaces. Finally, you'll want to handle run-time errors, if only to stop a script before it generates additional errors. The first step is to check the return code of any program you run:

```
lRetcode = rShell.Run(...)
If lRetcode <> 0 Then
   WScript.Echo "**Error: ..., script halted."
   WScript.Quit(1)
End If
```

The second step is to enable error trapping at the top of the script, and then check Err.Number after every statement:

```
On Error Resume Next
   .
   .
   .
lRetcode = rShell.Run(...)
If Err.Number <> 0 OR lRetcode <> 0 Then
   WScript.Echo "**Error: ..., script halted."
   WScript.Quit(1)
End If
```

Note that if you enable error trapping, you must also commit to checking Err.Number. Failure to do so may allow errors to go unreported, because the only error trapping option in VBScript is currently `Resume Next` (i.e., silently continue execution).

At this point the use of WSH may look too much like application building. And to some degree it is. But keep in mind that you can also simplify your automation needs by combining the ease of makefiles with the power of WSH. For completeness, here's a compelling example of a makefile and a script that work together to compile and install COM components under Windows 2000. The makefile manages the task of compilation, but then calls on a script to handle the installation within COM+:

```
TARGETS = C1.dll C2.dll
VB = "C:\Visual Studio\vb98\VB6.exe"
components: $(TARGETS)

C1.dll: C1.vbp Class1.cls Class2.cls
    $(VB) /make "C1.vbp"
    cscript install.vbs "C1" "C1.dll"

C2.dll: C2.vbp Class3.cls Class4.cls Class5.cls
    $(VB) /make "C2.vbp"
    cscript install.vbs "C2" "C2.dll"

.SUFFIXES: .vbp .frm .cls .bas
```

The script `install.vbs` takes an application and filename, and then interacts with the COM+ administration objects to (1) delete the COM+ application if present, (2) create the COM+ application, and (3) install the Compiled Com Objects (DLL) as a component of this application. For brevity, error handling has been omitted:

```
'** install.vbs ApplicationName FileName
Set rScriptArgs = WScript.Arguments
sApp = rScriptArgs(0)
sFile = rScriptArgs(1)

Set rCatalog = WScript.CreateObject( _
                    "COMAdmin.COMAdminCatalog")
rCatalog.Connect "localhost"
```

```
Set rApps = rCatalog.GetCollection("Applications")
rApps.Populate     '** get all installed applications...

For i = 0 To rApps.Count-1     '** (1) is COM+ app already installed?
    If rApps.Item(i).Name = sApp Then        '** yes, so delete...
        rApps.Remove i
        Exit For
    End If
Next

Set rApp = rApps.Add()         '** (2) create COM+ app
rApp.Value("Name") = sApp
rApps.SaveChanges

rCatalog.InstallComponent sApp, sFile, "", ""   '** (3) install
WScript.Echo sFile + " installed in " + sApp
```

For more information on COM+ scripting, see "Automating COM+ Administration" (*MSDN Magazine,* September 2000 15(19):135–145).

Makefiles and scripting may seem a little daunting at first, but after automating a few tasks you'll soon find yourself working in VB with a command window open nearby. :-) Also, note that if you prefer type checking and IntelliSense (and who doesn't), you can code against WSH using VB proper. Simply create a standard EXE project, set a project reference to the Windows Scripting Host Object Model, and code much like before:

```
Dim rShell As IWshShell_Class, lReturn As Long

Set rShell = New IWshShell_Class
lReturn = rShell.Run(...)
```

You can also set a project reference to the Microsoft Scripting Run-time for programmatic access to the `FileSystem` object, and to the COM+ Admin Type Library for programmatically administering COM+.

Chapter 2

Designing, Building, and Working with COM-Based Components

2-1 Think in terms of interfaces.

2-2 Use custom interfaces.

2-3 Define custom interfaces separately, preferably using IDL.

2-4 Avoid the limitations of class-based events with custom callbacks.

2-5 Be deliberate about maintaining compatibility.

2-6 Choose the right COM activation technique.

2-7 Beware of `Class_Terminate`.

2-8 Model in terms of sessions instead of entities.

2-9 Avoid ActiveX EXEs except for simple, small-scale needs.

Microsoft's Component Object Model is an important technology for sharing class-based code. The beauty of COM is that it is language independent, allowing developers to work in the language of their choice. It was VB, however, that first opened the door to widespread COM development.

The design of COM centers around the concept of an *interface:* Classes expose interfaces, and clients communicate with objects via these interfaces. Although VB can hide most aspects of interface-based programming, it's far better to be informed and to decide for yourself how much VB hides—and how much you explicitly embrace. If you are new to interfaces, rule 2-1 will get you started. We then encourage you to embrace fully interface-based design (rules 2-2 and 2-4), and to do so using tools outside VB (rule 2-3). Once defined, an interface is considered immutable to maintain compatibility as the component evolves. Compatibility is a subtle issue, and is the subject of rule 2-5.

The remaining rules focus on other important but less traveled techniques with respect to COM: proper COM activation and termination (rules 2-6 and 2-7), high-level class design (rule 2-8), and the move away from ActiveX EXE servers (rule 2-9).

Note that you may come across some COM-related terms that aren't defined in great detail: *in-process* DLL, *GUID*s, *registering* a server, COM *activation*, and everyone's favorite *IUnknown*. Some of the rules assume a basic COM background, so readers new to COM may need to consult one of the many available COM texts. Or, you can review the free online tutorial designed for VB programmers at www.develop.com/tutorials/vbcom.

Rule 2-1: Think in Terms of Interfaces

An *interface* defines a communication protocol between a class and a client (a user of that class). When a client references an object, the interface associated with this reference dictates what the client can and cannot do. Conceptually, we depict this relationship as shown in Figure 2.1. Note that an interface is represented by a small "lollipop" attached to the object. This symbolizes the fact that an interface is separate from, but a conduit to, the underlying implementation.

But what exactly is an interface? Consider the following employee class CEmployee:

```
'** CEmployee: class
Private sName As String
Private cSalary As Currency

Public Property Get Name() As String
   Name = sName
End Sub
Public Property Get Salary() As Currency
   Salary = cSalary
End Salary
```

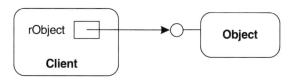

Figure 2.1 Client accessing an object through an interface

```
Public Sub ReadFromDB()
    ...         '** read from a database into private members
End Sub
Public Sub IssuePaycheck()
    ...         '** issue employee's paycheck
End Sub
```

Clients have access only to the public members—in this case, Name, Salary, ReadFromDB, and IssuePaycheck. These members constitute what is called the default interface of CEmployee. In general, an interface is simply *a set of signatures denoting the public properties and methods.* Because a class must expose at least one public member to be useful, this implies that every class in VB has at least one interface—its default.

The key point is that once an interface is published and in use by one or more clients, you should never change it. Doing so will break compatibility with your client base. For example, suppose our CEmployee class is compiled in a stand-alone COM component. Now consider the following client code written against CEmployee's default interface:

```
Dim rEmp As CEmployee      '** reference to default interface
Set rEmp = New CEmployee

rEmp.ReadFromDB
txtName.Text = rEmp.Name
txtSalary.Text = Format(rEmp.Salary, "currency")
```

If you were to change the name of CEmployee's public methods or properties and rebuild the COM component, this client code would no longer compile. If the client code was already compiled into an EXE, changing the type of

`Name` or `Salary` and rebuilding the COM component would cause a run-time failure when executing the client. In fact, any change to a public signature represents a change to an interface, and leads, ultimately, to some kind of error in code using that interface.

As a class designer, what changes can you safely make to your components over time? Because clients do not have access to private members, these can be changed at will. Of course, implementation details can also be modified, as long as the result is semantically equivalent. Lastly, note that although you cannot delete public members from an interface, you can *add* properties and methods without breaking compatibility (see rule 2-5 for a complete discussion of compatibility).

Thinking in terms of interfaces, and thus separating interface from implementation, helps you focus on a critical aspect of software development: maintaining compatibility as a system evolves. The next rule encourages you to take this one step further and actually design your classes in terms of explicit, custom interfaces. The result is that your systems become more open to change.

Rule 2-2: Use Custom Interfaces

COM is more than just a technology for building software—it is also a philosophy for building systems that evolve more easily over time. The designers of COM recognized that excessive *coupling* hinders evolution, and thus sought a mechanism that minimized the coupling between components. For example, VB clients typically reference a class directly:

```
Dim rEmp As CEmployee    '** class-based reference = default interface
```

As we know from rule 2-1, this declaration *implicitly* couples the client code to the default interface of class `CEmployee`. Because an interface represents a binding contract between client and class, this coupling prevents the class from evolving. But what if you really need to make an interface change (e.g., to extend a class's functionality or to repair a design oversight)?

The COM solution is to embrace *explicitly* interfaces in both the clients and the classes—an approach known as *interface-based programming.* Instead of presenting a single default interface, classes now publicize one or more *custom* interfaces. Clients then decide which custom interface they need, and couple to this interface much like before. The key difference, however, is that classes are free to introduce new custom interfaces over time. This allows the class to evolve and to serve new clients, yet remain backward compatible with existing clients. Interface-based programming is thus a design technique in which interfaces serve as the layer of abstraction between clients and classes. As shown in Figure 2.2, this minimizes coupling on the class itself.

How do you define a custom interface? Like classes, custom interfaces are created in VB using class modules. Unlike classes, they contain no implementation because a custom interface is simply a set of method signatures. For example, here's the default interface of CEmployee (from rule 2-1) rewritten as a custom interface named IEmployee:

```
'** class module IEmployee
Option Explicit

Public Property Get Name() As String
End Sub

Public Property Get Salary() As Currency
End Sub

Public Sub ReadFromDB()
End Sub

Public Sub IssuePaycheck()
End Sub
```

Note the absence of implementation details (i.e., private members and code). A custom interface thus represents an *abstract* class, which is conveyed in VB by setting the class's Instancing property to PublicNotCreatable. This also prevents clients from mistakenly trying to instantiate your interfaces at runtime.

Figure 2.2 Two views of an interface

Once defined, custom interfaces must be *implemented* in one or more class modules. For example, here is the class `CConsultant` that implements our custom interface `IEmployee`:

```
'** class module CConsultant
Option Explicit

Implements IEmployee

Private sName As String
Private cSalary As Currency

Private Property Get IEmployee_Name() As String
    IEmployee_Name = sName
End Sub

Private Property Get IEmployee_Salary() As Currency
    IEmployee_Salary = cSalary
End Sub

Private Sub IEmployee_ReadFromDB()
    ...         '** read from a database into private members
End Sub

Private Sub IEmployee_IssuePaycheck()
    ...         '** issue employee's paycheck
End Sub
```

Observe that every member in the class is labeled private! Clients thus cannot couple to `CConsultant` in any way, allowing it to evolve freely. Compatibility is maintained by continuing to implement `IEmployee`.

In general, clients now have a choice when accessing a class: to use its default interface or to use any one of the custom interfaces it implements. This choice is expressed by declaring your reference variables of the appropriate interface. For example, here we are accessing a `CConsultant` object through the `IEmployee` interface:

```
Dim rEmp As IEmployee          '** reference to custom interface
Set rEmp = New CConsultant     '** class that implements this interface
```

```
rEmp.ReadFromDB
txtName.Text = rEmp.Name
txtSalary.Text = Format(rEmp.Salary, "currency")
```

This situation is depicted in Figure 2.3. Note that the `CConsultant` object publicizes two interfaces: a default and `IEmployee`. VB classes always define a default interface, enabling clients to use class-based references:

```
Dim rEmp2 As CConsultant    '** class-based reference = default interface
Set rEmp2 = ...
```

This is true regardless of whether the interface is empty, which it is in the case of `CConsultant` because the class contains no public members. The variable `rEmp2` is thus useless, because there are no properties or methods to access.

Now that we can define, implement, and use custom interfaces, you may be wondering: How exactly does all this help me evolve my system more easily? Whenever you need to change a private implementation detail, merely recompile and redeploy the component (be sure to read rule 2-5 before recompiling COM components in VB). And when you need to make an interface change, simply introduce a new custom interface. In other words, suppose you want to evolve the `CConsultant` class by applying some bug fixes as well as by making a few interface changes. You would define a new interface, `IEmployee2`, implement it within `CConsultant`, apply the other bug fixes, recompile, and redeploy.

When existing clients come in contact with instances of the revised class, the result is shown in Figure 2.4 (notice the third lollipop).

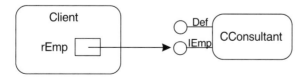

Figure 2.3 Referencing an object through a custom interface

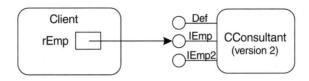

Figure 2.4 An existing client referencing a new version of class `CConsultant`

By introducing new interfaces, classes evolve to support new clients while remaining compatible with existing ones. Note that you have two choices when defining a new interface: It is completely self-contained or it works in conjunction with other interfaces. For example, suppose the motivation for `IEmployee2` is to add parameters to the method `ReadFromDB`, and also to add a method for issuing a bonus. In the first approach, you redefine the entire interface:

```
'** class module IEmployee2 (self-contained)
Option Explicit

Public Property Get Name() As String          '** unchanged
End Sub

Public Property Get Salary() As Currency      '** unchanged
End Sub

Public Sub ReadFromDB(rsCurRecord As ADODB.Recordset)
End Sub

Public Sub IssuePaycheck()                    '** unchanged
End Sub

Public Sub IssueBonus(cAmount As Currency)
End Sub
```

And then your classes implement both. For example, here's the start of the revised `CConsultant` class:

'** *class module CConsultant* (version 2)
```
Option Explicit

Implements IEmployee
Implements IEmployee2
   .
   .
   .
```

Although the class contains some redundant entry points (`Name`, `Salary`, and `IssuePaycheck` are identical in both interfaces), the advantage is that clients need to reference only one interface—either `IEmployee` or `IEmployee2`. The alternative approach is to *factor* your interfaces, such that each new interface includes only the changes and the additions. In this case, `IEmployee2` would contain just two method signatures:

'** *class module IEmployee2* (factored)
```
Option Explicit

Public Sub ReadFromDB(rsCurRecord As ADODB.Recordset)
End Sub

Public Sub IssueBonus(cAmount As Currency)
End Sub
```

This eliminates redundancy in the class, but requires more sophisticated programming in the client. For example, here's the revised client code for reading an employee from a database and displaying their name and salary:

```
Dim rEmp  As IEmployee           '** one reference var per interface
Dim rEmp2 As IEmployee2

Set rEmp  = New CConsultant      '** create object, access using IEmp
Set rEmp2 = rEmp                 '** access same object using IEmp2

rEmp2.ReadFromDB ...             '** read from DB/RS using IEmp2
txtName.Text = rEmp.Name         '** access properties using IEmp
txtSalary.Text = Format(rEmp.Salary, "currency")
```

This is depicted in Figure 2.5. Note that both variables reference the same object, albeit through different interfaces.

As your system evolves, different versions of clients and classes may come in contact with one another. For example, it's very common for classes to gain functionality over time, and thus for a single client to interact with numerous iterations of a class. This implies the need for a mechanism by which a compiled client, already deployed in production, can determine what functionality an object provides; i.e., what interfaces it currently implements. Such a mechanism, based on run-time type information (RTTI), is provided by every COM object and is accessed using VB's `TypeOf` function.

Suppose our system contains a number of different employee classes: `CConsultant`, `CTechnical`, `CAdministrative`, and so forth. All such classes implement `IEmployee`, but currently only a few have been revised to implement `IEmployee2`. Now, suppose the task at hand is to send out a bonus to every employee who is not a consultant. Assuming the employee objects are stored in a collection, we can iterate through the collection and simply check the interfaces published by each object:

```
Public Sub SendOutBonuses(colEmployees As Collection, _
                         cAmount As Currency)
   Dim rEmp As IEmployee, rEmp2 As IEmployee2

   For Each rEmp in colEmployees
      If TypeOf rEmp Is CConsultant Then  '** no bonus for you
         '** skip
      Else  '** issue this employee a bonus...
         If TypeOf rEmp Is IEmployee2 Then  '** use interface
            Set rEmp2 = rEmp
            rEmp2.IssueBonus cAmount
```

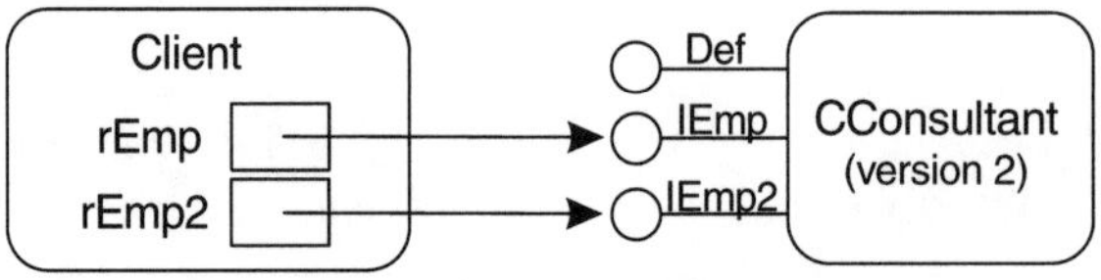

Figure 2.5 Each interface requires its own reference variable in the client

```
            Else '** issue bonus the old-fashioned way
                <human intervention is required>
            End If
        End If
    Next rEmp
End Sub
```

Even though the default interface `CConsultant` is empty, we use it as a *marker interface* to identify consultants uniquely. Of the remaining employees (all of whom receive a bonus), we check for the `IEmployee2` interface and apply the `IssusBonus` method if appropriate. Failing that, human intervention is required because the employee object does not provide an automatic mechanism. The beauty of `TypeOf` is that it is a run-time mechanism: The next time you execute it, it will respond `True` if the class has been revised to implement that interface. Thus, as more and more classes implement `IEmployee2` over time, `SendOutBonuses` will demand less and less human intervention.

The previous discussion reveals another advantage of custom interfaces—*polymorphism* (see rule 1-7 for a more precise definition). If you think of custom interfaces as reusable designs, then it makes perfect sense for different classes to implement the same interface. This leads to plug-compatible components, and a powerful, polymorphic style of programming in the client in which code is (1) reusable across different classes and (2) resilient to change as classes come and go. For example, consider once again a system with numerous employee classes that all implement `IEmployee`. As implied by Figure 2.6, our client-side code is compatible with any of these employee classes. Thus, if we need to pay everyone, this is easily done using the `IssuePaycheck` method implemented by each class:

```
Public Sub PayEveryone(colEmployees As Collection)
    Dim rEmp As IEmployee

    For Each rEmp in colEmployees
        rEmp.IssuePaycheck
    Next rEmp
End Sub
```

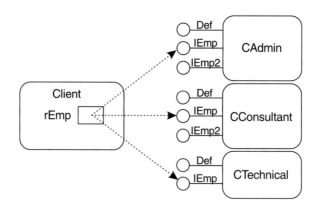

Figure 2.6 Custom interfaces encourage polymorphism

In other words, `IssuePaycheck` is polymorphic and can be applied without concern for the underlying object type. Furthermore, if new employee classes are added to the system, as long as each class implements `IEmployee`, then the previous code will continue to function correctly *without recompilation or modification.* As you can imagine, given a large system with many employee types and varying payment policies, polymorphism becomes a very attractive design technique.

Lest we all run out and start redesigning our systems, note that custom interfaces come at a price. They do require more effort, because each interface is an additional entity that must be maintained. Custom interfaces also complicate the compatibility issue, in the sense that default interfaces are easily extended (as a result of built-in support from VB) whereas custom interfaces are immutable (see rule 2-5 for a detailed discussion of maintaining compatibility in VB). Finally, scripting clients such as Internet Explorer (IE), Active Server Pages (ASP), and Windows Scripting Host (WSH) cannot access custom interfaces directly. They are currently limited to a class's default interface. This last issue is problematic given the importance of scripting clients in relation to the Web. Thankfully, a number of workarounds exist (see rule 4-5) until compiled environments (such as ASP.NET) become available.

Generally, however, the benefits of custom interfaces far outweigh the costs. Custom interfaces force you to separate design from implementation, encouraging you to think more carefully about your designs. They facilitate design reuse as well as polymorphism. Of course, custom interfaces also serve to minimize coupling between clients and classes, allowing your classes to evolve more freely while maintaining compatibility. As a result, you'll be able to "field-replace" components as business rules change or bug fixes are applied, insert new components of like behavior without having to revisit client code, and define new behavior without disturbing existing clients. You should thus consider the use of custom interfaces in all your object-oriented systems, but especially large-scale ones in which design and coupling have a dramatic effect.

Custom interfaces are so important that COM is based entirely on interfaces. Clients cannot access COM objects any other way. Hence, COM programmers are interface-based programmers. In fact, there exists a language, the Interface Description Language (IDL), solely for describing interfaces. Often called "the true language of COM," IDL is what allows a COM object developed in programming environment X to be accessed from a client written in programming environment Y. Although typically hidden from VB programmers, there are definite advantages to using IDL explicitly to describe your custom interfaces. Read on; we discuss this further in the next rule.

Rule 2-3: Define Custom Interfaces Separately, Preferably Using IDL

Interface-based programming is a powerful mechanism for building systems that evolve more easily over time. The importance of this programming style is evident in the design of Java, which raised interfaces to the same level as classes. Of course, COM is another compelling example of the significance of interfaces.

A custom interface is nothing more than a set of method signatures defined as a stand-alone entity. As discussed in the previous rule, however, this simple concept enables a wide range of advantages—in design, reuse, and evolution. The proposal here is to take this one step further and to define the interfaces separately.

In VB interfaces are typically defined as `PublicNotCreatable` class modules and are then implemented in `MultiUse` class modules within the same project (see the previous rule if you have never worked with custom interfaces). Although this is a perfectly adequate approach to implementation, there is a significant drawback: When you hand out your interfaces as class modules, you are essentially giving out the source code. This opens up the possibility that others may change your interfaces, thus altering your design and breaking compatibility with your clients. Whether the changes are accidental or intentional, this is a dangerous loophole.

As shown in Figure 2.7, the simplest precaution is to define your interfaces in a separate ActiveX DLL project, compile and hand out the resulting DLL file. Class implementers then create a *separate* VB project, set a project reference to this DLL, and implement the custom interfaces as before. Likewise, the client (typically denoted by a standard EXE project) must also set a reference to the interface's DLL. This scenario is depicted in Figure 2.8. Note that the client project actually references both the interface's DLL and the class's DLL. The former is needed to declare variables referencing a custom interface, whereas the latter is necessary to instantiate classes using New. For example,

```
Dim rEmp As IEmployee        '** need interface information
Set rEmp = New CConsultant   '** new class information
```

Keep in mind that a COM-based DLL must be *registered* on your machine before it can be referenced from a VB project. This can be done using the Windows utility RegSvr32, or through the Browse button available off the Project >> References menu item in VB.

Although separating your interfaces into a separate VB project is an improvement, it is somewhat confusing to use an executable DLL to represent

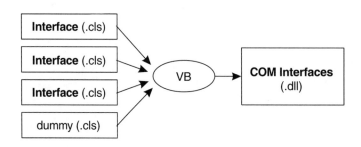

Figure 2.7 Defining custom interfaces separately in VB

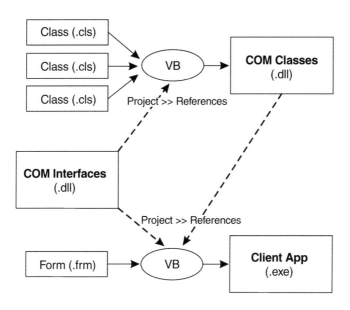

Figure 2.8 Accessing the custom interface's DLL in other VB projects

entities that contain no implementation! Furthermore, because ActiveX DLL projects must contain at least one public class, to make this work you must define a dummy `MultiUse` class along with your `PublicNotCreatable` interface classes (see Figure 2.7).[1] However, the most significant disadvantage to this approach is that VB allows you to extend your custom interfaces, without warning, even though the result breaks compatibility with your clients. For example, accidentally adding a method to an interface and recompiling the interface's DLL will break both the class implementer and the client application. This is true regardless of VB's *compatibility mode* setting when working with your interfaces (see rule 2-5).

The alternative, and better approach, is to do what C++ and Java programmers have been doing for years: defining their interfaces separately using IDL. IDL is a small C-like language solely for describing interfaces, and is often called "the true language of COM" because it is what enables clients and COM

---

[1] This is not true of ActiveX EXE projects, so you can avoid dummy classes if you want.

DESIGNING, BUILDING, AND WORKING WITH COM-BASED COMPONENTS

components to understand each other. Thus, the idea is to abandon VB, define your interfaces as a text file using IDL, compile this file using Microsoft's IDL compiler (MIDL), and deploy the resulting binary form, known as a *type library* (TLB).[2] This is outlined in Figure 2.9. Once you have a TLB definition of your interfaces, your clients simply set a project reference to the TLB file instead of the interface's DLL file (Figure 2.10). Note that TLBs are registered using the *RegTLib* utility, or via the Browse button under VB's Project >> References.[3]

The advantage to using IDL and MIDL is that you, and only you, can change an interface or break compatibility. You have complete control over your design, and exactly when and how it evolves. The drawback is that you have to learn yet another language. The good news is that we'll show you a way to generate automatically 98 percent of the IDL you'll need. But first, let's take a peek at what IDL looks like. As an example, consider the following VB interface IEmployee:

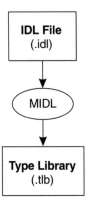

Figure 2.9   Defining custom interfaces separately using IDL

---

[2] MIDL is a command-line utility that ships as part of Visual Studio (newer versions are available in the Win32 SDK). Another tool, MkTypLib, performs the same function but accepts a slightly different interface language. We recommend the use of MIDL.

[3] Unless otherwise specified, all utilities mentioned here ship with Visual Studio. To provide easy access in a command window, run VCVars32.BAT to set up you path.

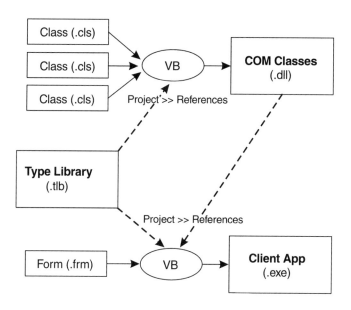

Figure 2.10 Accessing the custom interface's TLB in other VB projects

```
Public Name As String

Public Sub ReadFromDB(rsCurRecord As ADODB.Recordset)
End Sub

Public Function IssuePaycheck() As Currency
End Function
```

To make things more clear, let's first rewrite this as a custom interface (no data members), with parameter passing explicitly defined:

```
Private Property Get Name() As String
End Property

Private Property Let Name(ByVal sRHS As String)
End Property

Public Sub ReadFromDB(ByRef rsCurRec As ADODB.Recordset)
End Sub
```

DESIGNING, BUILDING, AND WORKING WITH COM-BASED COMPONENTS

```
Public Function IssuePaycheck() As Currency
End Function
```

Now, here is the equivalent COM-based interface in IDL:

```
[
    uuid(E1689529-01FD-42EA-9C7D-96A137290BD8),
    version(1.0),
    helpstring("Interfaces type library (v1.0)")
]
library Interfaces
{
    importlib("stdole2.tlb");

    [
        object,
        uuid(E9F57454-9725-4C98-99D3-5F9324A73173),
        oleautomation
    ]
    interface IEmployee : IUnknown {
        [propget] HRESULT Name([out, retval] BSTR* ps);
        [propput] HRESULT Name([in] BSTR s);

        HRESULT ReadFromDB([in, out] _Recordset** pprs);
        HRESULT IssuePaycheck([out, retval] CURRENCY* pc);
    };
};
```

This IDL description defines a TLB named Interfaces, which is tagged with three *attributes* (values within square brackets). When registered, the helpstring attribute makes the TLB visible to VB programmers as "Interfaces type library (v1.0)," whereas internally it is represented by the *globally unique identifier (GUID)* E1689529-01FD-42EA-9C7D-96A137290BD8 because of the uuid attribute. The library contains one interface, IEmployee, uniquely identified by the GUID E9F57454-9725=4C98-99D3-5F9324A73173. The remaining attributes define the version of IDL we are using (object) and enable automatic proxy/stub generation (oleautomation). IEmployee consists of four method signatures, each of which is defined as a function returning a 32-bit COM error code (HRESULT). Note that VB functions (such as

`IssuePaycheck`) are redefined to return their values invisibly via an additional `out` parameter. Finally, for each method, the VB parameter type is translated to the equivalent IDL data type, and the parameter-passing mechanism (`ByVal` versus `ByRef`) is transformed to its semantic equivalent (`in` versus `in/out`). The most common mappings from VB to IDL data types are shown in Table 2.1.

In general, a TLB may contain any number of interface definitions. When writing IDL, the first step is to assign the TLB and each interface a GUID. GUIDs can be generated using the `GuidGen` utility: Select Registry Format, press New GUID, then Copy, and paste the resulting GUID into your IDL file. Next, assign the TLB and interfaces the same set of attributes shown earlier. Finally, define each interface. Once you have the IDL file, simply run MIDL to compile it (see Figure 2.9). For example, here's the compilation of `Interfaces.idl`:

midl Interfaces.idl

Table 2.1   VB-to-IDL data type mappings

VB	IDL
Byte	unsigned char
Integer	short
Long	long
Single	float
Double	double
Array	SAFEARRAY(<type>) *
Boolean	VARIANT_BOOL
Currency	CURRENCY
Date	DATE
Object	IDispatch *
String	BSTR
Variant	VARIANT

This produces the TLB `Interfaces.tlb`. The interfaces are now ready for use by your clients (see Figure 2.10).[4] Note that your clients do not have to be written in VB. For example, class implementers can use C++ if they prefer. In fact, another advantage of using IDL is that MIDL can automatically generate the additional support files needed by other languages.

Although writing IDL is not hard, it is yet another language that you must learn. Furthermore, you must be careful to use only those IDL constructs and types that are compatible with VB. This is because of the fact that IDL is able to describe interfaces for many different object-oriented programming languages (C++, Java, and so on), but only a subset of these interfaces are usable in VB. Thus, writing IDL from scratch is not a very appealing process for VB programmers.

Luckily, Figure 2.11 presents an easy way to generate VB-compatible IDL automatically. Given a VB ActiveX DLL (or EXE), the `OLEView` utility can be used as a decompiler to reverse engineer the IDL from the DLL's embedded TLB (put there by VB). Obviously, if we start with a DLL built by VB, the resulting IDL should be VB compatible! The first step is to define your interfaces using VB, as discussed earlier (see Figure 2.7). Then, run `OLEView` (one of the Visual Studio tools available via the Start menu) and open your DLL file via File >> View TypeLib. You'll be presented with the reverse-engineered IDL. Save this as an IDL file. Edit the file, defining a new GUID for the TLB as well as for each interface, Enum, and UDT. Now compile the IDL with MIDL, unregister the VB DLL, and register the TLB. In a nutshell, that's it.

Figure 2.11 Reverse-engineering IDL using `OLEView`

---

[4] Note that class implementers should continue to work in *binary compatibility* mode. See rule 2-5.

Unfortunately, `OLEView` is not perfect: You will want to modify the resulting IDL file before compiling it with MIDL. If your interfaces use the VB data type `Single`, the IDL will incorrectly use `Single` as well. Search the file and change all occurrences of `Single` to `float`. Also, if your interfaces define a UDT called `X`, the equivalent IDL definition will be incorrect. Manually change `struct tagX {...}` to `struct X {...}`. Finally, you'll want to delete some unnecessary text from the IDL file. In particular, it will contain one or more *coclass* (or COM class) definitions, including the dummy class you may have defined for VB to compile your interfaces classes. For example, suppose `Interfaces.DLL` contains the `IEmployee` interface class we discussed earlier, as well as a `CDummy` class. Decompiling the DLL with `OLEView` yields

```
// Generated .IDL file (by the OLE/COM Object Viewer)
//
// typelib filename: Interfaces.DLL
[
    uuid(E1689529-01FD-42EA-9C7D-96A137290BD8),
    version(1.0),
    helpstring("Interfaces type library (v1.0)")
]
library Interfaces
{
    // TLib :   // TLib : Microsoft ADO : {...}
    importlib("msado15.DLL");
    // TLib :   // TLib : OLE Automation : {...}
    importlib("stdole2.tlb");

    // Forward declare all types defined in this typelib
    interface _IEmployee;
    interface _CDummy;

    [
        odl,
        uuid(E9F57454-9725-4C98-99D3-5F9324A73173),
        version(1.0),
        hidden,
        dual,
        nonextensible,
        oleautomation
    ]
```

```
interface _IEmployee : IDispatch {
    [id(0x40030000), propget]
    HRESULT Name([out, retval] BSTR* Name);
    [id(0x40030000), propput]
    HRESULT Name([in] BSTR Name);
    [id(0x60030000)]
    HRESULT ReadFromDB([in, out] _Recordset** );
    [id(0x60030001)]
    HRESULT IssuePaycheck([out, retval] CURRENCY* );
};

[ ... ]
coclass IEmployee {
    [default] interface _IEmployee;
};

[ ... ]
interface _CDummy : IDispatch {
    [id(0x60030000)]
    HRESULT foo();
};

[ ... ]
coclass CDummy {
    [default] interface _CDummy;
};
};
```

At the very least, your IDL file must contain the code shown in boldface and italic. The rest can be safely deleted. Note that VB defines the name of an interface by starting with the _ character (e.g., _IEmployee). Delete this character as well. Next, you should change each interface `odl` attribute to `object`, and `IDispatch` reference to `IUnknown`. Finally, consider adding `helpstring` attributes not only to your interfaces, Enums, and UDTs, but to their individual elements as well. This information is visible when others browse your TLB, yielding a convenient form of documentation.

You are now ready to begin using IDL for defining your interfaces, and to reap the advantages that C++ and Java programmers have been enjoying for years: separating design from implementation, and retaining complete control over when and how your interfaces change. No one else can alter your design, and only you can break compatibility with clients. The many advantages of custom interfaces rely on your ability to maintain compatibility, and IDL is the best way to go about doing this.

Rule 2-4: Avoid the Limitations of Class-Based Events with Custom Callbacks

The notion of *events* and *event handling* has been a central feature of VB since its inception. The most common case is graphical user interface (GUI) building, which typically requires the programming of form `Load` and `Unload` events, command button `Click` events, and text box `Validate` events. But you can also define and raise your own custom, *class-based* events. For example, the class `CConsultant` could raise a `Changed` event whenever one or more data fields in the object are updated:

```
'** class module CConsultant
Option Explicit

Implements IEmployee

Private sName As String

Public Event Changed()     '** event definition: Changed

Private Property Get IEmployee_Name() As String
    IEmployee_Name = sName
End Sub

Private Property Let IEmployee_Name(ByVal sRHS As String)
    sName = sRHS
    RaiseEvent Changed     '** name was changed, so raise event!
End Sub
    .
    .
    .
```

Any client that holds a reference to a `CConsultant` object now has the option to handle this event, and thus be notified whenever *that* employee's data changes:

```
'** form module denoting client
Option Explicit

Private WithEvents employee As CConsultant    '** client reference

Private Sub employee_Changed()                 '** event handler
    <update form to reflect change in employee object>
End Sub
```

In essence, events enable an object to *call back* to its clients, as shown in Figure 2.12.

Unfortunately, VB's class-based event mechanism has a number of limitations. For the client, the `WithEvents` key word can be applied only to module-level reference variables; arrays, collections, and local variables are not compatible with events. For the class designer, events must be defined in the class that raises them, preventing you from defining a single set of events for reuse across multiple classes. In particular, this means you cannot incorporate events in your custom interfaces, such as `IEmployee`:

```
'** class module IEmployee
Option Explicit

Public Name As String

Public Event Changed()    '** unfortunately, this doesn't work...

Public Sub ReadFromDB(rsCurRecord As ADODB.Recordset)
End Sub

Public Function IssuePaycheck() As Currency
End Function
```

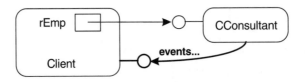

Figure 2.12 Events are really just a callback mechanism

Although VB accepts this event definition, you'll be unable to raise this event from any of your classes.

The solution to these limitations is to design your own event mechanism based on custom interfaces. Consider once again Figure 2.12. Notice that events represent nothing more than an interface implemented by one or more clients. For example, here is a custom interface `IEmployeeEvents` that defines the `Changed` event:

```
'** class module IEmployeeEvents
Option Explicit

Public Sub Changed(rEmp As IEmployee)
End Sub
```

The difference is that events are represented as ordinary subroutines; in this case, with an explicit parameter providing a reference back to the object for ease of access. To receive events, the client now implements the appropriate interface, such as `IEmployeeEvents`:

```
'** form module denoting client
Option Explicit

Implements IEmployeeEvents

Private Sub IEmployeeEvents_Changed(rEmp As IEmployee)
    <update form to reflect change in rEmp.Name, etc.>
End Sub
```

However, we must mention one little detail: How does the object get that reference back to the client, as shown in Figure 2.12? The *object* will raise the event by making a call like this:[5]

```
rClient.Changed Me
```

But who sets this `rClient` reference variable?

---

[5] If the object executing this code is configured for MTS, you must pass SafeRef(Me).

The client does, by calling the object to set up the callback mechanism. Thus, before any events can occur, the *client* must first call the object and *register* itself:[6]

```
rObject.Register Me      '** register a reference back to ME, the client
```

This means the object must expose a `Register` method. Likewise, the object should expose an `Unregister` method so that clients can stop receiving events:

```
rObject.Unregister Me    '** unregister ME, the client
```

Because every object that wishes to raise events must provide a means of client registration, the best approach is to define these methods in a custom interface and to reuse this design across all your event-raising classes. The following interface `IRegisterClient` summarizes this approach:

```
'** class module IRegisterClient
Option Explicit

Public Enum IRegisterClientErrors
    eIntfNotImplemented = vbObjectError + 8193
    eAlreadyRegistered
    eNotRegistered
End Enum

Public Sub Register(rClient As Object)
End Sub

Public Sub Unregister(rClient As Object)
End Sub
```

Now, every class that wishes to raise events simply implements `IRegisterClient`.

As shown in Figure 2.13, the end result is a pair of custom interfaces, `IRegisterClient` and `IEmployeeEvents`. The object implements

---

[6] Likewise, if the client executing this code is configured for MTS, pass SafeRef(Me).

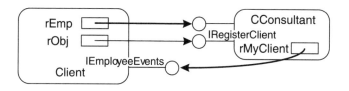

Figure 2.13 An event mechanism based on custom interfaces

`IRegister Client` so that a client can register for events, whereas the client implements `IEmployeeEvents` so the object can call back when the events occur. For completeness, here's the `CConsultant` class revised to take advantage of our custom event mechanism:

```
'** class module CConsultant
Option Explicit

Implements IRegisterClient
Implements IEmployee

Private sName As String
Private rMyClient As IEmployeeEvents    '** ref back to client

Private Sub IRegisterClient_Register(rClient As Object)
    If Not TypeOf rClient Is IEmployeeEvents Then
        Err.Raise eIntfNotImplemented, ...
    ElseIf Not rMyClient Is Nothing Then
        Err.Raise eAlreadyRegistered, ...
    Else
        Set rMyClient = rClient
    End If
End Sub

Private Sub IRegisterClient_Unregister(rClient As Object)
    If Not rMyClient Is rClient Then
        Err.Raise eNotRegistered
    Else
        Set rMyClient = Nothing
    End If
End Sub
```

DESIGNING, BUILDING, AND WORKING WITH COM-BASED COMPONENTS

```
    Private Property Get IEmployee_Name() As String
        IEmployee_Name = sName
    End Sub

    Private Property Let IEmployee_Name(ByVal sRHS As String)
        sName = sRHS

        On Error Resume Next    '** ignore unreachable/problematic clients
        rMyClient.Changed Me    '** name was changed, so raise event!
    End Sub
        .
        .
        .
```

The first step is to save the client's reference in a private variable (`rMyClient`) when he registers. Then, whenever we need to raise an event, we simply call the client via this reference. Finally, when the client unregisters, we reset the private variable back to `Nothing`. Note that the `Register` and `Unregister` methods perform error checking to make sure that (1) the client is capable of receiving events, (2) the client is not already registered, and (3) the correct client is being unregistered. Furthermore, to handle multiple clients, also note that the previous approach is easily generalized by replacing `rMyClient` with a collection of client references.

To complete the example, let's assume on the client side that we have a VB form object that instantiates a number of employee objects (`CConsultant`, `CTechnical`, `CAdministrative`, and so on) and displays them on the screen. The client's first responsibility is to implement the custom `IEmployeeEvents` interface so it can receive the `Changed` event:

```
    '** form module denoting client
    Option Explicit

    Private colEmployees As New Collection    '** collection of object refs

    Implements IEmployeeEvents

    Private Sub IEmployeeEvents_Changed(rEmp As IEmployee)
        <update form to reflect change in rEmp.Name, etc.>
    End Sub
```

Here the `Changed` event is used to drive the updating of the form. Before the client can receive these events however, it must register with each employee object *that supports "eventing."* In this case we assume the employees are created during the form's `Load` event based on records from a database:

```
Private Sub Form_Load()
    <open DB and retrieve a RS of employee records>

    Dim rEmp As IEmployee, rObj As IRegisterClient

    Do While Not rsEmployees.EOF
        Set rEmp =CreateObject(rsEmployees("ProgID").Value)

        If TypeOf rEmp Is IRegisterClient Then '** event based
            Set rObj = rEmp      '** switch to register interface...
            rObj.Register Me     '** and register myself to receive events
        End If

        rEmp.ReadFromDB rsEmployees
        colEmployees.Add rEmp
        rsEmployees.MoveNext
    Loop

    <close DB and RS>
End Sub
```

Lastly, the client is also responsible for unregistering when it no longer wishes to receive events. This task is performed during form `Unload` (i.e., when the form is no longer visible):

```
Private Sub Form_Unload(Cancel As Integer)
    Dim rEmp As IEmployee, rObj As IRegisterClient
    Dim l As Long

    For l = colEmployees.Count To 1 Step -1
        Set rEmp = colEmployees.Item(l)
        colEmployees.Remove l
```

```
        If TypeOf rEmp Is IRegisterClient Then  '** event based
            Set rObj = rEmp           '** switch to register interface...
            rObj.Unregister Me        '** and unregister myself
        End If
    Next 1
End Sub
```

Note that unregistering is important to break the cyclic reference formed between the client and the object.

Although custom callbacks require more effort to set up than VBs built-in event mechanism, the benefits are many: reusable designs, better callback performance, and more flexibility during implementation.[7] For example, an object with multiple clients can apply a priority-based event notification scheme if desired. In the greater scheme of things, custom callbacks also illustrate the power of using interfaces to design flexible solutions to everyday problems.

Rule 2-5: Be Deliberate About Maintaining Compatibility

In a COM-based system, clients communicate with objects via interfaces. These interfaces must be well-defined, registered, and agreed on by all parties for your system to run properly (Figure 2.14). The good news is that this is relatively easy to ensure in your first release: Recompile the COM servers, then recompile the clients and deploy.

However, at some point you will be faced with recompiling and redeploying one of your COM servers—perhaps to apply bug fixes or to add new functionality. In this case, what happens to the clients? You can either (1) redeploy all new clients to match or (2) ensure that your COM server maintains *compatibility* with the existing clients. Although the latter is typically preferred (and certainly less work), it requires that you have a solid understanding of COM's rules for *versioning,* and how VB applies those rules. Otherwise, recompiling a COM server can lead to all sorts of errors on the client side, from "Can't create object" and "Type mismatch" to the dreaded GPF.

---

[7] Keep in mind that security may be an issue if raising events across processes/machines, because the object needs permission to call the client.

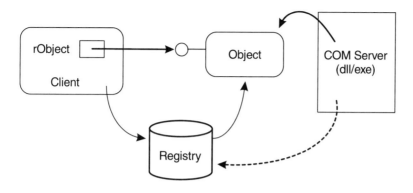

Figure 2.14 COM requires that servers (and their interfaces) be registered

Before we start, let's review some important concepts in COM. A typical COM server is a DLL/EXE that defines one or more classes, one or more interfaces, and a TLB that summarizes this information. Every class, interface, and TLB is assigned a unique 128-bit integer called a *GUID*. These are referred to as *CLSIDs*, *IIDs*, and *LibIDs*, respectively. GUIDs are compiled in the COM server that defines them, make their way into the registry when the COM server is registered, and usually get compiled in the clients as well. COM *activation* is the process of creating an instance of a class from a COM server, triggered, for example, when a client executes New. To activate, COM requires both a CLSID and an IID, locates the COM server via the registry, asks the COM server to create the instance, and then obtains the proper interface reference for return to the client. As discussed in rule 2-3, you can use the OLEView utility to view the contents of a server's TLB and to see the GUIDs firsthand.

Lastly, it's very important to understand the difference between a default interface and a custom one. Review rules 2-1 and 2-2 if necessary.

To maintain compatibility with clients, the short answer is that when recompiling a COM server, you need to focus on three things: functionality, interfaces, and GUIDs. Obviously, although implementation details may change, the server's overall functionality must be compatible from one version to the next. Second, the interfaces exposed by each class should not change in any way. Methods cannot be deleted, their names cannot differ, and their parameters cannot vary (not in number, type, or order). Finally, the identifying GUIDs should not change (i.e., the CLSIDs, IIDs, and LibID). Let's look at these compatibility issues in more detail.

Scripting Clients

The first step is to understand your clients. There are two types: *scripting* and *compiled.* Scripting clients are typically written in VBScript or JavaScript and are executed in environments such as ASP, IE, or WSH. The key characteristic of a scripting client is its use of generic object references:

```
Dim rObj        '** As Variant / Object
```

This typeless variable represents a *late-bound* (indirect, less efficient) connection to an object's *default interface.*[8,9] In addition, scripting clients typically create objects using VB's CreateObject function, passing the appropriate ProgID (a string denoting the TLB followed by a class name):

```
Set rObj = CreateObject("Employees.CConsultant")
```

CreateObject first converts the ProgID to a CLSID (via the registry), and then performs a standard COM activation.[10] Once activated, a scripting client may call any method in the object's default interface. For example,

```
rObj.IssuePaycheck
```

This assumes that IssuePaycheck is a public subroutine within class CConsultant.

Thus, maintaining compatibility in your COM server amounts to preserving the ProgIDs and the default interfaces. The ProgIDs are easy to deal with: Simply do not change the name of your TLB or your classes. When building COM servers in VB, note that your TLB's name is derived from your VB project's

---

[8] Every method call typically requires two calls (lookup then invoke), with variants used to pass parameters. This approach is based on COM's IDispatch interface.

[9] As discussed in rule 4-2, scripting clients cannot access custom interfaces.

[10] Where does CreateObject get the IID? It uses the well-known IID for IDispatch, COM's predefined late-bound interface. This maps to the default interface of a VB class.

name (a project property). As for the default interfaces, for each class you cannot delete any public subroutine or function, nor can you change its method signature. However, note that because clients are late-bound and parameters are thus passed as variants, it is possible to change a parameter's type in some cases and still maintain compatibility. For example, suppose a class originally contained the following method:

```
Public Sub SomeMethod(ByVal iValue As Integer)
```

This can evolve to

```
Public Sub SomeMethod(ByVal lValue As Long)
```

without breaking compatibility because `Integer` is upward compatible with `Long`.

Finally, it is worth noting that compiled environments also behave like a scripting client when object references are generic. In VB, this occurs whenever clients use the `Variant` or `Object` data type:

```
Dim rObj2 As Object     '** this says I want to be late-bound
Dim rObj3 As Variant    '** likewise...
```

Each reference denotes a late-bound connection to an object, regardless of how that object is created:

```
Set rObj2 = New Employees.CConsultant
Set rObj3 = CreateObject("Employees.CConsultant")
```

In this case, the same compatibility rules apply, with the exception that the client's use of `New` requires that the COM server's CLSIDs and default IIDs also remain unchanged. This is discussed in the next section.

Compiled Clients

Compiled clients are characterized by object references of a specific interface type, for example:

```
Dim rObj4 As Employees.IEmployee    '** a custom interface
Dim rObj5 As Employees.CConsultant  '** the default interface
```

These variables represent a *vtable-bound* (direct, efficient) connection to a specific interface of an object. These interface types must be defined by your COM server—or more precisely, in its TLB—which the client must reference. Object creation is typically done using `New` or `CreateObject`:

```
Set rObj4 = CreateObject("Employees.CConsultant")
Set rObj5 = New Employees.CConsultant
```

Regardless of how the objects are created, at this point the reference `rObj4` can be used to call methods in the custom interface `IEmployee`, whereas `rObj5` can be used to call methods in `CConsultant`'s default interface.

From the perspective of compatibility, the key observation about compiled clients is that they refer to interfaces and classes by name. As a result, when the client code is compiled, the corresponding IIDs and CLSIDs are embedded into the resulting EXE. Thus, maintaining compatibility with compiled clients requires that you preserve not only the ProgIDs and the interfaces, but the GUIDs as well.

Much like scripting clients, the ProgIDs and interfaces are under your control. However, VB is in charge of generating the necessary GUIDs whenever you compile your COM server. So how can you prevent VB from changing these values during recompilation? By manipulating your project's *version compatibility* setting, as shown in Figure 2.15.

The first setting, No Compatibility, means precisely that. If you recompile, all GUIDs will be changed, thereby breaking compatibility with compiled clients. This setting lets you intentionally break compatibility (e.g., when you need to begin a new development effort). The second setting, Project Compatibility, is meant to preserve compatibility with other *developers*. In this case the LibID and CLSIDs are preserved, but the IIDs change. This allows references to your TLB to remain valid (i.e., references to your COM server from other VB projects), as well as class references embedded in Web pages. However, the IIDs continue to change, reflecting the fact that the server is still under construction. The rationale for this setting is team development, and thus the setting should be used when you are developing classes that you must share with others before the design is complete. To help track versions, note that VB changes the version number of your COM server's TLB by a factor of one each

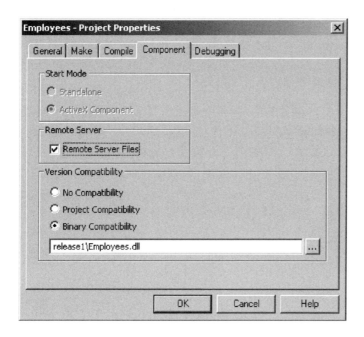

Figure 2.15 VB's version compatibility settings

time you recompile. The third and final setting is Binary Compatibility, in which all GUIDs are preserved from one compilation to the next. This is VB's "deployment" setting, because it enables you to maintain compatibility with compiled clients out in production. Thus, you should switch to binary compatibility mode (and remain there) as soon as you release the first version of your COM server. Note that binary compatibility is necessary even if your interfaces and IIDs are defined separately, because of the fact that your clients may be dependent on the default interfaces generated by VB.[11]

When working in binary compatibility, it's important to understand that VB needs a copy of your released DLL/EXE to maintain compatibility when you recompile. Notice the reference in Figure 2.15 to "release1\Employees.DLL." VB simply copies the GUIDs from the referenced file and uses them to generate the new COM server. It's considered good practice to build each release in

---

[11] For example, see using IDL as discussed in rule 2-3.

a separate directory (release 1, release 2, and so on) so that you can always recompile against an earlier version if necessary.[12] In general, however, make sure your binary compatibility setting always references the most recent production release. To prevent accidental overwriting, it's also a good idea to keep your release DLLs/EXEs in a version control system for read-only checkout.

Besides retaining GUIDs, binary compatibility mode also protects your interfaces. In particular, VB prevents you from making any changes that might break compatibility. For example, changing a method's parameter type from `Integer`

```
Public Sub SomeMethod(ByVal iValue As Integer)
```

to `Long`

```
Public Sub SomeMethod(ByVal lValue As Long)
```

yields the warning dialog shown in Figure 2.16. At this point, unless you are absolutely sure of what you are doing, you should *cancel* and then either restore the method signature, switch compatibility mode, or define a new interface containing your change.[13] Note that variants can be used as parameter types to give you some flexibility for future evolution without the need to change explicitly the type in the interface.

Version-Compatible Interfaces

The COM purist would argue that when you need to change an interface, you do so by defining a completely new one. This makes versioning easier to track, because each interface will have a distinct name (and IID). Although this may lead to more work within your COM servers, it enables a client to differentiate between versions, and thus remain backward compatible with your earlier COM servers. For example, a client can test for version 2 of the `IEmployee` interface before trying to use it:

---

[12] For example, if you accidentally break compatibility, you can rereference the proper release version in binary compatibility mode to restore compatibility.

[13] The option to Break compatibility causes all the IIDs to change (much like project compatibility), whereas Preserve compatibility retains the IIDs. Either way, the physical interface is changed. The latter could be selected, for example, if no one is calling `SomeMethod`.

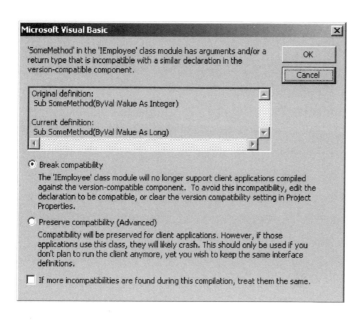

Figure 2.16 VB's warning dialog that an interface has changed

```
If TypeOf rEmp Is IEmployee2 Then '** is v2 available in this object?
    Dim rEmp2 As IEmployee2
    Set rEmp2 = rEmp

    <use rEmp2 to access v2 of IEmployee interface>

    Set rEmp2 = Nothing
End If
```

As a result, new clients can be released before servers are upgraded, or can continue to function properly if servers are downgraded for some reason.

However, although COM purists argue in favor of maintaining *version-identical* interfaces, VB implements a more flexible (but dangerous) notion known as *version-compatible* interfaces. In short, VB's binary compatibility mode actually allows one type of interface change: You may *add* methods to the default interface. When you do so, VB is careful to add the new methods to the end of the class's underlying vtable, generating a single default interface that is compatible with both old and new clients. Note that VB increases the version number of your COM server's TLB by 0.1 to reflect the fact that the interface changed.

Interestingly, VB isn't breaking the rules of COM, because it generates a new IID to identify the resulting interface. To maintain compatibility, VB must produce code within the COM server so that objects recognize both the new and the old IIDs when queried at run-time. Likewise, the registry must be reconfigured to support the fact that multiple IIDs map to the same physical interface. In particular, the original interface *forwards* to the new interface, as shown in Figure 2.17. Note that interface forwarding is direct. If you add a method from release 1 to release 2, and then add another method in release 3, releases 1 and 2 both forward to release 3.

Why does VB offer this feature? To make it easier for your classes to evolve. Why is this feature dangerous? First of all, there is only one version of an interface from the perspective of the client—the most recent one. VB clients thus cannot use `TypeOf` to determine which version of an interface is available. This makes it harder for clients to achieve backward compatibility with earlier versions of your COM server. Second, VB only provides support for extending the default interface. You cannot add methods to custom interfaces such as `IEmployee`. In fact, adding methods to a custom interface yields no warning from VB, yet breaks compatibility with your clients (even in binary compatibility mode!). Finally, some client-side setup programs fail to register properly the necessary interface forwarding information, leading to COM activation errors at run-time. This is a known problem (e.g., with MTS's `export` command).[14]

Figure 2.17 Forwarding to a version-compatible interface

---

[14] See Microsoft Knowledge Base (KB) article Q241637 in the MSDN library.

The safer alternative is that of the COM purist: Use custom interfaces, and define a new interface whenever changes are needed from one release to another. Note that avoiding these dangers is also one of the reasons we recommend defining your custom interfaces outside VB. See rule 2-3 for more details.[15]

COM is a somewhat fragile system, requiring that all participants agree—servers, clients, and registries alike. Because most applications live beyond version 1, maintaining compatibility in the presence of evolution and recompilation becomes one of the most important aspects of COM programming. Although the nuances may be complex, the overall solution is straightforward: Develop in project compatibility, deploy in binary compatibility, and use custom interfaces whenever possible.

Rule 2-6: Choose the Right COM Activation Technique

In VB, the traditional mechanism for creating an object is the `New` operator. For example,

```
Set rEmp = New Employees.CConsultant
```

creates a new instance of the `CConsultant` class. However, this is not the only alternative. If the class is registered as a COM component, you can also use `CreateObject` and `GetObject`:

```
Set rEmp2 = CreateObject("Employees.CConsultant")
Set rEmp3 = GetObject("", "Employees.CConsultant")
```

On the other hand, if the class is configured to run under MTS, then you should probably be using `CreateInstance` instead:

```
Set rEmp4 = GetObjectContext.CreateInstance( _
                         "Employees.CConsultant")
```

---

[15] See also Microsoft KB articles Q190078, Q190967, and Q191214.

Finally, as if this wasn't enough, when you are writing server-side ASP code you will want to use `Server.CreateObject`:

```
Set rEmp5 = Server.CreateObject( _
                     "Employees.CConsultant")
```

Do you know when to use each technique? If not, then read on . . .

First off, let's clear up a common misconception about how clients bind to objects at run-time.[16] Logically, the situation is depicted in Figure 2.18. Clients hold references to interfaces and use these references to access objects. Physically, however, the binding mechanism used between client and object can vary, *depending on how the reference variables are declared in the client.* There are two main approaches: *vtable-binding* and *late-binding.* The former is more efficient, because the client is bound directly to an interface's implementation. This is available only in compiled environments such as VB, VC++, and soon ASP.Net. For example, the following two declarations dictate vtable-binding (1) to the default interface of class `CConsultant` and (2) to the custom interface `IEmployee`:

```
Dim rEmp1 As Employees.CConsultant    '** (1) default interface
Dim rEmp2 As Employees.IEmployee      '** (2) custom interface
```

This is true regardless of how the objects are created. Regardless of whether the client uses `New` or `CreateObject` or some other mechanism,

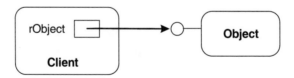

Figure 2.18 A client holding a reference to an object

---

[16] This discussion is a summary of the more detailed scripting client versus compiled client discussion held earlier in rule 2-5. Rule 2-5 should be read first if COM is new to you.

rEmp1 and rEmp2 are vtable-bound to the objects they reference. In contrast, consider the following declarations:

```
Dim rEmp3 As Variant
Dim rEmp4 As Object
Dim rEmp5                    '** implies Variant
```

These references all dictate late-binding, a less efficient mechanism based on COM's IDispatch interface (and one that always maps to the object's default interface). Again, this is true regardless of how the objects are created. For example, any use of rEmp5 is late-bound, even if the object is created using New:

```
Set rEmp5 = New Employees.CConsultant
rEmp5.SomeMethod    '** this implies a lookup of SomeMethod, then invoke
```

Although late-binding is possible in compiled environments like VB (using the previous declarations), it is the only binding technique available in scripting environments such as IE, ASP, and WSH.

Note that the object being created must support the type of binding requested by the client; otherwise a run-time error occurs. Objects built with VB automatically support both vtable-binding and late-binding.

COM Activation

COM activation is the process by which a client creates a COM object at run-time. It is a somewhat complex process that involves the client, GUIDs, the COM infrastructure, one or more registries, and the COM server. Although the details are interesting, what's important here are the goals of activation: (1) create the object and (2) obtain the necessary interface references.[17] Keep in mind that objects can be activated across process and machine boundaries, a daunting task that is automatically handled by the COM infrastructure.

---

[17] The interested reader is encouraged to read one of the many good books on COm, e.g., *Programming Distributed Applications with COM+ and VB6* by our own Ted Pattison, (MS Press, 2001).

The New Operator

The most important characteristic of New is that it does not always trigger COM activation. In some cases, a call to New results in an optimized form of object creation performed entirely by VB.[18] How the New operator behaves depends on whether the class is internal or external, *from the perspective of the client creating the object.* For example, consider the following client code:

```
Dim rObj1 As IInterface
Set rObj1 = New CClass
```

The call to New results in VB's optimized creation if the class is internal, (i.e., CClass is either (1) part of the same VB project/DLL/EXE as the client, or (2) part of the same VB group as the client [and you are running that group inside the VB IDE]). Otherwise, the class is considered external, and COM activation is performed in an attempt to instantiate the object.

Being aware of New's optimized behavior is important for two reasons. First, it is much more efficient than COM activation, and thus is preferable for performance reasons. But, second, it is incorrect in certain situations, for example, when the class being instantiated is configured to run under MTS or COM+. In this case, COM activation is required for the class to receive the necessary MTS/COM+ services, but if the class is internal then New bypasses COM activation, creating an object that may not run properly. For this reason, the conservative programmer should avoid the use of New.

Note that the New operator can be applied in two different ways: *traditional* and *shortcut*. With the traditional approach, you declare a reference and then create the object separately as needed:

```
Dim rObj2 As IInterface
    .
    .
    .
Set rObj2 = New CClass
rObj2.SomeMethod
```

---

[18] This is analogous to calling New in other object-oriented programming languages like C++, versus calling CoCreateInstanceEx in Windows to perform COM activation.

This allows your references to be of any interface type, and makes object creation visible in the code. The second alternative is the shortcut approach, in which you embed the `New` operator in the variable declaration:

```
Dim rObj3 As New CClass
    .
    .
    .
rObj3.SomeMethod
```

In this case, VB automatically creates an object on the first use of the reference variable (`rObj2`). Although this requires less typing, this approach restricts you to a class's default interface, and can lead to interesting runtime behavior. For example, consider the following code fragment:

```
Set rObj3 = Nothing
rObj3.SomeMethod          '** traditionally, this would fail
    .
    .
    .
Set rObj3 = Nothing
If rObj3 Is Nothing Then   '** traditionally, this would be true
    Msgbox "you'll never see this dialog"
End If
```

Each time you use a shortcut reference in a statement, VB first checks to see if the reference is `Nothing`. If so, it creates an object before executing the statement. Not only does this result in additional overhead, but it also prevents you from checking whether an object has been destroyed (the act of testing re-creates another object!). For these reasons, we generally recommend that you avoid the shortcut approach.

CreateObject

Unlike `New`, the `CreateObject` function always creates objects using COM activation. You supply a string-based ProgID, and `CreateObject` converts this to a CLSID (via a registry lookup) before performing a standard COM activation. Here's a generic example:

```
Dim rObj1 As TLibName.IInterface
Set rObj1 = CreateObject("TLibName.CClass")
```

The advantage to this approach is flexibility. First, because `CreateObject` is based on strings and not class names, the class to be instantiated can be computed at run-time based on user input, configuration files, or records in a database. Second, `CreateObject` has an optional parameter for specifying *where* to create the object (i.e., on which remote server machine). This overrides the local registry settings, once again providing more flexibility at run-time. For example, this feature can be used to implement simple schemes for fault tolerance:

```
On Error Resume Next
Dim rObj2 As TLibName.IInterface
Set rObj2 = CreateObject("TLibName.CClass", "Server1")

If rObj2 Is Nothing Then      '** server1 is down, try server2...
    Set rObj2 = CreateObject("TLibName.CClass", "Server2")
End If

If rObj2 Is Nothing Then      '** both servers are down, give up...
    On Error Goto 0           '** disable local error handling
    Err.Raise ...             '** inform the client
End If

On Error Goto Handler   '** success, reset error handler and begin...
    .
    .
    .
```

Note that the machine names are also string based, and thus can be read from configuration files or a database.

Because `CreateObject` only performs COM activation, it cannot instantiate `Private` or `PublicNotCreatable` VB classes. The class must be a registered COM object. Furthermore, whether you are using vtable-binding or late-binding, instantiation via `CreateObject` requires that the object support late-binding.[19] If the object does not, VB raises error 429. In these cases, the only way to instantiate the object is via `New`.

GetObject

As the name implies, `GetObject` is designed to gain access to existing objects; for example, an MS Word document object in a file:

```
Dim rDoc As Word.Document     '**set a reference to MS Word Object Library
Set rDoc = GetObject("C:\DOCS\file.doc", "Word.Document")
rDoc.Activate
```

However, it can also be used to create new objects. For example,

```
Dim rObj1 As TLibName.IInterface
Set rObj1 = GetObject("", "TLibName.CClass")
```

In this sense, `GetObject` is equivalent to `CreateObject`, albeit without the ability to specify a remote server name.

Interestingly, as we'll see shortly, there's a version of `GetObject` that is more efficient than `CreateObject`, yet it is rarely used for this reason. Instead, it is commonly used to access MS Office objects or Windows services such as Active Directory, Windows Management Instrumentation (WMI), and the Internet Information Server (IIS) metabase. It is also used in conjunction with Windows 2000-based queued components (i.e., objects with method calls that are translated into queued messages for asynchronous processing). For example, suppose the class `CQClass` is configured as a queued component under COM+ on Windows 2000. The following gains access to the appropriate queue object for queuing of method calls (versus creating a traditional COM object that executes the method calls):

```
Dim rQObj As TLibName.CQClass
Set rQObj = GetObject("Queue:/new:TLibName.CQClass")
```

---

[19] In other words, the object must implement `IDispatch`; some ATL components do not.

```
rQObj.SomeMethod                          '** call to SomeMethod is queued
rQObj.SomeMethod2 "parameter"             '** call to SomeMethod2 is queued

MsgBox "client is done"
```

In this case, the calls to `SomeMethod` and `SomeMethod2` are queued for later processing by some instance of `CQClass`. This implies that a `MsgBox` dialog appears on the screen long before the actual method calls take place.

`GetObjectContext.CreateInstance` and `Server.CreateObject`
Suppose you have two classes configured to run under MTS, `CRoot` and `CHelper`. If `CRoot` needs to create an instance of `CHelper`, then there is exactly one way for `CRoot` to instantiate this class properly—via `GetObjectContext.CreateInstance`:

```
'** code for configured class CRoot
Dim rObj1 As TLibName.IInterface
Set rObj1 = GetObjectContext.CreateInstance( _
                                  "TLibName.CHelper")
```

Likewise, if `CRoot` is an ASP page, then the proper way to instantiate `CHelper` is using `Server.CreateObject`:

```
'** code for ASP page
Dim rObj2
Set rObj2 = Server.CreateObject("TLibName.CHelper")
```

These methods are essentially wrappers around `CreateObject`, accepting a ProgID and performing COM activation. However, they enable the surrounding environment (MTS and ASP respectively) to recognize and to participate in the creation of the COM object. Direct calls to `New` and `CreateObject` bypass the surrounding environment, leading to slower or incorrect execution.[20]

---

[20] With COM+, it is safe to use `CreateObject` as well as `CreateInstance`. With ASP, use `CreateObject` in cases in which `Server.CreateObject` is designed to fail. See Microsoft knowledge base (KB) article Q193230 in the MSDN library.

For more details on the rationale and proper use of `CreateInstance`, see rule 3-3.

Performance Considerations

Most discussions involving the performance of COM objects focus on two things: (1) the type of binding (vtable versus late) and (2) the marshaling characteristics of any parameters. Although these are very important, little attention is paid to the cost of COM activation. Thus, assuming there is no compelling design reason to choose between `New`, `CreateObject`, and `GetObject`, is there a performance reason?

First, keep in mind that `New` is optimized for internal classes, so it is always the most efficient mechanism when COM activation is not needed. However, let's assume our goal is COM activation. There are three types of activation: *in-process, local,* and *remote.* In-process activation means the resulting object resides in the same process as the client. Both local and remote activation represent *out-of-process* activation, in which the object resides in a process separate from the client—either on the same machine (local) or a different one (remote). Examples of in-process activation include classes packaged as an ActiveX DLL and then registered as COM objects, and classes configured to run under MTS as a library package. Examples of local and remote activation include classes packaged in an ActiveX EXE, and classes configured to run under MTS as a server package.

In the case of in-process activation, `New` is always the most efficient: It is 10 times faster than `CreateObject` and is 10 to 20 times faster than `GetObject`. This is mainly the result of the fact that `CreateObject` and `GetObject` require additional steps (e.g., the conversion of the ProgID to a CLSID). Interestingly, in the out-of-process cases, the best performer varies: `New` is more efficient (10 percent) when you plan to use vtable-binding against the object's default interface, whereas `CreateObject` and `GetObject` are more efficient when you plan to use late-binding against the default interface (two times) or vtable-binding against a custom interface (10 to 15 percent). Let's discuss why this is so.

As noted earlier, COM activation has two goals: (1) create the object and (2) acquire the necessary interface references. The `New` operator is essentially optimized for vtable-binding against an object's default interface. In one API call, New creates the object and acquires four interface references: the default interface, IUnknown, IPersistStreamInit, and IPersistPropertyBag. On the other hand, CreateObject and GetObject are optimized for late-binding, because they acquire a slightly different set of interface references: IDispatch, IUnknown, IPersistStreamInit, and IPersistProperty-Bag. Note that CreateObject and GetObject also take longer to create the object and to acquire these references (two API calls and three method calls).

So why is New slower in some cases? Recall that out-of-process activation yields proxy and stub objects to handle the communication between client and object (Figure 2.19). A proxy/stub pair is created during activation for each interface that is acquired, and thus forms part of the activation cost. Assuming the object does not perform custom marshaling,[21] the proxy-stub pair associated with its default interface is much more expensive to create than those associated with predefined COM interfaces such as IDispatch. As a result, if the client ends up using the default interface, then New is faster because it automatically acquires a reference to the object's default interface. However, if the client needs IDispatch (late-binding) or a custom interface, then CreateObject and GetObject are faster because time is not wasted building an expensive proxy/stub pair that will never be used. The results are summarized in Table 2.2.

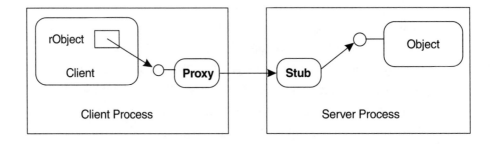

Figure 2.19 COM out-of-process activation yields proxy and stub objects

---

[21] In other words, the object uses COM's standard marshaling infrastructure. By default, VB objects rely on standard marshaling.

Table 2.2 Maximizing performance of COM objects

Activation Type	Interface Client Will Use	No. of Calls Client Will Make	Best Performance Activation	Binding
In-process	—	—	New	vtable
Local	default	< 10	CreateObject	late
		³ 10	New	vtable
	custom	—	CreateObject	vtable
Remote	default	< 3	CreateObject	late
		³ 3	New	vtable
	custom	—	CreateObject	vtable

What's fascinating is that activation is not the complete picture. The conventional wisdom for best overall performance is to access the object using vtable-binding because it requires fewer actual calls to the object and passes parameters more efficiently. However, vtable-binding implies the direct use of an object's interface (default or custom), and hence the need for an expensive proxy/stub pair in the out-of-process case. For example, assume the following client-side code is activating an out-of-process COM object:

```
Dim rObj1 As TLibName.CClass    '** implies default interface
Set rObj1 = CreateObject("TLibName.CClass")
```

Even though `CreateObject` avoids the expensive proxy/stub pair, the `Set` statement will trigger their creation because the type of the variable being assigned is one of the object's interfaces. Therefore, to get the full benefit of using `CreateObject`, it turns out that you must also use late-binding! In other words,

```
Dim rObj2 As Object    '** implies IDispatch to default interface
Set rObj2 = CreateObject("TLibName.CClass")
```

is roughly twice as fast as the previous code fragment. Of course, late-binding is more expensive per call, and thus the advantage of this approach diminishes as the number of calls increases. This explains the results in Table 2.2, in which there exists some threshold at which point vtable-binding becomes more efficient. Note that the exact threshold will vary in different situations (based on network speeds and distances, interface designs, and so on).

Lastly, if you are running Windows 2000 and are truly concerned with performance, you might consider using `GetObject` in place of `CreateObject`. `GetObject` is slightly more efficient when used as follows:

```
Dim rObj As ...
Set rObj = GetObject("new:TLibName.CClass")
```

In this case, `GetObject` acquires only two interface references instead of four; namely, `IDispatch` and `IUnknown`. Although this speeds up activation by reducing the number of method calls (which may be traversing across the network), it prevents the proper activation of "persistable" objects because `IPersistStreamInit` and `IPersistPropertyBag` are no longer available.

Fortunately or unfortunately, VB offers a number of different techniques for creating objects. Some always perform COM activation (`CreateObject` and `GetObject`); some do not (`New`). Some are more flexible (`CreateObject` and `GetObject`), whereas others must be used in certain cases for correct execution (`GetObjectContext.CreateInstance`, `Server.CreateObject`, and `New`). And some are more efficient than others, although one must take into account the type of activation, the interface being used, and the number of calls the client plans to make.

If you do not need COM activation, use `New` and vtable-binding. Otherwise, consult Table 2.2 to maximize performance. Although it may be counterintuitive, if your design involves "one-shot" objects (i.e., create, call, and destroy), then `CreateObject` with late-binding may be the most efficient approach. However, keep in mind that you lose IntelliSense and type checking with late-binding. For this reason, the conservative programmer should consider sticking with vtable-binding.

Rule 2-7: Beware of `Class_Terminate`

Two of the most heavily used classes in VB are probably `Connection` and `Recordset`, members of the ADO object model. Like most object-oriented classes, these two classes have destructors similar to `Class_Terminate`. In other words, they have methods that are automatically triggered when an instance of the class is about to be destroyed. Destructor methods are typically used to clean up before an object's state is lost forever, which would seem like the perfect place to handle things like saving changes to a database. So why is it, then, that `Connection` and `Recordset` have explicit `Close` methods that we have to call ourselves?

The answer is that some resources are too important to leave open until the client (or the run-time environment) gets around to triggering the object's destructor.[22] In other words, in VB, the destructor is triggered when an object is no longer referenced by any client:

```
Dim rs As ADODB.Recordset
Set rs = New ADODB.Recordset
   .
   .
   .
Set rs = Nothing    '** destructor is triggered at this point, assuming
                    '**   we didn't pass the reference to anyone else
```

This occurs when all references have been set to `Nothing`. For database classes like `Connection` and `Recordset`, which may be allocating memory and setting locks in the database, unnecessary delay in performing cleanup may waste precious resources and may hurt performance. Hence the explicit `Close` method:

```
Dim rs As ADODB.Recordset
Set rs = New ADODB.Recordset
rs.Open ...
   .
   .
   .
```

---

[22] The ideas in this rule will become even more important in .NET, which uses garbage collection and thus unpredictably delays object destruction.

```
rs.Close              '** cleanup performed here
Set rs = Nothing      '** destructor triggered here
```

Even though the client is responsible for calling `Close` (and thus may forget), its use can be documented as necessary for correct behavior. Regardless, it provides a solution to the problem of timely cleanup for those able to use it properly.

What does this mean to you? First of all, as a consumer of objects, you must be careful to use other classes properly. Look for methods entitled `Close` or `Dispose`, and be sure to call them as soon as you are done using that object. In particular, be careful to call these in your error handlers as well. For example, here's the proper way to ensure that both a connection and a recordset are closed, even in the presence of errors:

```
Public Sub SomeTask()
    On Error Goto errHandler
    Dim dbConn As ADODB.Connection
    Dim rs As ADODB.Recordset

    Set dbConn = New ADODB.Connection
    Set rs = New ADODB.Recordset
       .
       .
       .
    rs.Close : dbConn.Close
    Set rs = Nothing : Set dbConn = Nothing
    Exit Sub

errHandler:
    If rs Is Nothing Then
    Else
        If rs.State <> adStateClosed Then rs.Close
        Set rs = Nothing
    End If

    If dbConn Is Nothing Then
    Else
        If dbConn.State <> adStateClosed Then dbConn.Close
        Set dbConn = Nothing
```

```
        End If

        Err.Raise ...
End Sub
```

Second, as a producer of classes, you need to decide whether VB's `Class_Terminate` event is sufficient for your cleanup needs. If not, then you need to incorporate an explicit `Close` or `Dispose` method in your class design.

The current convention is to provide a `Close` method if your design allows an object to be reopened or reused after it has been closed. Otherwise, provide a `Dispose` method, which implies to your clients that the object is no longer usable once `Dispose` has been called. Implementing these methods is easy; the hard part is deciding when your classes need them.

The obvious examples are classes that open and hold on to operating system or other resources: files, shared memory, network connections, and ADO `Connection` and `Recordset` objects. If you find yourself opening these types of resources in your class's `Class_Initialize` event (or in an explicit `Open` method) and accessing them via private class variables, then you most likely need a `Close` or `Dispose` method. For example, you may design a data access class that automatically logs every access via a private ADO connection:

```
'** class module: CDataAccess
Option Explicit

Private dbLog As ADODB.Connection    '** for logging accesses

Public Sub Open()
    Set dbLog = New ADODB.Connection
    dbLog.Open "<proper connection string>"
End Sub
    .
    .
    .
Public Sub Close()
    dbLog.Close
    Set dbLog = Nothing
End Sub
```

DESIGNING, BUILDING, AND WORKING WITH COM-BASED COMPONENTS

```
Private Sub Class_Terminate()
    Close    '** in case client forgets...
End Sub
```

Of course, keep in mind that although maintaining a dedicated logging connection may be efficient, it is certainly wasteful of an important (and usually limited) resource. In fact, we do not recommend the previous design for objects that may live in the middle tier, and thus need to scale (e.g., see rule 5-3). However, if such a design is appropriate in your case, then remember to think twice before relying solely on `Class_Terminate` for cleanup.

Rule 2-8: Model in Terms of Sessions Instead of Entities

When it comes to designing the object model for your system, you should consider whether to design your classes around *sessions* or *entities*. Entities represent a more traditional object-oriented approach, in which classes are based on real-world entities in your system—customers, orders, products, and so forth. In contrast, sessions represent the set of expected interactions between clients and your objects. Although session-based class designs may deviate from pure OODs, the motivation is performance over elegance. Session-based systems strive to streamline client interactions, which is particularly important when objects are out-of-process (e.g., in distributed applications).[23]

Obviously, the issue of design is no small matter. For example, consider a multi-tier system with business and data layers. How should the data access layer behave?[24] Should it model each table as a class? If so, where do queries over multiple tables fit in? Perhaps there should be just one class per database. And what about the business layer? Are lots of smaller classes better than a few larger ones? How should they be grouped to take advantage of polymorphism in the client? Each of these questions may have different answers, based on system goals.

At a high level, most business systems are the same: They gather information from their users and submit this information for processing. The system is thus divided into at least two parts, the front-end user interface and the back-

---

[23] If you are new to out-of-process COM or why it is important, read rule 2-9 first.
[24] The interested reader should also see rule 5-2.

end processor. Each communication from the front-end to the back-end represents a unit of work and constitutes a *round-trip*. Session-based designs model user scenarios in an attempt to minimize round-trips. Traditional OODs often don't take into account the cost of a round-trip, yielding less than optimal performance.

For example, consider the traditional entity-based design of a `CCustomer` class. The class models the state and behavior of a customer in the system; in particular, allowing easy access to customer information:

```
'** class module: CCustomer (traditional OOD)
Option Explicit

Public Name As String
Public StreetAddr As String
Public City As String
Public State As String
Public Zip As String

Public Property Get CreditLimit() As Currency
    '** return customer's credit limit for purchases
End Property

Public Sub PlaceOrder(ByVal lProductNum As Long, _
                     ByVal lQuantity As Long)
    '** code to place an order for this customer
End Sub
```

Although straightforward to understand, consider what the client must do to change a customer's address:

```
Dim rCust As CCustomer
Set rCust = ...

With rCust
    .StreetAddr = <new street address>
    .City = <new city>
    .State = <new state>
    .Zip = <new zipcode>
End With
```

The cost is four round-trips, one per datum. Likewise, placing an order for *N* different products requires $N + 1$ trips, one to check the customer's credit limit and another *N* to order each product.

A better approach, at least from the perspective of performance, is to redesign the `CCustomer` class based on the expected user scenarios: getting the customer's information, updating this information, and ordering products. This leads to the following session-based result:

```
'** class module: CCustomer (revised session-based design)
Option Explicit

Private Name As String              '** no public access to data
Private StreetAddr As String
Private City As String
Private State As String
Private Zip As String

Public Sub GetInfo(Optional ByRef sName As String, _
           Optional ByRef sStreetAddr As String, _
           Optional ByRef sCity As String, _
           Optional ByRef sState As String, _
           Optional ByRef sZip As String)
    sName = Name
    sStreetAddr = StreetAddr
    sCity = City
    sState = State
    sZip = Zip
End Sub

Public Sub Update(Optional ByVal sName As String = "?", _
           Optional ByVal sStreetAddr As String = "?", _
           Optional ByVal sCity As String = "?", _
           Optional ByVal sState As String = "?", _
           Optional ByVal sZip As String = "?")
    If sName <> "?" Then Name = sName
    If sStreetAddr <> "?" Then StreetAddr = sStreetAddr
    If sCity <> "?" Then City = sCity
    If sState <> "?" Then State = sState
    If sZip <> "?" Then Zip = sZip
End Sub
```

```
Public Sub PlaceOrder(laProducts() As Long)
    '** confirm that client passed a 2D array (products times quantities)
    Debug.Assert UBound(laProducts, 1) = _
                 UBound(laProducts, 2)

    '** code to check that credit limit is sufficient
    '** code to place entire order for this customer
End Sub
```

First of all, notice there is no public access to customer data. All reads and writes must be done via methods. As a result, an address change now takes only one round-trip call to `Update`. Likewise, `PlaceOrder` is redesigned to accept an array of product numbers and quantities, allowing an entire order to be placed via one round-trip call. In short, the class contains one entry for each task that the user may need to perform. Although the class's interface is arguably more cumbersome for clients to use, the potential increase in performance is significant, especially across a network.

Session-based designs are usable at every level of a system. For example, in a standard multi-tier application, your business objects would model client sessions, whereas your data access objects model business object sessions. For the latter, your data access design may be as simple, and as efficient, as two methods: one to read and one to write:

```
'** class module:  CDataAccess (minimal session-based design)
Option Explicit

Public Function ReadDB(sConnectionInfo As String, _
                       sSQL As String) As ADODB.Recordset
    '** code to open DB, build recordset, disconnect, and return it...
End Function

Public Function UpdateDB(sConnectionInfo As String, _
                         sSQL As String)
    '** code to open DB and update via SQL...
End Function
```

Obviously, good design is the proper balance of usability, maintainability, extensibility, and performance.

Rule 2-9: Avoid ActiveX EXEs Except for Simple, Small-Scale Needs

When you create a new project in VB, you are presented with a list of project types from which to choose: Standard EXE, ActiveX EXE, ActiveX DLL, ActiveX Control, Addin, IIS Application, and so forth. The ActiveX project types are used when you want to create a COM server—a set of classes in a DLL or EXE that can be activated using COM. If your goal is a user-interface component, select ActiveX Control. However, if your goal is a traditional object-oriented, non-user interface component, then you should select either ActiveX DLL or ActiveX EXE. But which one?

The answer depends on two factors: the type of COM activation you desire, and whether you plan to use MTS or COM+. Let's review the three types of COM activation: *in-process*, *local*, and *remote*. An in-process activation means the COM object resides in the same process as the client that created the object. In this case, you must create an ActiveX DLL project, and the resulting DLL must be installed on the client's machine. Both local and remote COM activation represent *out-of-process* activation, in which the object resides in a process separate from the client—on either the same machine (local) or a different one (remote). With this scenario you have a choice. You can create an ActiveX EXE project, and the resulting EXE serves as a stand-alone process for hosting your objects, or you can create an ActiveX DLL and configure it to run within MTS or COM+ as a server process.

In-process objects are much more efficient, because calls are typically 10 to 100 times faster than calls out of process. The trade-off is that out-of-process objects offer

- Fault isolation (object can crash without crashing the client, and vice versa)
- Separate security identity (object runs under an identity separate from the client)
- Multi-threaded behavior (clients can concurrently activate objects/execute calls)
- The ability to run objects on a machine separate from the clients

The last is perhaps the most important, because it enables the construction of distributed, multi-tier applications. Assuming you want out-of-process activation, the question is should you use ActiveX EXEs or should you turn to MTS/COM+?

In short, VB's ActiveX EXEs are designed to support small-scale needs. They provide basic out-of-process activation, nothing more. On the other hand, MTS and COM+ support large-scale designs, in addition to providing a host of other services: security, resource sharing, distributed transactions, and configuration/process management. When in doubt, the general consensus is to use MTS or COM+, because you never know when you may need to handle additional clients, share resources among your objects, or implement security. However, if your needs are simple, then VB's ActiveX EXEs are a viable option. Because Chapter 3 focuses entirely on MTS and COM+, we discuss ActiveX EXEs here.

VB's ActiveX EXEs enable you to build multi-threaded server applications with relative ease. Like many features of VB, multi-threading is presented through the IDE with the utmost consideration for productivity. In this case, your ActiveX EXE's threading strategy is determined by two option buttons and a text box, not by coding. These Threading Model settings are found in your project's properties, under the General tab as shown in Figure 2.20.

An ActiveX EXE is compiled to follow one of three threading model approaches. The default is Thread Pool of 1 (shown in Figure 2.20), which gives you a single-threaded application. This means that a single-thread is shared by all objects living in this server process, and thus only one client request can be processed at a time. Although this type of server consumes very few resources, it should be used only when you are supporting a single client.

The second approach is Thread per Object, which represents the other end of the threading spectrum. Now, instead of one thread, every object has its own thread.[25] The result is maximum concurrency, because no client request blocks that of another. However, even though the server process supports an unlimited number of concurrent clients, does it maximize throughput? Not likely. At some

---

[25] Assuming the object was activated by a client outside the server process. If the client lives inside the EXE, then the new object lives on the same thread for better performance. Note that setting a class's instancing property to `SingleUse` has a similar effect—an entirely new EXE is started for each instance of that class.

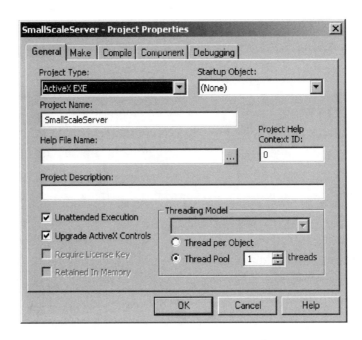

Figure 2.20 Project properties for an ActiveX EXE

point, the rising number of threads begins to hurt performance, because the operating system spends more time switching from one thread to another than it does letting a thread run. Thus, if you want to maximize both concurrency and throughput, you need to either *scale up* (add more hardware to the existing machine) or *scale out* (add more machines and load balance). You'll also need to cap the size of the thread pool—the motivation for the third approach.

The third (and best) approach for multi-threading is a thread pool more than 1. The idea is to limit concurrency by restricting the number of threads, thereby guaranteeing some base amount of throughput as the load on your server process increases. For example, Figure 2.21 shows a VB ActiveX EXE compiled with a thread pool of 3. The threads are depicted as circles with arrowheads, and each thread is assigned to a single *apartment* within the process (hence the term single-threaded apartment, or STA). When VB objects are created, they are likewise assigned to an apartment, and remain in that apartment until they are destroyed. Although the ActiveX EXE can support an unlimited

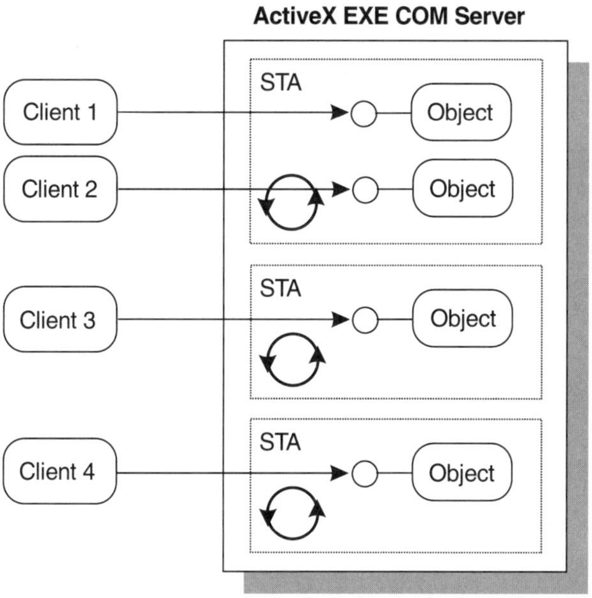

Figure 2.21 ActiveX EXE server with four clients and a thread pool of 3

number of objects (and hence an unlimited number of clients), in this example only three client requests can be processed concurrently. In particular, note that clients 1 and 2 have objects assigned to the same thread. Thus, if both submit a request (i.e., make a method call) at the same time, one request is processed and the other is blocked.

The idea of a fixed-size thread pool is not unique to VB. MTS and COM+ also take this approach: MTS 2.0 on WinNT has a thread pool of 100, whereas COM+ (i.e., MTS 3.0) on Windows 2000 has a thread pool per processor ranging in size from 7 to 10. Notice that the size of the pool was reduced significantly in COM+, acknowledging the tension between concurrency and throughput.

Even though their thread pooling strategies are the same, note that MTS and COM+ provide a more sophisticated implementation, yielding better performance than VB's ActiveX EXEs. MTS and COM+ provide other distinct advantages as well. For example, consider the problem of objects trying to share data such as configuration information or a set of database records. In VB, the standard approach is to use global variables declared in a BAS module. However, in an ActiveX EXE, global variables are not truly global: A BAS module is replicated so that each apartment has its own copy. The result is that "global" variables are global only within an apartment.[26] This implies that you must use an alternative mechanism to share state, such as a file or database, or the memory-based Shared Property Manager within MTS and COM+.

With regard to security, VB's ActiveX EXEs rely on COM's security model. Using the `dcomcnfg` utility, you can configure the identity under which an ActiveX EXE runs, as well as who may start up, access, and configure the EXE. This also applies to the authentication level (frequency of authentication and network packet integrity/privacy).

In summary, ActiveX EXEs provide a quick-and-dirty mechanism for out-of-process COM activation, and thus are a basis for application designs requiring fault isolation, security, concurrency, or distributed processing. However, keep in mind that Microsoft is moving away from ActiveX EXEs, and is encouraging developers to build ActiveX DLLs and to let MTS or COM+ serve as your EXE. This allows Microsoft to provide services that are difficult to implement yourself, and the ability to evolve these services without the need for you to recompile your code. Applications based on MTS and COM+ will scale, offer better concurrency and resource sharing, allow more flexible configuration of the server, and yield faster time-to-market for multi-tier systems. In the end, you'll spend your time more productively, working on business logic rather than infrastructure.

---

[26] Why did the designers of VB do this? Consider the alternative: If global variables were shared across apartments, then programmers would need to worry about synchronization—a slippery slope that leads to subtle, error-prone code. Another side effect: If you start up via a `Sub Main`, it is run *each* time a new apartment is created.

Chapter 3

MTS, COM+, and VB— The Middle Tier

3-1 Understand the design of MTS and COM+.

3-2 Don't use singletons in MTS or COM+.

3-3 Know when to use `New` versus `CreateObject` versus `GetObjectContext.CreateInstance`.

3-4 Understand the real motivation for `SetComplete`.

3-5 Consider an AutoAbort style with transactions.

3-6 Don't reinvent the DBMS.

3-7 Don't feel obligated to configure all your components.

3-8 Avoid compiling things into DLLs that you'll later regret.

3-9 Best practices for porting MTS code into COM+.

3-10 Best practices for writing code that runs on MTS and COM+.

MTS and COM+ provide a home for running COM objects on the middle tier. In addition, these frameworks also provide many of the services commonly needed by distributed applications, such as security, process management, distributed transactions, and configuration support. MTS 2.0 is available as an option pack for Windows NT4; COM+ (i.e., MTS 3.0) is built into Windows 2000.

In this set of rules, we address a series of best and worst practices associated with surrogate-based deployments. We give equal time to MTS and COM+, because the community is pretty evenly split between the two frameworks at the time of this writing. We discuss fundamentals early on, then tackle many of the common questions flooding the landscape these days, such as the ramifications of choosing `New` versus `CreateObject` versus `CreateInstance` to instantiate your objects in MTS/COM+. The chapter closes with a few tips to help those who must deploy to both MTS and COM+, or for those who are deploying today in anticipation of porting tomorrow. MTS and COM+ provide tremendous benefits, and we hope you'll be able to realize them more effectively after you have finished reading this chapter.

Rule 3-1: Understand the Design of MTS and COM+

If you're building a distributed system, one of your leading challenges is how to manage shared resources. You'll have to decide how to share things like threads, database connections, state, and objects, often from within a single server-side application that is shared among many calling clients. Fortunately for us as developers, there are some existing products that offer a framework for managing our resources, namely, MTS and COM+.

MTS was originally designed to target the management of distributed transactions. It is a layer over Microsoft's Distributed Transaction Coordinator (DTC), which serves as a transaction manager. However, the process space—called MTX.EXE in MTS and DLLHOST.EXE in COM+—has the same kinds of resource management issues as any distributed system. Microsoft included several sharing mechanisms for this, and MTS quickly grew in scope from a distributed transaction manager to a middle-tier surrogate, which is its primary role today.

MTS manages threads using a pool of STAs.[1] This pool grows as needed to accommodate client requests, up to a maximum of 100 threads. Once allocated, an STA lives for the life of its process. Note that MTS supports an unlimited number of clients; the thread pool controls the maximum number of requests that can execute concurrently.

The COM+ thread-pooling scheme is a little more complex and is better suited for enterprise solutions. It includes an STA thread pool with a size that varies with the number of processors on the server. The thread pool limits are determined by the following formulas:

---

[1] What is a single-threaded apartment? See rule 2-9.

```
Minimum no. STAs = 7 + (no. of processors)
Maximum no. STAs = 10 * (no. of processors)
```

COM+ also includes a multi-threaded apartment (MTA) pool, and a thread neutral apartment (TNA) area in which components may be accessed from any other thread. VB6 (and earlier) components, however, can live only in STAs because they have thread affinity. In COM+, STAs are gradually reclaimed by the system when they are no longer used, down to the minimum value.

In both cases, you may notice that during high user volumes, one thread could be required to service multiple clients simultaneously. In this scenario, it is important to be able to keep user A out of user B's state, and vice versa.[2] *Activities* serve to isolate one user's resources from another's. Activities are, effectively, wrappers around logical threads, much like apartments wrap physical threads. Because logical threads may span physical threads and even processes, activities also may span them.

You could also view an activity as housing for a set of objects created on behalf of a single client. When a client makes a call to a properly designed system, all objects created on the client's behalf should live in the same activity.[3] Additionally, because a transaction should be specific to a user request, a transaction will live within a single activity. Transactions are always subsets of activities in an MTS/COM+ system. The relationship between activities and the STA thread pool is shown in Figure 3.1.

Activities always exist when you are using MTS. With COM+, you can turn them off with the Synchronization attribute, but as a VB developer you should not. If you turn off activities, you are removing one of your serialization techniques within the middle tier. VB compensates for the loss of serialization by running all instances of the non-synchronized component in the main STA, which severely limits scalability.

Synchronization is one of many attributes available in a COM+ system. But what exactly are attributes, and how do they fit into the MTS/COM+ model? Perhaps the easiest way to describe attributes is by comparison with an older but similar technique. Each of your configured components has conditions and

---

[2] For a discussion of why this is important, see rule 3-2.
[3] See rule 3-3 for more information on properly designing your systems.

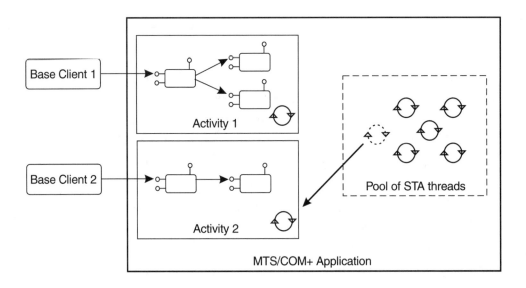

Figure 3.1 Relationship between the STA thread pool and activities in MTS/COM+

settings that describe how it is to be used. In the long-forgotten days of Windows 3.1, we used initialization (INI) files to maintain these settings outside the binary. You can think of attributes as a set of INI file settings for each of your configured components. Attributes can be set for each class, application, interface, and method. These settings are kept in the Registry (for MTS) or in RegDB (for COM+), instead of in an INI file.

Attributes allow you to change the run-time conditions for your components without having to recompile your code. When a client calls an instance of your component, the call is intercepted, attributes are applied, and the call is then forwarded to the object. On exiting the component's code, the return is again intercepted and "cleaned up." The process of pre- and post-processing is called *interception,* and is fundamental to MTS/COM+ development. Interception allows an administrator to change the run-time conditions without touching the code base. It also simplifies the code by allowing developers to reduce the number of system calls from within their code that would otherwise be necessary.

If you're going to program with MTS/COM+, there are three primary concepts you need to understand: apartments, activities, and interception. Now that you've seen at a high level how all three of these are used in a configured system, let's look at how to make the best use of these concepts in your MTS/COM+ solutions as you read the rest of this chapter. Keep in mind that the term *configured component* is used to denote a class installed in MTS or COM+, whereas *nonconfigured* refers to a standard COM object.

Rule 3-2: Don't Use Singletons in MTS or COM+

You may find yourself reading the title of this rule and asking, "What's a singleton?" A singleton is nothing more than a single instance of a class that is used by multiple clients, and is sometimes used by developers to share state among clients. Perhaps a better title to this rule is "Don't share server objects among clients." Why not?

Software systems often need to share state among clients. The most obvious technique for sharing state is a database. Databases, however, require configuration, passwords, and trips to other processes, often on other machines. Sometimes an optimal design requires shared state among clients from within a common process space, perhaps within the business tier. Singletons are one way to achieve this, exposing shared state and behavior among clients. Although sharing data among clients is reasonable, it is critical to recognize the difference between sharing state and sharing an actual object.

VB does not explicitly encourage the use of singletons, largely because of the increased responsibilities of multiplexing your code. However, there are times when you may have the need to share state between multiple clients. You can do this independently with VB or with the aid of the MTS/COM+ environment. As you will see, sharing state with the MTS/COM+ environment has many advantages over using VB directly. In either case, it is probably state that you really want to share, and not a VB object.

It turns out that the concurrency model of MTS/COM+ actually discourages the creation of a shared VB object. In MTS 2.0, all objects are created inside a synchronization boundary referred to as an *activity*. Activities isolate users from other users (see rule 3-1 for an introduction to activities), which by design deters clients from sharing state. Doing so causes excessive blocking because apartment boundaries are crossed to access the shared object. The COM+ environment allows activities to be turned off through its `Synchronization` setting, but this is an unwise decision for VB developers, because then the objects all live in the same apartment (no concurrency). Thus, if you need to share state among your clients, the best approach is to use the Shared Property Manager (SPM) within MTS/COM+. The SPM lets you name and group your state by creating *property groups,* which contain sets of name/value pairs that are accessible by name from anywhere within the process. For example, this means that all clients requesting the `LastReportRun` field from the `Reports` group will operate on the same piece of data.

The SPM (discussed in more deatil in rule 4-2) can be programmatically accessed from MTS by setting a reference to the Shared Property Manager Type Library. The same components are available in COM+ by referencing the COM+ Services Library. In either case, the code to create a shared property is fairly straightforward, as shown here:

```
Dim rManager As SharedPropertyGroupManager
Dim rGroup As SharedPropertyGroup
Dim rProperty As SharedProperty
Dim bExists As Boolean

Set rManager = New SharedPropertyGroupManager

'** create a Group for name/value pairs
Set rGroup = rManager.CreatePropertyGroup("Reports", _
                    LockSetGet, Process, bExists)

If Not bExists Then   '** create a name/value pair
    Set rProperty = rGroup.CreateProperty _
                        ("LastReportRun", bExists)
    If Not bExists Then   '** initialize property
        rProperty.Value = Format$(Date(), "mm-dd-yy")
    End If
End If
```

Note that in this code, the `CreatePropertyGroup` method is used to create a group of name/value pairs, and the individual name/value pairs are created using the `CreateProperty` method. In both cases, a variable `bExists` is passed in and returned with the value `True` if the property or group already exists. `LockGetSet` specifies a lock duration during access, and

`Process` specifies that the property group live as long as the process lives. Once created, you can fetch `LastReportRun` on behalf of any client that invokes the following server-side code:

```
Dim rManager As SharedPropertyGroupManager
Dim rGroup As SharedPropertyGroup
Dim rProperty As SharedProperty
Dim sVal as String

Set rManager = New SharedPropertyGroupManager

'** reference the existing group
Set rGroup = rManager.Group("Reports")

'** reference the name/value pair
Set rProperty = rGroup.Property("LastReportRun")
sVal = rProperty.Value
```

These code fragments show how to achieve the benefits of a singleton without all the drawbacks. Note that a value in the SPM is a variant, and thus can hold any VB data type. Although this means you can store an object reference in the SPM, don't. Doing so yields a singleton object. Instead, store non-reference types in the SPM, such as strings.

If you choose to build your components with VB, there are no reasonable ways to create a safe, scalable singleton object when using MTS or COM+. Most developers who think they want a singleton really just want to share state. Concentrate on sharing data, not objects, and leave the job of sharing data to the SPM.

Rule 3-3: Know When to Use `New` versus `CreateObject` versus `GetObjectContext.CreateInstance`

When you're writing the code for DLLs that are going to be deployed in an MTS or COM+ environment, things can get a little confusing when you need to create an object.[4] VB provides two primary ways to create an object: the `New` operator and the `CreateObject` function. The TLBs for MTS and COM+ supply a

---
[4] This item is a continuation of the discussion started in rule 2-6.

third technique via the `CreateInstance` method of the `ObjectContext` interface. Knowing when to use the appropriate object creation technique isn't all that intuitive. However, using the wrong technique can adversely affect not only performance, but the correctness of your code as well.

Let's begin by looking at a VB project that references neither the MTS nor the COM+ TLB. One possible example of a project that meets this criterion is a client application that users will run on a Windows 98 desktop. In this type of project you have to choose between the `New` operator and the `CreateObject` function when creating a COM object.

When a client application creates a COM object from your server using either `New` or `CreateObject`, it results in standard activation through COM's Service Control Manager (SCM). The `New` operator is a little bit faster than the `CreateObject` function because the client application doesn't need to resolve the ProgID to a CLSID at run-time. When you use the `New` operator, VB also provides a compile-time type check on the name of the class you're using to create the object. However, when you use the `CreateObject` function, VB cannot verify whether the ProgID is valid at compile-time because it's merely a string argument. This means you won't know whether you have a bad ProgID until you run your code.

On the other hand, the `CreateObject` function can offer a little more flexibility than `New` does. This is because you don't have to commit to a specific CLSID at compile-time. It's not that difficult to devise a design in which a client application dynamically chooses one ProgID from a set of compatible components at run-time. This is a great option when you'd like to design an application in terms of plug-compatible components.

As you can see, a *base client* (meaning a client running *outside* the MTS/COM+ run-time) can create objects using either `New` or `CreateObject`. Each technique has one or two advantages over the other, and both work fine. However, once you start running your components inside an MTS or COM+ application, things get more complicated. In this case, using `New` or `CreateObject` can get you into trouble. Things get more complicated because of the interception scheme and concurrency models built into MTS and COM+. For now, let's concentrate on writing code for MTS and Windows NT4. We'll bring COM+ and Windows 2000 into the picture a little later.

MTS and Windows NT4

Concurrency in MTS is based on activities. An activity is a logical thread of execution created by the system on behalf of a single client (a broader definition of an activity is given in rule 3-1). When a client activates an object from a component in an MTS server package, the MTS run-time transparently creates a new activity, as shown in Figure 3.2. In fact, every MTS object activated from a configured component is created inside an activity. It's also important to note that once an object is created inside a specific activity, it spends its entire lifetime there.

The MTS concurrency model is based on the premise that each client gets its own activity. This means there should be only one activity for each client, and every object belonging to the same client should run in one and only one activity. Activities are a valuable abstraction because programmers can think in terms of a *logical thread per client* while the MTS run-time worries about the details of managing a pool of physical threads. When you follow the rules of keeping a one-to-one relationship between clients and activities, the MTS run-time manages an efficient thread-pooling scheme for you behind the scenes.

When a remote client activates an object from a configured component that's been installed in an MTS server package, the MTS run-time creates a new activity that will host the object. Because this new activity only represents a logical thread, MTS must supply a physical thread to the activity to execute any code. The MTS run-time binds each new activity to an STA thread when the activity is created. MTS 2.0 maintains a thread pool on a per-process basis that can hold as many as 100 STA threads. MTS is able to supply each new activity with its own exclusive STA thread until the thread pool reaches capacity.

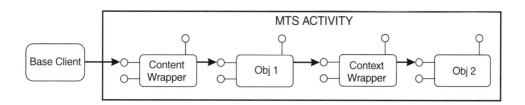

Figure 3.2 An MTS activity is a logical thread of execution created by the MTS run-time on behalf of a single client.

When the number of activities begins to exceed the number of STA threads, the MTS run-time begins to assign multiple activities to the same physical STA threads.

When two clients' activities map to the same STA thread, the code executing on behalf of one client can potentially block the call of another. However, this isn't something you should worry about too much as an MTS programmer. You're supposed to think in terms of activities and let the MTS run-time manage the physical threads as it sees fit. The designers of MTS have tried to make their concurrency model as simple as possible. The abstraction of the STA thread in COM relieves you from worrying about synchronization. The abstraction of the activity in MTS is even more valuable because it also relieves you from worrying about the complexities of thread pooling.

Let's review the rules you should keep in mind when you're writing an MTS application. Each activity should represent a set of all objects that belong to a single client. From this rule, we can draft two other rules. First, no two clients should ever be connected to the same activity, and therefore, to the same object (see rule 3-2 for alternative ways to share state). In MTS and COM+, you should never design a middle-tier application in which a singleton is shared across multiple clients. Second, you should avoid creating objects in different activities when they belong to the same client. In MTS, you have to write code explicitly to propagate new objects into the activity of their creator. If you do not, your new object may be created in a different activity and, therefore, may run on a different physical thread.

When you write code in a configured component to create an object from another configured component, you should do so by sending the activation request directly to the MTS run-time. You do this by calling the `CreateInstance` method on the `ObjectContext` interface. `CreateInstance` takes a single parameter for the ProgID. The following code demonstrates the proper technique:

```
'** method in ComponentA (rMyObj1)
Dim rMyObj2 As ComponentB
Set rMyObj2 = _
   GetObjectContext.CreateInstance("MyDLL.ComponentB")
```

As in the case of the `CreateObject` function, VB cannot verify the ProgID you pass to `CreateInstance` at compile-time. Be extra careful and make sure you always pass valid ProgIDs when calling `CreateInstance`.

When a configured component calls `CreateInstance`, it is telling the MTS run-time to create the new object in the current activity. The MTS run-time creates the new object and places a context wrapper between it and its creator, as we saw in Figure 3.2. Because the two objects are running on the same STA, there's no need for a thread-switching proxy/stub layer between them. Also, the context wrapper is inserted between the two objects, so the MTS interception scheme is set up properly.

Although you can activate objects in an MTS server package from a remote client application using `New` or `CreateObject`, you should be cautious when using these techniques inside the MTS. Using `New` and `CreateObject` can result in several undesirable situations. Take a moment to examine the following code:

```
'** method in ComponentA (rMyObj1)
'** NOTE: we are assuming ComponentB is compiled in the same DLL as A.
Public Sub CreateSecondaryObjects()

    '** the correct way to instantiate an MTS object
    Dim rMyObj2 As ComponentB
    Set rMyObj2 = _
      GetObjectContext.CreateInstance("MyDLL.ComponentB")

    '** incorrect --- introduces a proxy/stub layer and another activity
    Dim rMyObj3 As ComponentB
    Set rMyObj3 = CreateObject("MyDLL.ComponentB")

    '** incorrect --- MTS interception scheme isn't set up properly
    Dim rMyObj4 As ComponentB
    Set rMyObj4 = New MyDLL.ComponentB

End Sub
```

Figure 3.3 shows how the objects are allocated inside the process of an MTS server application. Assume that `rMyObj1` is the creator of the other objects. First, note that `rMyObj2` has been created correctly using the

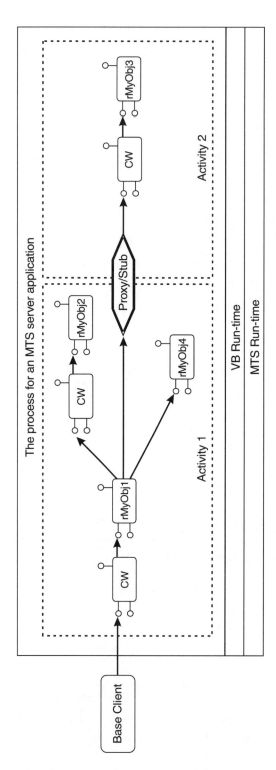

Figure 3.3 The result of creating objects from a configured component in MTS using the three different activation techniques. Note that this assumes the objects are instantiated from classes in the same DLL.

`CreateInstance` method: The new object has been created in the activity of its creator, and the context wrapper has been set up correctly. However, there are problems with both `rMyObj3` and `rMyObj4`. Let's start by examining the problem with `rMyObj3` and look at what happens when you try to create one MTS object from another using the `CreateObject` function.

When an MTS object calls `CreateObject`, the activation request bypasses the MTS run-time and is sent down to the SCM. The SCM, in turn, calls back into the process of the MTS server package to forward the same activation request. However, the SCM in NT4 doesn't know anything about MTS and, therefore, does not pass on any contextual information about the creator's activity. The MTS run-time assumes this is just another base client and creates `rMyObj3` in a new and separate activity.

The key point is that when you use the `CreateObject` function, the MTS run-time doesn't know that the creation request is coming from an existing activity. Instead, MTS assumes that another external client is creating an object. MTS thus creates the new object in a new activity, and always (if possible) on a different STA thread. The two objects are now bound together across a thread-switching proxy/stub layer. This significantly degrades performance and unnecessarily consumes another STA thread from the pool. Also, because these two objects are running in separate activities, they can't be part of the same MTS transaction, because every MTS transaction must be scoped inside the context of a single activity.

The `CreateObject` function isn't the only culprit that causes trouble. You can also get into trouble in MTS when creating an object from a configured component using `New`, as shown in Figure 3.3. When you use the `New` operator, there are two scenarios you need to consider. In the first scenario, the creator component and the component used to instantiate the new object live in separate DLLs. In this case, `New` behaves exactly as `CreateObject` does. As we have already seen, this situation is undesirable.

In the second scenario, the creator calling `New` and the component from which the object is being instantiated are compiled in the same DLL. The problem here is more subtle, but it can lead to even greater frustration. When a VB object calls `New` on a class name that's compiled in the same DLL, the VB run-time creates and binds the object on its own without involving either the MTS run-time or the SCM. The new object gets loaded on the same STA thread as the creator, but the MTS run-time has no idea that the new object exists. It isn't a valid MTS object because it doesn't get its own context wrapper, and hence the MTS interception scheme is not in place.

Look again at rMyObj4 in Figure 3.3. Neither COM nor MTS knows that a new object has been created. If rMyObj4 calls GetObjectContext, it's given a reference to the object context of its creator, rMyObj1. When rMyObj4 tries to use the object context of rMyObj1, your code will exhibit strange and mysterious behavior. An example demonstrates one of the potential problems you may encounter.

Let's assume you're writing an MTS transaction using rMyObj1 and rMyObj4. If rMyObj1 (*the root object*) creates rMyObj4 (*the secondary object*) using the New operator, then rMyObj4 will not have its own context wrapper. If rMyObj4 calls SetAbort, it's voting to roll back the transaction. In the MTS programming model, any object that calls SetAbort should be capable of rolling back the transaction. However, if rMyObj1 calls SetComplete after rMyObj4 calls SetAbort, the transaction will be committed.

The problem here is not readily obvious: rMyObj4 was created by the VB run-time instead of the MTS run-time. Consequently, rMyObj4 doesn't get its own context wrapper. When rMyObj4 votes to abort the transaction by calling SetAbort, its transaction vote is stored in the object context for rMyObj1. Then rMyObj4's vote is overwritten when rMyObj1 calls SetComplete. In the MTS programming model, any object should be able to roll back a transaction. However, if you have an object that calls SetAbort, the transaction still commits. The New operator is wreaking havoc on the correctness of your code. The good news is that once you change the call to New to a call to CreateInstance, everything starts to behave properly.

As it turns out, there are times when you can use the New operator when writing the code for a configured component in MTS. You can use the New operator whenever you create objects from nonconfigured components.[5] For example, you can and should use the New operator when you create new ADO

---

[5] Recall that a nonconfigured component is any class that's registered with COM but not with MTS or COM+.

objects. ADO components aren't registered with MTS. ADO objects never need a context wrapper and they don't rely on things that are part of the MTS programming model such as the object context. Objects created from nonconfigured components can be safely created by the SCM.

From what you've seen here, you can conclude that an MTS application can run a mixture of configured components and nonconfigured components.[6] An object created from a configured component in MTS requires a context wrapper. An object created from a nonconfigured component does not.

When you write a method implementation for a configured component to create an object from a nonconfigured component, you can use the New operator or the CreateObject function. The new object is created in the same activity and on the same STA thread as the creator. However, once a component has been programmed against the MTS TLB, it picks up a dependency on its object context. A component with such a dependency must be registered as a configured component in an MTS package and must be properly created as an MTS object. As a rule in MTS, one configured component must always create objects from another configured component using CreateInstance.

There is one more important point to consider when creating objects in MTS and NT4. It has to do with creating a VB object from an ASP page. If you're writing code in an ASP page with VBScript, you can use the CreateObject method of the ASP Server object or you can use the CreateObject function. It's important to note that a call to Server.CreateObject is like a call to CreateInstance in the sense that it passes contextual information about the ASP page's activity to the new object. If you're creating an object from a component in an MTS library package, the object and the ASP page that created it will run in the same activity and on the same STA thread. However, if you create the object using the VBScript CreateObject function, the contextual information about the creator's activity does not flow to the new object. Therefore, the new object is created in a new activity and most likely on a different STA thread. As you can see, using the CreateObject function when you should call Server.CreateObject can result in unnecessary proxy/stub layers that will definitely impact application performance.

---

[6] More information on whether to configure your components is found in rule 3-7.

COM+ and Windows 2000

COM and MTS represent two different run-time layers in Windows NT. Things are much better in Windows 2000 because COM and COM+ have been integrated into a single run-time. The SCM for Windows 2000 has been rewritten to be aware of context and activities. This eliminates the problems of having to decide between calling to the MTS run-time versus calling to the SCM. In Windows 2000, the SCM is part of the COM+ run-time.

A call to VB's `CreateObject` function under Windows 2000 always produces the same results as a call to `CreateInstance` under Windows NT. With either creation technique, the object will always be properly created in the activity of its creator.[7] However, in Windows 2000, `CreateObject` is preferred over `CreateInstance`, primarily because it eliminates confusion. `CreateInstance` is no longer needed and is only included under the COM+ programming model for backward compatibility with MTS components. However, there is no drawback to using `CreateInstance`; in fact, you should continue to use `CreateInstance` if you want to run your DLLs in both MTS and COM+.

Even though the `CreateObject` function doesn't get you into trouble under Windows 2000, the `New` operator continues to cause problems. If one configured component calls `New` on another configured component that has been compiled in the same DLL, the VB run-time creates and initializes the new object without the help of the SCM and COM+. This scenario produces unfortunate results in COM+ just as it does in MTS. COM+ cannot properly set up its interception scheme between the two objects.

Calling `New` to create an object from a configured component that's part of the same DLL is always bad. The new object gets created without its own context. This means the new object cannot reliably call `GetObjectContext` or use the `ObjectContext` interface. Doing so can result in the same types of problems that were discussed when using `New` with MTS. For this reason, you should prefer the `CreateObject` function instead of the `New` operator in situ-

---

[7] This assumes that the component's COM+ `Synchronization` setting is set to `Required`, the default (and proper) setting for VB objects.

ations when one configured component is creating an object from another configured component in the same DLL.

More Problems With New

You already know that it's incorrect to call New on a configured component that's compiled in the same DLL. It gets even worse. The New operator causes even more problems when you're trying to debug configured components inside the VB IDE. Inside the VB debugger, the rules for when to avoid New are even more restrictive. You must avoid the New operator when the code creating the object and the configured component being used to instantiate the object are both inside the same VB project *group.* This is true even when calling the New operator across project boundaries. In other words, the call to New and the configured component you're using to instantiate the object can't be running inside the same session of the VB debugger. We'll provide a little background to illustrate why this is such a problem.

Let's say you have a VB project for a client application and a project for an ActiveX DLL with your configured component in the same project group. Your motivation for adding them to the same project group is to debug both projects in a single session of the VB IDE. When the client application calls New on the configured component in the DLL, VB creates the new object without the assistance of the SCM. The result is that the new object doesn't get created by the COM+ run-time in a valid context.

This situation has unfortunate side effects that are often easy to recognize. All of your calls to GetObjectContext will return a null reference, which typically results in a series of run-time errors. If you repeatedly see error 91 ("Object variable or With block variable not set"), the cause is likely that your code is trying to invoke methods using a null reference that was returned from a call to GetObjectContext.

The bottom line is that you can't properly debug the project for your client application and the project for your ActiveX DLL in the same project group when the client application is using the New operator. It also doesn't work if you try to debug two ActiveX DLL projects in the same project group and code in one DLL is using the New operator to create objects from a configured component in the other DLL. If you want to be sure that the SCM properly creates your objects in a valid context, you must either use the `CreateObject` function instead of `New`, or use a second session of the VB IDE to house your calling code during debugging.

There are many times in COM+ when you should use the `CreateObject` function instead of the `New` operator. Remember there are times when it's OK and a little bit faster to use the `New` operator (see rule 3-7), such as when you're creating an ADO object. However, remember these rules. In COM+, you should use `CreateObject` or `CreateInstance` when creating objects from a class you intend to use as a configured component. In MTS, you must use `CreateInstance` when creating objects from a class you intend to use as a configured component. Knowing which activation technique to use will save you considerable headaches down the road.

Rule 3-4: Understand the Real Motivation for `SetComplete`

There's a lot of misinformation floating around about why the programming models for MTS and COM+ provide the `SetComplete` method. During the last few years we've met quite a few programmers who call `SetComplete` in every method of every component they're targeting for MTS or COM+. They're not sure why they're calling `SetComplete`, however for some mystical reason they believe that their applications will scale to new heights if they do. The purpose of this topic is to clarify when calls to `SetComplete` are appropriate and when they're not.

A call to `SetComplete` tells the MTS/COM+ run-time that you'd like to deactivate your object as soon as possible. Internally, `SetComplete` sets an object's *done bit* to `True`. When the done bit is set to `True`, it instructs the MTS/COM+ run-time to deactivate the object when the current method call returns control back to the interception layer.

This transparent deactivation of MTS/COM+ objects has been termed *stateless programming*. In the short history of MTS and COM+, there has been a good deal of confusion about why statelessness is an essential aspect of the programming model. Some books and articles have even gone so far as to suggest that stateless programming is primarily about reclaiming memory on an

MTS/COM+ server. They argue that destroying objects and reclaiming memory results in higher levels of scalability as a result of more efficient resource usage. This argument is both confusing and inaccurate.

As it turns out, there are two compelling arguments for calling `SetComplete`. One argument has to do with controlling the outcome of a transaction and the other has to do with object pooling. However, if your component isn't involved in a transaction and doesn't support object pooling (*which VB objects currently do not*), a call to `SetComplete` has either no effect or a negative effect. Blindly following the advice of other programmers without an understanding of the issues at hand isn't a very sound programming practice.

MTS and COM+ provide two important transactional methods: `SetComplete` and `SetAbort`. These methods are critical for controlling the outcome of an MTS/COM+ transaction. Although it's important to know the specifics of how and when to call these methods to vote on a transaction's outcome, this rule does not cover those issues (see rule 3-5). Instead, let's focus on what happens at the end of a transaction. Regardless of whether the transaction is committed or rolled back, every object involved is deactivated when the transaction is released.

When you're writing an MTS/COM+ transaction, your objects will be acquiring and releasing locks on various *resource managers*. The MTS/COM+ runtime provides support to acquire locks as late as possible and to release them as quickly as possible. Minimizing the lock times for transactions is one of the most effective ways to optimize throughput and to increase scalability in a distributed online transaction processing (OLTP) system. One very popular and efficient way to write MTS/COM+ transactions is to add a call either to `SetComplete` or to `SetAbort` in every possible execution path for each method in a component that serves as the root object.

When a method in the root object returns after calling either `SetComplete` or `SetAbort`, the MTS/COM+ interception layer releases the transaction and all the locks that it has acquired. The interception layer also deactivates every object associated with the transaction as part of the cleanup process. Furthermore, if the objects inside the transaction do not support object pooling, deactivation also results in the objects' destruction. This means that the root object and any secondary objects will be created and destroyed inside the scope of a single method call from the client.

It's important to note that the client can't tell that the root object is being deactivated and destroyed. In the case of MTS, the client holds a persistent connection to the root object's context wrapper. Things are similar in COM+, in which the client holds a reference to a context-aware proxy associated with the object. Every time the client calls another method, a new root object and possibly a set of secondary objects are created and destroyed inside the scope of a new transaction. This transparent creation and destruction of objects is a side effect of the MTS/COM+ just-in-time activation (JITA) scheme.

So why is it important for MTS/COM+ to deactivate all the objects inside a transaction? It deactivates all the objects to ensure the proper semantics of the transaction. The idea is that an object in a declarative transaction can see a data item in a consistent state only while the resource manager (for example, a database management system [DBMS]) is holding a lock. If an object in a transaction were to hold a copy of a data item in the middle tier after the lock has been released, another transaction could modify the original data item inside the resource manager. The original data item and the copy would thus be out of sync and would violate the "ACID" (atomic, consistent, isolated, durable) rules of a transaction.

The reason that MTS/COM+ requires the deactivation of objects at transactional boundaries is that any copy of a data item must be thrown away when the resource manager releases its locks. MTS and COM+ require you to deactivate every transactional object so you don't compromise the consistency of your application's data. A call to SetComplete simply forces the end of the transaction and the inevitable deactivation of your objects as soon as possible.

A call either to SetComplete or to SetAbort informs the interception layer that you'd like to deactivate your object when the current method call returns. In MTS, objects are always destroyed by the system immediately after they have been deactivated. COM+, on the other hand, provides object pooling for those objects *that support it.* This means that when an object is deactivated, it can be placed in a pool rather than destroyed, and can be reused later by other clients. Object pooling introduces a second motivation for calling SetComplete (or any other method that sets the done bit to True). A call to

`SetComplete` can speed up deactivation and return an object back to the pool more quickly.

The primary motivation behind object pooling is that some middle-tier objects are expensive to create and initialize continually. If a set of these "expensive" objects can be created once and recycled across a set of clients, an application can conserve the processing cycles associated with this ongoing object creation and initialization. Think of a pooled object as you would think of any other shared server-side resource. By calling `SetComplete` in a pooled object, you can acquire the resource as late as possible and release it as early as possible.

Object pooling is particularly valuable for recycling objects in which initialization is both expensive and generic. If a component meets these criteria, object pooling and calls to `SetComplete` can increase an application's response times and overall throughput. However, it's important to remember that a component will not really benefit from object pooling if it doesn't meet these criteria.

A configured component must meet a fairly rigid set of requirements to support object pooling. Unfortunately, VB6 is not capable of creating components that meet these requirements. VB can only create components that reside in STAs. Furthermore, all VB objects exhibit thread affinity because of the VB's usage of thread local storage (TLS). These threading limitations, along with a few other shortcomings, prevent VB6 objects from participating in the object pooling scheme of COM+.

When you install a VB component in a COM+ application, the object pooling settings will always be disabled. There's nothing you can do to make COM+ pool your objects. Using C++ along with the Active Template Library (ATL) is the easiest and most straightforward way to create configured components that support object pooling.

Until the day when VB components meet the requirements for object pooling, a call to `SetComplete` will always result in the destruction of your VB objects. If you're programming in VB6 (or earlier versions), your only motivation for calling `SetComplete` or `SetAbort` is to control the outcome of a transaction. If you have an object that isn't involved in a transaction, there's no reason to call `SetComplete` or `SetAbort`.

If you set a component's Transaction support property to Doesn't Support Transactions and don't call `SetComplete` or `SetAbort`, your objects remain alive and thus can maintain client-specific state across method calls. This type of component is called a *stateful component.* There are many people who believe that it's never acceptable to create stateful components for MTS or COM+. Quite simply, these people are wrong.

The people who suggest that stateful components shouldn't be used in MTS or COM+ are simply repeating the mantra they've heard from others. Don't let anyone convince you that stateful components don't have a place in MTS and COM+ application design. The most common misconception is that stateless components scale better as a result of a more efficient utilization of middle-tier resources.

Some people argue that calling `SetComplete` is beneficial because it aggressively reclaims memory in the middle tier. As it turns out, when you call `SetComplete` and deactivate a server-side object, you're not releasing the memory required to hold open the connection. With MTS, server-side residue such as the stub and the context wrapper continue to consume approximately 1K of memory even after a VB object has been deactivated. The amount of memory used for a COM+ connection is fairly similar.

In many cases the memory you reclaim from deactivating an object is much smaller than the ongoing memory requirements keeping the connection alive. For example, if you call `SetComplete` on a VB object that's 250 bytes (a medium-size object in VB terms), you're really only reclaiming 20 percent of the memory that the client's consuming on the server computer. If you want to reclaim all the memory, you must tear down the connection by releasing the object reference from the client application.

Also note that calling `SetComplete` does nothing with respect to thread management to improve your application's performance or concurrency. Some programmers have been incorrectly convinced that a call to `SetComplete` breaks the client's association with a specific STA thread. That's absolutely not the case. The client's connection is pinned to a specific STA thread regardless of whether VB objects are being created and destroyed through the MTS/COM+ JITA scheme.

You can't break the association between a client and an STA thread simply by calling SetComplete. You can only do that by releasing the entire connection from the client. Once again, you have to tear down the entire connection by setting the client's object reference equal to Nothing. Releasing the object reference from the client application is the only thing that actually releases all server-side resources.

There are some situations in which stateful components make sense. Let's look at a common example. Assume you have an MTS/COM+ application in which clients are creating objects from across the local area network (LAN). In this scenario, stateful components have many advantages over a stateless component.

Consider the disadvantages of calling SetComplete and destroying your object every time you call a method. First, you're wasting processing cycles because of the ongoing need to tear down and re-create objects. Second, you can't maintain client-specific state in server-side objects. You must pass initialization parameters and reinitialize one or more objects in every method call. This doesn't sound like an efficient practice in times when it's not required.

For example, if you are designing a stateless customer component, you must pass the primary key or some other logical ID for the customer in each method call. Not only is this tedious when it comes to defining methods, but it has a definite run-time cost that impacts performance. Method calls require more parameters, which result in more network traffic. Every call requires additional processing cycles on the server for object creation and initialization. If JITA requires complex calculations or database access, then calls to SetComplete can significantly reduce your application's performance.

From the design perspective, stateless programming is usually more difficult than stateful programming. If you can't maintain client-specific state inside the middle tier, your management of client sessions becomes far more complex. You must either bring all the state back to the client, or you must go to the database more often. A stateful middle-tier object allows you to maintain a reasonable amount of client-specific state in the middle tier.

We don't mean to suggest that you can always maintain client-specific state in the middle tier. In many situations such as Web application development, you cannot get away with such a technique (see rule 4-2 for state management details). However, in LAN-based scenarios, in which caching client-specific state is appropriate, stateful components make the application's design much more straightforward. After all, you can simply calculate how much memory each client needs and then multiply that number by your expected number of clients. So go ahead and purchase more memory for your server computers and save yourself a few headaches during the design phase.

As you can see, you must carefully weigh the pros and cons when you decide whether you really need stateless components. Objects that are stateful definitely have a place in the MTS and COM+ programming model. A stateful object can hold the client-specific state and save valuable processing cycles required to create and initialize new instances. You can also use stateful objects to accomplish many programming tasks that are impossible with stateless objects.

The bottom line is that you ought to know when you should and shouldn't call `SetComplete`. Don't call it simply because some weird-looking guy at a conference told you it's a surefire way to maximize your application's scalability.

Rule 3-5: Consider Auto-Abort Style with Transactions

When moving into the world of MTS/COM+ transactional programming, there is a period of readjustment for most of us in the VB community. Transactions have traditionally been things we've programmed, not things we've declared. It's hard to see how a transaction can be committed or rolled back when we don't explicitly request either.

With the new concept of declarative transactions comes a new set of coding practices. We have to start thinking in terms of settings and votes, and which of each represents the best style of coding. Our transactional objects (Figure 3.4) set flags that impact the final outcome of a transaction.

When designing your transactional objects, you must first guarantee that a root object sets its done bit to `True` before returning control back to the base client. Setting the done bit guarantees deactivation, and deactivation of the root object initiates the commit/rollback of the transaction. Second, you must ensure that if a transaction becomes doomed (i.e., a component has voted that it is unhappy and done), no additional work will be performed against that trans-

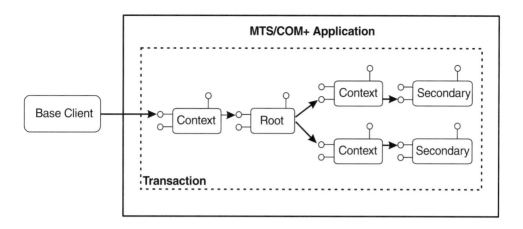

Figure 3.4 An MTS/COM+ transaction involving root and secondary objects

action. This is important because once a transaction has been doomed, the work performed will be rolled back, so continuing the task is futile.

It's your responsibility as a developer to ensure that these two conditions are always met, even in the presence of run-time errors. This becomes more difficult when secondary objects are involved, because one object is unable to determine directly the vote of another. Furthermore, you need to do this in a way that allows your secondary objects to behave identically to your root objects (i.e., a single design that is easy to understand, implement, and yields objects that can function in either capacity). Ultimately, you want to make sure it is crystal clear to the base client when a transaction is committed versus rolled back.

The solution is a conservative style of transactional programming we call *Auto-Abort*. It is based on two key observations: (1) All objects must vote if secondary objects are to be equivalent to root objects, and (2) the best way to communicate an unhappy vote among all parties involved is to raise run-time exceptions (see rule 1-4 for other considerations when raising errors). This translates into the following implementation style for transactional methods:

```
Public Sub PerformTaskTransactionally(...)
    On Error Goto errHandler
```

```
        Dim rObjCtx As ObjectContext
        Set rObjCtx = GetObjectContext()

        '** Initially vote unhappy & done in case something happens...
        If rObjCtx.IsInTransaction Then rObjCtx.SetAbort

        '** Perform task(s)...
            •
            •
            •

        '** if we got here, we're OK, so change vote and return!
        If rObjCtx.IsInTransaction Then rObjCtx.SetComplete
        Exit Sub

    errHandler:
        '** deal with error
            •
            •
            •
        '** tell caller we voted to abort
        Err.Raise ...
    End Sub
```

The idea is that *every* object, root or secondary, implements its methods using this same Auto-Abort style. Let's take a closer look at the code.

First, note that control can only leave the method in two ways: either the method returns normally or a run-time error occurs. Because one of the first steps is a tentative vote to roll back (`rObjCtx.SetAbort`), the object is guaranteed to have cast a vote no matter how control eventually exits. This satisfies the first design requirement that a root object should always vote done before returning to the base client. By the way, the name Auto-Abort is derived from the conservative nature of this voting scheme, which aborts a transaction by default.

Second, assuming the only `Exit Sub` statement is the one shown, then a normal return means that the object must have voted to commit. A run-time error would mean that the object must have voted to roll back. This is based on the fact that the only way to return normally is to reach the `Exit Sub`, in which case the tentative vote to roll back is changed to a commit.[8] As a result, if object A calls another object B, object A can always determine how B voted. Because local error trapping is enabled via `On Error Goto`, if B votes to roll back, control immediately transfers to the handler, stopping all transactional work. As long as the error handler does not try to resume execution in this case (and instead raises the error further up the call chain), the second and final design requirement has also been met: No additional work is performed against a transaction, *by any object,* once it is doomed. Note that if an error is caused by a nontransactional object or statement, the error handler is free to attempt recovery.

Lastly, not only does the code satisfy both requirements; it does so using a design that is identical for both root and secondary objects. And although an object may be secondary today and a root tomorrow, the base client can always determine the final outcome of a transaction in the same, predictable way, via error handling.

If you are working with COM+ under Windows 2000, you should be aware of two issues. There is a bug in the original release version of Windows 2000 that manifests itself as follows: If a secondary object votes that it is done (e.g., `rObjCtx.SetAbort`) and then raises an error, its error description will be replaced by the infamous "Method ~ of object ~ failed." Because the Auto-Abort design presented here dictates that you call `SetAbort` in secondary objects, you will encounter this bug on Windows 2000 release versions. You can take the easy way out and apply service pack 1 or higher for Windows 2000, or you can rewrite your secondary objects so they don't vote to abort before returning an error. The latter works fine because secondary objects convey their votes to the root object anyway (based on how they return), and the root eventually casts the necessary vote in accordance with the secondary objects. The disadvantage is that your secondary objects are now coded differently than your root objects, and thus are no longer reusable as root objects. This bug is not present in MTS, only in COM+ and only on Windows 2000 machines in which no service pack has been applied to the operating system.

---

[8] Changing one's vote is perfectly legal, as long as it is done before control leaves the method. The vote is not officially counted until the call passes back through the object's context proxy.

One other item of note with COM+ is that you can now declaratively vote as well as programmatically vote, if you want to. After configuring a component via Component Services, drill down to the method level. For each transactional method, display its properties, and check "Automatically deactivate this object when this method returns." If the method returns normally, the behavior is equivalent to calling `SetComplete`. If the method raises a run-time error, the behavior is equivalent to calling `SetAbort`. Note, however, that this is merely a default behavior. Any programmatic votes cast at run-time will always override the declarative setting. This feature is only available in COM+.

Moving from a world of programmatic transactions to declarative transactions takes some time and thought. However, using a simple, consistent style like Auto-Abort can save a lot of time and trouble, especially when translating results from secondary components to root components.

Rule 3-6: Don't Reinvent the DBMS

When it comes to designing a multitier system such as a Web application built with VB components, you are often confronted with state management issues relating to reading, writing, and caching data. Some client requests require one or more trips to the DBMS. However, there are times when you can avoid DBMS round-trips by caching in-memory data on the Web server. Eliminating DBMS round-trips often results in better performance and faster response times. In-memory caching techniques can also increase response times by eliminating the overhead of the database query engine and disk input/output (I/O).

You're probably aware of a few different techniques that allow you to cache data on the server. VB allows you to cache thread-level data using BAS modules (see rule 2-9). MTS and COM+ allow you to cache process-wide data items using the SPM (see rule 3-2). The ASP framework allows you to cache a single user's data items in the `Session` object and application-wide data items using the ASP `Application` object (discussed further in rules 4-2 and 4-3). There are certain situations in which each of these techniques offers benefits over the other. However, there are other situations in which none of these caching techniques provides an acceptable solution.

Sometimes it makes sense to avoid round-trips to the DBMS. There are other times when it's foolish to avoid the DBMS in an attempt to achieve better performance. Some reasons to consider incorporating a DBMS into your application design include the following:

- Data needs to be persisted for durability and recoverability.
- Read locks are needed for improved concurrency.
- Updates need to be rolled back in the event of an error condition.
- Locks need to be synchronized with locks from other data sources.
- Data needs to be shared across process and machine boundaries.

When you design a caching scheme, it typically means you're making a copy of frequently used data items and storing them in a place that provides faster access. As long as the real data items (ones that live in the DBMS) and the copies (ones that live in the server's memory) stay in sync, things are fine. However, when cached data needs to be updated, there are consistency issues. For example, if another application makes changes to the DBMS, the copies in the server's memory can become inconsistent. It's much easier to design a caching scheme for read-only data than for updatable data.

Let's look at an example of designing a caching scheme for a Web application. Imagine you need to generate a Web page that displays product inventory levels to your users. You decide to cache these product inventory levels in ASP `Application` variables to reduce round-trips to the DBMS. Now assume that another application is updating these inventory levels directly to the DBMS at periodic intervals. The product levels you're caching on the Web server are going to get out of sync with the live data in the DBMS. Consequently, you need to add some type of refresh logic to your application.

One strategy is to cache a timestamp value along with the product inventory levels. When a client request sees that the cached data is older than some configurable refreshing interval (perhaps five minutes), you make another round-trip to the DBMS to retrieve and cache the latest values. For the next five minutes, no other client request requires a round-trip to the DBMS.

The refreshing technique that has just been described can offer a measurable performance win if your application can tolerate small inconsistencies between what's actually in inventory and what's perceived to be in inventory. However, there's always a chance a user will retrieve an inconsistent value. If you need to guarantee that your application always retrieves consistent values, you may be required to make a round-trip to the DBMS for each client request. There's a definite trade-off between performance and data consistency. The best solution for one application may be totally inappropriate for another.

Now let's consider a more difficult scenario. Imagine you're writing a method implementation for a client request that's required to update a cached data item. Remember, when you modify an in-memory data item in the SPM or the ASP `Application` object, nothing is written to disk. This means updates are not recoverable (a.k.a. lost) in the event of an application crash. In most applications, losing updated data in this manner is unacceptable. When your method returns without raising an error, the client should be guaranteed that its changes have been stored in some durable format and that its changes are recoverable in the event of an application crash.

You can attempt to solve the problem of durability without a DBMS by finding another manner in which to persist updated data to disk. VB makes simple file I/O a trivial undertaking using built-in functions such as `FreeFile`, `Open`, and `Write`. The initial challenge you have with this technique is structuring a way to write updates to an unstructured text file. You could take a more progressive approach and persist updates to disk using an extensible markup language (XML) parser. An XML parser abstracts the structure of the underlying text file and allows you simply to insert, update, and retrieve data items as nodes in an XML document.

Although implementing a simple scheme to persist updates to disk may not prove too difficult, adding code to recover after an application crash or to optimize response times during larger updates is far more challenging. For example, how would you answer the following questions?

When your application starts up, how does it know whether there has been an application crash and, therefore, whether it needs to recover data from disk? How do you back up and reload persisted data to protect against hard disk failure? When there's an update, how much data do you need to write out to disk before returning control back to the client? Is it possible to perform an optimization by writing the minimal amount of data that represents the delta between the old data and the new data? (The transaction log in a SQL Server DBMS provides this type of optimization.)

All the issues you've just seen are relevant and must be considered when designing a durability scheme for a multitier application. Think about how much time it will take to design, implement, test, and debug the code to make your data durable and recoverable. Now compare that investment with the licensing fee for an installation of SQL Server. If SQL Server can offer comparable performance to a custom caching scheme, it's going to save you a great deal of time and money. However, before you make a judgment on whether you need a DBMS, there are a few more important issues that we need to talk about.

A noteworthy limitation with both the SPM and the ASP `Application` object is their inability to use shared locks. Both the SPM and the ASP `Application` offer exclusive locking only. Once a client request acquires an exclusive lock for a particular data item, it blocks every other client until the lock is released. In many situations, exclusive locking is overkill. Shared locks can offer the required levels of consistency with significantly less impact on an application's concurrency.

A DBMS provides an optimized form of concurrency by complementing exclusive locks with shared locks. A client with a shared lock blocks another client attempting to perform a write operation. However, a shared lock does not block other clients that are attempting a read operation on the same data item. This additional level of locking granularity can provide faster response times and higher levels of throughput because it prevents readers from blocking one another.

Because of to their simplistic locking schemes, the SPM and the ASP `Application` object are best used for read-only data that's loaded at application start-up. They can be used to a lesser extent in scenarios in which data changes are infrequent. As discussed earlier, periodic data refreshing can boost performance by reducing DBMS round-trips. However, in a large-scale application with frequent updates, you need more sophisticated locking support. Neither the SPM nor the ASP `Application` object provides a satisfactory solution.

What are your options? Although you could create a custom C++ implementation that's similar to the SPM, and includes the logic to use shared locking in addition to exclusive locking, it would be a pretty expensive undertaking and it may require expertise that your company doesn't possess. Alternatively, you could save yourself lots of time and money by leveraging the sophisticated locking behavior that's built into a DBMS such as SQL Server.

You'd be surprised at how well SQL Server performs when it's installed on the same computer as a Web application. Although accessing data in a local SQL Server database requires cross-process calls, it's not that much slower than accessing in-memory data with the SPM or the ASP `Application` object. You should try running your own benchmarks because the performance differences are far less than most developers expect. SQL Server's internal data-caching scheme is very fast, and its use of shared locks may improve your application's performance.

Although the SPM and the ASP `Application` object provide isolation through exclusive locking, they are unlike a DBMS because they cannot enforce the ACID rules. You've already seen that neither the SPM nor the ASP `Application` object provides durability. Now, let's consider the issue of atomicity. Neither the SPM nor the ASP Application object provides any type of rollback facilities. For example, what happens if you modify data in the SPM from inside a COM+ transaction and then roll back the transaction? The changes you've made to SPM data are not automatically reversed. That means you have to provide custom code to detect error conditions, and undo changes by hand. However, if you write your changes to a DBMS, reversing those updates is as easy as aborting the current transaction. This is a huge benefit because it eliminates the need to write code for undoing changes.

Additionally, the locks held by the SPM and the ASP `Application` object are never coordinated with any other data source. For example, if you make a change to a data item in the SPM and another change to a data item in an Oracle database from within a COM+ transaction, the locks on these two data items are not synchronized. The SPM typically releases its locks as soon as the current method call finishes, which happens before the DTC starts to run the two-phase commit protocol. This lack of synchronization can lead to violations of the ACID rules.

How would moving data items from the SPM over to a local SQL Server database change the scenario that's just been described? Because SQL Server is a resource manager, you can use a COM+ transaction to synchronize locks held across multiple resource managers. For example, from within a COM+ transaction you could establish a local connection to a SQL Server database and another remote connection to an Oracle database. Because both connections are auto-enlisted in a single distributed transaction, the DTC synchronizes the locks held by both data sources to enforce the ACID rules.

The last important thing to note about the SPM and the ASP `Application` object is that neither provides a way to share data *across* process boundaries. Two VB objects can only see the same SPM data when they are running inside the same process. Two VB objects (or ASP pages) can only see the same ASP `Application` object data when they are running inside the same process and the same ASP `Application`.

How do you share data between VB objects that are running in different processes on the same computer? One possible approach is to use a low-level Win32 programming technique such as memory-mapped files. Unfortunately, this approach isn't very practical in VB. This means you'd be better off resorting to another language better suited for the task, such as C++.

Alternatively, you could share data between processes by writing it out to a file on disk. For example, VB objects running in different processes can share data by reading and writing to a common file. However, with this approach you'd have to deal with the issues of persistence and durability that were discussed earlier. You'd also more than likely have to incorporate a locking scheme to deal with concurrency issues. As you can imagine, it's tough to design and to implement a locking strategy that allows multiple processes to access the same file concurrently without compromising data consistency.

As you can see, sharing data across processes on the same computer is not an easy problem to solve. However, sharing data across computer boundaries is even more difficult. Moreover, sharing data across computer boundaries is a very common application requirement. This is especially true when the code is designed for a Web farm for which client requests are arbitrarily redirected to different Web servers on a request-by-request basis. Your code must be able to access application data and session data from any one of several Web servers in the farm.

Let's walk through one possible solution for maintaining session state in a Web farm environment without using a DBMS. You could dedicate one computer (a COM+ application server) to hold the session state for every user. When processing a client request on one of the Web servers in the farm, you can activate an object on the COM+ application server. Objects running on the COM+ application server all run in the same process and can, therefore, read and write shared data using the SPM. When a second request from the same client is redirected to another Web server in the farm, it too could activate an object on the COM+ application server to access data written during the previous request. This approach provides a foundation for reading and writing cached data in a Web farm environment.

Once you've gone this far, you probably want to add the logic to persist all updates and to make them durable to protect against system failures. If concurrent access exposes your application data to inconsistency, you'll need to add a locking scheme. If you need rollback support, you'll have to devise an update buffer to build in support for automatic rollback. If your locks need to be synchronized with other data sources, you may even be required to add the support to make your application a resource manager that can interoperate with the DTC. Is this starting to look suspiciously like a DBMS to you?

What does this example demonstrate? It shows that many of today's multitier applications present complex problems that have already been solved by the DBMS. There is no reason to reinvent the DBMS. To a large extent, it doesn't really matter whether you use SQL Server, Oracle, or DB2. All these DBMS vendors have already invested millions of dollars and thousands of man-years solving the same problems that we encounter time after time. Their code has gone through many generations of design, implementation, testing, and debugging. When you purchase a license for a DBMS, you get lots of value for your money.

Here's something to keep in mind. When you try to design and implement a sophisticated caching scheme, you're starting down the same road that's already been traveled by DBMS vendors such as Microsoft, Oracle, and IBM. However, these vendors are a few decades ahead of you and they have invested literally thousands of man-years designing, implementing, testing and debugging their code. In most cases, your efforts are not going to be as cost-effective as simply purchasing a license for SQL Server.

Rule 3-7: Don't Feel Obligated to Configure All Your Components

MTS and COM+ are great environments that provide a lot of features and services that in many cases would be very difficult for us to write. The benefits of decoupling services from business logic should not be overlooked. Additionally, the prebuilt surrogate framework can save weeks of coding, letting you focus on business logic instead. Of course, although these services are beneficial, they come with a price. You may want to think twice before configuring components just for the sake of configuration.

MTS/COM+ programming relies heavily on intercepting a client's calls to a component. Components are configured, meaning that settings are applied when instances are created. This extensible loading mechanism makes it possible for administrators to change run-time characteristics of your solutions without having to recompile your code. If these services would benefit your solutions, then you should leverage MTS and COM+, and thus configure your components to run inside them.

Sometimes, however, you don't need to apply configuration to all your components in a solution. If that is the case, you have to decide if you should incur the expense of the MTS/COM+ environment. By now you are well aware of proxies, stubs, contexts, and interception. These things are expensive, and if you can avoid them you should. The addition of context in COM+ is significant for VB developers. Two configured components written with VB will *always* live in separate contexts. This means that any time two configured components communicate, there is context switching, which adds overhead.

To run your components in a surrogate, the root object must be configured. The idea, however, is that secondary objects don't have to be configured to load into the same process, *as long as they are instantiated by the root object.* In fact, if your secondary component is not making use of attributes, its context proxy is simply overhead. If you were to have a configured component call a nonconfigured component, then they can run in the same context and eliminate the proxy. Eliminating the proxy means direct communication between your components, which in turn means faster response times. The easiest way to remove the proxy is simply not to deploy your secondary component within MTS/COM+. Instead of using MTS or COM+, simply register your component with REGSVR32.EXE, and it will be instantiated as a nonconfigured component.

It's one thing to register a component as nonconfigured, but it's another thing altogether to understand *when* and *why* you should or shouldn't do this. Although not configuring a component may speed up your application somewhat, failing to configure a component that should be configured could be disastrous! A simple rule is this: When in doubt, configure the component. However, a classic example when you may consider nonconfigured components is for data access. If your design on the middle tier calls for a business layer with an underlying data access layer, you can configure the business components to require the services of MTS and COM+. However, the data access layer can remain nonconfigured, thereby reaping the benefits of MTS/COM+ (including transactions) without the cost of interception and context. Note that these costs are typically a factor of ten in terms of call time, and 4K in terms of memory.

In short, any component that could be a root under some scenario *must* be configured. You should only consider nonconfigured components if they are to be exclusively used as secondary components. The drawback to nonconfigured components is that your objects cannot be explicitly written to take advantage of MTS/COM+ services (e.g., object constructor strings), nor can they vote. Likewise, nonconfigured components will not be a part of the client and server setup files exported by MTS/COM+.

Another way you can avoid an unwanted context proxy is by placing a secondary component in the same DLL as the root component that will call it. If you deploy this way *and* you instantiate the secondary component using the New key word, this triggers a fast internal allocation of memory rather than a COM-based activation. Because COM is unaware of the instance, it will also not place a proxy between the root and secondary component, yielding direct efficient access between the two.

In general, if you know your component is going to function properly as a nonconfigured component, then you may have a case for running them this way. The important point is to think through the use of your components and deploy them in their proper place. Don't necessarily configure all your components, only when you explicitly need one or more features of MTS or COM+.

Rule 3-8: Avoid Compiling Things into DLLs That You'll Later Regret

As a developer you're probably familiar with the procedure when it's time to upgrade a DLL that's in production. First, you open the project that contains the DLL's source code. This may involve checking the project out of a source code management system such as Visual SourceSafe. Once opened, you modify your code and recompile the DLL. Finally, you (or the administrator) redistributes the DLL to the production servers.

It's important to remember that upgrading your DLL code in production usually requires shutting down the hosting application. For example, if the old version of the DLL has been loaded into the IIS Web server process (INETINFO.EXE), you may have to shut down the Web site to upgrade the DLL. This requires an interruption in service that most companies would rather avoid.

As you can see, it can be a fairly painful and intrusive undertaking to upgrade DLL code that's already in production. There are times when upgrading a DLL in production is an absolute necessity. However, with some extra work during the design phase, you can significantly reduce the number of times you'll be forced to go through this recompilation and redeployment cycle. The key is to determine what things are vulnerable to change when you're designing your components and then to avoid compiling those things into your DLLs.

Let's start with a common example. Let's say you're writing data access code that uses the ADO library and you need an OLE DB connection string to establish a connection to a DBMS. One option is to hard code the connection string into a DLL using a module-level constant:

```
Const sCONNECT = "PROVIDER=SQLOLEDB;" & _
                 "SERVER=MyComputer;" & _
                 "DATABASE=MyDB;" & _
                 "UID=MyAccount;" & _
                 "PWD=Waldo;"
```

Think about what aspects of this connection string are likely to change. The database administrator (DBA) may decide to rename the database or move it to another computer. The DBA may decide it's necessary to change the password for the user account because a disgruntled employee has compromised it. Whatever the case, a change to any part of the connection string requires you to go through the recompilation/redeployment cycle to get your changes into production.

Using a data source name (DSN) or a universal data link (UDL) file in a connection string offers more flexibility. As you probably know, a DSN is a set of Open Database Connectivity (ODBC) configuration values in the Windows registry that holds the connection information for a specific database. A UDL file is roughly the OLE DB equivalent of an ODBC DSN. One difference is that a UDL file exists in the file system instead of the registry. Here's an example of what the connection string looks like when it references a UDL file:

```
Const sCONNECT = "file name=c:\myapp\myconnection.udl"
```

Whenever the database needs to be renamed or moved, or whenever a password needs to be changed, it's easy for the DBA to modify a DSN or a UDL file at the same time. In most cases, modifying a DSN or a UDL file is much easier than modifying a connection string that's been compiled into a production DLL.

Over the past decade, many VB programmers have avoided the use of DSNs and resorted to DSN-less connection strings. However, it's important to understand that this bias against DSNs was formed in a two-tier world. When data access code runs on the client's computer, it's necessary to create and configure a DSN on each user's desktop. The DSN-per-desktop requirement is expensive to set up, and an overly curious user can break an application by fooling around in the ODBC section of the Windows control panel.

A multitier application doesn't require a DSN or a UDL file on the client desktop. Instead, the DSN or UDL file is placed on the server. It's not as difficult to set up because there will always be far fewer server computers than desktop computers. You also don't have the problem of careless users doing something to a DSN or a UDL file.

ODBC and OLE DB provide DSNs and UDL files so you can avoid compiling things that frequently change in your DLLs. However, what if you have something other than a database connection string that frequently changes? For example, what if your DLL is dependent on a uniform resource locator (URL) used to download an XML file from across the Internet. During the design phase you decide this URL is something that will change on a somewhat regular basis. Therefore, you don't want to compile the URL into your DLL. Moreover, if you sell the DLL to ten different customers and they all require a different URL, you don't want to compile ten different DLL builds that only differ with regard to this URL.

To avoid compiling the URL into your DLL you can write it into the Windows registry or to a custom configuration file. Both approaches require you to devise a way to write the URL data to the server computer when the DLL is installed. If you want your software to have a polished appearance, you should also provide a way for an administrator to adjust the URL on an ongoing basis. Some administrators may feel that a README.TXT file showing how to adjust registry settings with REGEDIT32.EXE is a less than elegant solution.

If you're designing a DLL for COM+ and Windows 2000, you have another option. You can use the declarative constructor string attribute. A separate constructor string can be associated with each configured class. COM+ stores constructor strings in RegDB and provides the class designer with an opportunity to load the string value into objects created from these configured components at activation time. Here's a simple example of a class that uses a constructor string:

```
'** required interface to receive the construct or string
Implements COMSVCSLib.IObjectConstruct
Private sMyURL As String

Sub IObjectConstruct_Construct(ByVal pCtorObj As Object)
   sMyURL = pCtorObj.ConstructString
End Sub
```

In addition to implementing the `IObjectConstruct` interface, the configured class must have its `ConstructionEnabled` attribute enabled and its `ConstructorString` attribute set to the desired string. It's very easy to configure these attributes in the COM+ Services administrative tool after the class has been installed in a COM+ application.

A constructor string has a few advantages over using a registry entry or a custom configuration file. If you create a server-side setup program for a COM+ application using the `Export` command, you can preconfigure a constructor string. After the DLL has been installed, the COM+ Services administrative tool makes it easy for other administrators to make changes. Furthermore, COM+ provides programmable administrative components that make it relatively simple to update a constructor string with an administrative script. You can even run a script to update a constructor string from across the network.

The use of a declarative constructor string can also provide performance benefits over writing and reading values to and from the registry or a custom configuration file. The COM+ run-time caches a constructor string the first time it's used in the lifetime of the hosting process. All subsequent uses of the constructor string use this cached value. However, if an administrator changes a constructor string after it's already been cached, the COM+ run-time knows to discard the old value and use the new one. If you wanted a similar caching scheme with values in the registry or a custom configuration file, you'd have to design and implement it yourself.

So far, this rule has discussed techniques using the registry, custom configuration files, and constructor strings. These techniques make your life easier by allowing you to avoid compiling important yet dynamic values into your DLLs. However, there's one other really popular place where programmers store data that's constantly changing—a database.

Let's look at an example of a poor software design to illustrate a point. Imagine you want to create a DLL for generating HTML pages dynamically at run-time. The motivation for creating such a DLL is to move content out of ASP pages to improve application maintainability. Examine the following method, which will be called from an ASP page:

```
Public Sub ProcessRequest()
    '** generate content
    Dim sContent As String
    sContent = "My content retrieved from a DBMS"

    '** generate HTML page
    Dim sPage As String
```

```
        sPage = "<html><title>Acme Industries Home " & _
                "Page</title>" & _
                "<body bgcolor='lightblue'>" & _
                "<h1>Welcome to my home page</h1>" & _
                sContent & _
                "</body><html>"

        '** write page back to client
        Dim rResponse As ASPTypeLibrary.Response
        Set rResponse = GetObjectContext("Response")
        rResponse.Write sPage
    End Sub
```

What's wrong with this code? The obvious problem is that the HTML tags that hold the page's layout details are compiled into the DLL. What's going to happen when you need to change the page's title or background color? You have to recompile and redistribute your DLL.

In a case such as this, you should strive for a more data-driven design. You definitely want your application's view of business data to be data-driven, but you can take the concept much further than that. You can also use a data driven approach with page titles, page formatting, and navigation. This sort of data isn't exactly business data. It's metadata that the user interface portion of your application needs to do its job.

To use a data-driven approach, you can create a framework that allows the site's Webmaster to add new pages by simply adding a new record to a database that holds your metadata. For example, you can create a database table named `Pages` that defines a set of fields such as `Title`, `Header`, and `Body`. The code in your framework can dynamically parse these elements into a Web page at run-time.

Likewise, you can easily make a site-wide change to such things as page formatting and the navigation toolbar if the metadata that defines them also lives in the database. If you get to a point where you can make site-wide formatting changes and add new pages without recompiling any code, you've done a good job.

As we've mentioned, if you take a data-driven approach, you should store all content and HTML metadata in a database. The DLL can then retrieve content and HTML metadata from the database at application start-up or on an as-needed basis. You can also optimize performance by caching data inside the Web server process. For example, when your ASP application starts, you can retrieve all the HTML metadata from the database and load it into ASP `Application` variables. This provides fast and easy access to your HTML metadata and lets you generate custom pages, on the fly, much faster.

This item has illustrated the key points of using a data-driven approach to improve application maintainability. One of the most important things you can do during the design phase is determine what elements are likely to change over the DLL's lifetime in a production environment. Many of these elements are the things that you may later regret having compiled into your DLLs.

Rule 3-9: Best Practices for Porting MTS Code to COM+

As developers, we are occasionally called on to move an existing software solution from one platform to another. With the gradual influx of Windows 2000 into the business world, one common occurrence of this is porting an MTS solution over to COM+. Although the move is largely transparent, there are a few things you need to know to execute a smooth transfer. The following features will help you write your code in such a way as to make a smoother transition, should you be called on to port MTS code to COM+.

In COM+ You No Longer Need to Call `GetObjectContext.CreateInstance`

The underlying COM functions `CoCreateInstance` and `CoCreateInstanceEx` have been updated to be aware of the COM+ Catalog (the database in which configuration information is stored for your configured components). As VB programmers, we don't need to make direct calls to these COM+ functions. However, when we call `CreateObject`, the run-time forwards the call to one of these functions. This allows the underlying activation infrastructure to place our objects in the appropriate context when being created and thus removes the need for calling `GetObjectContext.CreateInstance` (although `CreateInstance` still works in COM+ and is safe to use). On the other hand, be aware when you create objects using `New` that the VB run-time has not been updated and may internally service your call, meaning your object will not have the appropriate interception layer in place. (Note that activation architectural details are covered in detail in rules 2-6 and 3-3.)

You No Longer Need to Call `SafeRef` When Passing `Me` as a Parameter
With MTS, much of the interception layer was wedged into place by brute force. Thus we often needed to help MTS stay in the middle of things by letting it know when we were creating objects or handing references around. Most of this is because COM had no notion of MTS. Now that the low-level COM+ services have been updated to be MTS-aware, we don't have to force interception into the picture.

Under MTS, calls to `SafeRef` were used to ensure that a reference to the context wrapper was handed out as opposed to a direct reference to an object. Because MTS needed to intercept all calls to an object, this was a very important thing to remember and an often-overlooked piece of code. Again, thanks to the low-level changes in COM, `SafeRef` is no longer necessary.

Watch Out When Returning Errors from Secondary Objects in a Transaction; You May Get "Method ~ of Object Failed ~" Instead of the Rich Error Information You Specified Before Propagating the Error
This is one of those little bugs that can be a real problem for people who just move their components from MTS to COM+. Because this is not a problem when running under MTS, people are likely to have faith that it will work under COM+. The scenario for this error is rather specific, so the following example may help. First, a client creates an instance of a transactional object, called the *root object*. The root object then creates an instance of another transactional object, called the *secondary object*. The secondary object encounters an error, which it handles as follows:

```
' ** code dooms the transaction and raises an error
ErrorHandler:
    rObjCtx.SetAbort
    Err.Raise lErrNumber, sYourSource, sYourMessage
Exit Function
```

Notice first the call to `SetAbort`. This call is required to doom the transaction and to indicate failure of the method call. This also has another significant impact: It tells COM+ to destroy the object! (You can find more information about this in rule 3-4.) Under MTS, the previous code would propagate the specified error information back to the caller. However, under COM+, the error description specified with `Err.Raise` will be lost when the function returns. Instead, the caller sees "Method ~ of object ~ failed."

In actuality, the error number itself is maintained, but the description that accompanies it is lost. This is a result of the way COM+ deactivates and destroys your transactional object when the method call returns. When the object is deactivated, the error description that is associated with the method call is lost and thus the root object has nothing to read and you get the ugly message. To avoid this there are two options. The easiest and best solution is to install service pack 1 or higher for Windows 2000. Alternatively, you can change the code in the secondary object from calling `SetAbort` to call `DisableCommit`. This has the effect of keeping the transaction from committing but does not destroy the object when the method returns, allowing the error information associated with the object to be propagated.

Take Advantage of the `ObjectConstruct` String

There are many ways to initialize an object with some specific information when it first gets created. Techniques for doing this include reading registry settings, looking at some configuration file, or even taking advantage of a simple DSN. Under COM+ a new method has been added that allows you to pass a string to an object when created. If you're going to recompile your code anyway, it may be worth your time to decouple some of your hard-coded data and place it in a `ConstructString`. There are a few simple steps you need to complete for this to work. First, your object must implement the new `IObjectConstruct` interface. This interface can be found by making a reference to the COM+ Services TypeLib. The following code shows how to implement this interface:

```
Implements IObjectConstruct
Private sVar as String


Sub IObjectConstruct_Construct(ByVal pCtorObj As Object)
    '** cast to the construct string interface
    Dim rConString As IObjectConstructString
```

```
    Set rConString = pCtorObj
    sVar = rConString.ConstructString
End Sub
```

Once your object has the ability to receive the constructor string, you will then need to specify the string you wish to be passed to the object when it is activated. This can be found in the Component Services tool by selecting the properties for your configured component. On the Activation tab of the properties box, check the "Enable object construction" check box and then enter your string in the textbox provided.

Declarative Security Checks Can Now Be Checked When Intraprocess Calls Are Made in a COM+ Application

With COM+, we have seen a dramatic evolution of security features. Originally in COM we had very little control over who had access to an object or methods of an object within our ActiveX executable. All we could specify was whether a particular user had access to the application. Once the user gained access, he had access to all objects and methods within the application. MTS provided a much more granular level of security via *roles.* Roles provided both declarative and programmatic security.

With declarative security the concept is fairly simple: You create a role, place users and groups in it, then allow access to a component based on that particular role. When a call is made to the component, checks are performed automatically to ensure the user is in a permissible role. If the user is not in a permissible role, access is denied. The only issue was that declarative checks occurred only when a process boundary was crossed, not on intraprocess calls. Under COM+ you can specify component-level checks to enforce security on entrance to each component. To enforce this, on the Application property page, the Security tab, select the option button "Perform access checks at the process and component level."

The `Refresh Components` Command Is No Longer Necessary in COM+

With MTS, many modifications have to be made to the registry when your configured component is going to run under MTS's control. This can be a major problem for VB developers because every time you recompile your component, VB modifies the same sections of the registry as MTS. So a component that has been configured to run under MTS might get "unconfigured" if you simply recompile the source code.

The changes in your registry settings can be found under HKEY_CLASSES_ROOT\CLSID. Your CLSID entries are considerably different after configuring in MTS. When a component is configured for a server package, a `LocalServer32` entry is created and the entry points to MTX.EXE /P:*GuidofyourMTSPackage*. With a library package, the component's `InprocServer32` entry would point to MTXEX.dll. Of course, as soon as you recompile in the VB IDE, the `InprocServer32` entry reverts back to the normal COM activation settings. This boils down to a "last-one-in-wins" scenario. Developers always need to reregister a component with MTS after building it to ensure that the appropriate settings exist in the registry. For this reason, the MTS Explorer has a *Refresh* menu item on the *Components* folder that updates each component's registry entries to reflect their MTS configuration.

To make this problem less annoying, Microsoft created a VB add-in that provides automatic refreshing of each component's registry entries after you compile a project. The goal of this add-in is to ensure that once a component is configured to run under MTS's control, it remains there, even after compiling new versions of the component with VB. With COM+, the registry remains the same as COM, and configuration settings are stored separately in RegDB. As a result, you do not need to refresh after compiling with VB, nor do you need the add-in.

The COM+ Exported Client Setup Application Requires a Version of Microsoft Installer (MSI) on Pre-Windows 2000 Machines

This feature is fairly self-explanatory but it's included here for completeness. When you export an application in COM+, a setup program is created that can run on any client machine that wants to use that application. The catch is that the setup program requires a version of the Microsoft installation software known as Microsoft Installer (MSI) for pre-Windows 2000 machines. Office 2000 was one of the first applications to use this technology, and even if you've installed Office 2000, the version of MSI that installed on your machine with

Office 2000 is not the one you need. You'll need to get the newer version, which can be found on the Windows Platform Software Development Kit (SDK).

Rule 3-10: Best Practices for Writing Code That Runs on MTS and COM+

Making the switch to Windows 2000 and COM+ is not always as easy as running the setup program. Many companies are slow to adopt new technologies without first spending a large amount of time testing to make sure things will work properly in their new environments. As developers, we often push the technology envelope and expect those around us to do the same. This forces us down a path where we may be developing components today for MTS even though we expect to migrate to Windows 2000 and COM+ in the near term. We may also create applications that simply need to run on NT4 machines and Windows 2000 machines. So how do we create components that will work in either place without having to make a bunch of coding changes before we recompile? One simple rule sums it up best: Don't use any of the new COM+ features. Beyond this general rule, however, there are some more specific tips.

Stick With `GetObjectContext.CreateInstance` When Creating Objects

Because the MTS interception layer relies on you to make sure it's always in the middle of things, don't do anything in your code that would prevent MTS from stepping up to the plate. In COM+, the infrastructure for creating objects is now aware of the COM+ Catalog and therefore other configured components. This allows the interception layer, under COM+, always to be in place when it is required. Under MTS this is drastically different. Prior to Windows 2000, COM had no knowledge of MTS and didn't know about the MTS interception layer. As a result, it became your job as a developer to keep MTS in the loop. This was accomplished by creating MTS objects using `GetObjectContext.CreateInstance`. Now, under COM+, `CreateObject` does the "right" thing and you don't need to use `CreateInstance`. You are leaving yourself open, however, to potential errors if you use `CreateObject` to create secondary components in MTS. Avoid the use of `CreateObject` for code that needs to run in both MTS and COM+.

Use Programmatic Security for Checking Access Permissions Instead of Relying on Declarative Security

COM+ has the ability to perform component-level access checks within an application. This is not supported under MTS. The only way to be safe is to stick with programmatic security checks via calls to `IsSecurityEnabled` and `IsCallerInRole`. This is also critical when you need to perform method-level security checks under MTS, because COM+ supports method-level checks via declarative security.

Prefer `DisableCommit` to `SetAbort` in Secondary Objects When Failing a Method That's Transactional

This relates to a problem porting to COM+ in regard to error propagation. When a call is made to `SetAbort` in a transactional object, followed by a call to raise an error, the resulting behavior is different under MTS than in COM+. The problem only occurs under a particular sequence of events; however, this sequence happens to be one we at DevelopMentor have been preaching for years! The problem occurs when calls to `SetAbort` and `Err.Raise` are both performed in a secondary object during a COM+ transaction. Error information is not propagated appropriately under COM+ because of the way transactional objects are destroyed. Under MTS, object destruction was handled differently, so this was not a problem. If you instead call `DisableCommit` in your secondary objects, you can be sure things will work correctly under both environments. `DisableCommit` tells the MTS/COM+ run-time that the transaction cannot commit, but that you would like your object to hold state. This allows the error information that was created in the `Err.Raise` call to propagate back to the root object. If you see the error "Method ~ of object ~ failed" then this may be an indication that you have deactivated a secondary object and thrown an error from it. This feature/bug was corrected with service pack 1 for Windows 2000.

Don't Install Your DLL on the Client by Accident

One of VB's many production-oriented features is the built-in TLB it embeds in our ActiveX DLLs. Placing the TLB in the DLL is great for administering the server, because there is only one file to maintain. The client install, however, is another issue altogether. Although we want to give our clients a TLB, we don't want to install our DLL on the client machine.

VB gives us another option by allowing us to generate a second TLB (independent of the DLL) by selecting the Remote Server Files option under the project's properties (Component tab). These generated stand-alone TLBs can be added to an MTS package by dragging and dropping them into it. Under MTS, they can be exported successfully, meaning the stand-alone TLB (and not the DLL) will be installed on the client machine.

Under COM+, however, this approach no longer works when creating an application proxy for client-side setup. Installing both a TLB and a VB DLL in COM+ triggers an error on export. As a result, what worked in MTS no longer works under COM+.

To ensure that your DLL is not installed on the client, you need to either (1) use a different mechanism to configure client machines or (2) install the TLB as you did under MTS but hack your VB DLL (using VC++) and remove the TLB resource before running export in COM+. The latter is ugly, but it works.

Stick With the `ObjectContext` Interface

COM+ has introduced several new interfaces. Some of these don't add any features in comparison to MTS, whereas others add capabilities not formerly available. For example, `ObjectContext` can be used in MTS to deal with creating other objects, programmatic security, transaction control, and accessing framework objects (i.e., ASP objects). It can also be used in COM+. On the other hand, the `IContextState` and `IObjectConstruct` interfaces are unique to COM+, and thus should be avoided. Likewise for the new `SecurityCallContext` interface.

Keep Using `SafeRef` for Handing Out Object References

Under NT4, the COM infrastructure had no knowledge or awareness of MTS. This often caused problems for developers who were new to COM and MTS. Because MTS relies heavily on interception via the context wrapper, we must always ensure that clients hold references to the interception layer and not directly to the object. Under NT4, when an object reference is handed out, the

COM infrastructure doesn't know to hand out a reference to the context wrapper because it doesn't know that it exists. So, unless you force the issue by using `SafeRef`, as shown here, clients will hold a direct reference to an object and no interception will occur:

```
'** reference the wrapper, not myself directly!
Set rGoodRef = SafeRef(Me)
```

This can lead to "unexpected results" because the interception layer is bypassed. Under Windows 2000 the use of `SafeRef` is no longer a requirement because the COM+ infrastructure is now aware of the interception layer. However, you should continue to use it for backward compatibility with MTS.

Note that with COM+ there is still a `SafeRef`-like issue to keep in mind. If a configured component returns a reference to a nonconfigured component (e.g., back to a client), COM+ ends up building an interception object for the nonconfigured object. Calls to this nonconfigured object will now pass through an interception layer and receive COM+ services, potentially yielding incorrect execution. In general, when working in MTS or COM+, you must be very careful when passing object references or—avoid it altogether.

Chapter 4

The Web and VB

4-1 Understand the IIS architecture.

4-2 Manage application state to maximize efficiency.

4-3 Manage session state to maximize scalability.

4-4 Understand the differences between DCOM and HTTP.

4-5 Write COM components for scripting environments (like ASP).

4-6 Understand how your COM objects interact with ASP.

4-7 Use XML instead of proprietary data formats.

4-8 Be deliberate about presentation versus business logic.

4-9 Use XSLT to move from data to presentation.

The Web has had a profound impact on the way we design and create applications with VB. The opportunities to reach a wider audience through the Hypertext Transport Protocol (HTTP), HTML, and XML are part of today's landscape. To take advantage of these technologies, you need to learn not only how they work, but also how they interact with each other and with VB and COM. Toward this end, this chapter presents an overview of Microsoft's Web server technology—*IIS* (rules 4-1 through 4-3). We explain the principles behind ASP and its interaction with the protocol of the Web—HTTP (rules 4-4 and 4-5). We talk about the ways that Microsoft has integrated its component technologies with its Web strategy (rules 4-5 and 4-6), and how Microsoft uses open technologies like XML (rules 4-7 through 4-9). Lastly, we provide some pointers on maintaining a disciplined coding style, keeping your different application tiers separated, in the face of all these technologies coming together (rules 4-8 and 4-9).

Rule 4-1: Understand the IIS Architecture

The likelihood is that you already are writing or soon will write applications in VB that will be used over the Internet. With such a universally accepted distribution platform available, it is hard to resist the pull to write wide-distribution applications. To create efficient, scalable, stable applications on this platform, you should understand the infrastructure that girds it.

IIS is Microsoft's Web server technology. At its heart, it is not much more than a listening service. When installed, it registers itself against certain ports on your machine and listens for network traffic on those ports that conform to one of the network protocols it understands. Those protocols are

- Hypertext transport protocol (HTTP)
- File Transfer Protocol (FTP)
- Simple Mail Transport Protocol (SMTP)
- Network News Transfer Protocol (NNTP)

You will largely be concerned with the first, HTTP, because all Web traffic consists of HTTP requests and responses.

If IIS receives an HTTP request for static content, such as an HTML document or a JPEG image, it can natively respond to the request. Such files are loaded into memory, packaged as the body of an HTTP response, and shipped back to the calling client. To provide true services to your application's consumers, however, you need to provide more than fixed information. You need to be able to provide dynamic content based on user requests and run-time conditions. You need to provide extra services to IIS.

Microsoft originally provided for extending the services of IIS through Internet Services Application Programming Interface (ISAPI) filters and extenstions. ISAPI extensions are DLLs that provide code to handle requests for a specific type of dynamic content. IIS provides a way to map requests for documents with a given file extension to the DLL that can handle the request. If IIS receives a request for a static document (default.html, banner1.gif), it can then natively return the requested data. If IIS receives a request for a dynamic file (calculate.cgi, getrecords.pl), IIS loads the appropriate ISAPI DLL and passes on the request.

ISAPI extensions have drawbacks. The model itself is very complex and can only be used through C++. Even C++ developers find the model somewhat tedious to work with. Additionally, creating your own ISAPI extension also means creating a new file extension to be associated with it in HTTP requests. The model is fraught with difficult development and customized deployment.

Luckily for VB developers, something quickly came along to replace ISAPI extensions as the gateway to more power through IIS. Microsoft's ASP is an architecture that provides a much easier way to include new dynamic services through your Web server. ASP pages, combinations of static content and dynamic script code, provide a much simpler development environment for Web services. The code that makes up ASP is housed in ASP.dll, which is itself an ISAPI extension to IIS. IIS associates several file types with ASP; most important, the .asp file extension. When a request for such a page arrives, IIS loads ASP.dll to do the processing.

Under the Hood

The main process for the Web server is INETINFO.exe, as shown in Figure 4.1. This process hosts an object called the Web Application Manager (WAM), from WAM.dll. The WAM object is the undocumented controlling object of IIS. It acts as the gateway for inbound HTTP requests, dispatching them to whatever service will eventually provide the response. INETINFO uses a pool of MTA threads to receive the incoming requests.

If the request is for an ASP page, ASP.dll is loaded into the INETINFO process. ASP maintains its own request queue, separate from the MTA pool that stores requests for the WAM object. The WAM object forwards the original request to the ASP request queue and then gets out of the way. ASP maintains its own pool of STA threads to service ASP requests. These STA threads pull requests out of the queue in a first-in/first-out order. A thread switch is necessarily incurred as a result of this handoff (the original request is serviced by an MTA thread, whereas ASP uses STA threads only). Both the thread pool and the request queue have well-defined upper bounds. Under NT4, each INETINFO process has 10 STA threads for ASP requests, and the queue can reach a maximum of 500 pending requests before the user is told that the server is too

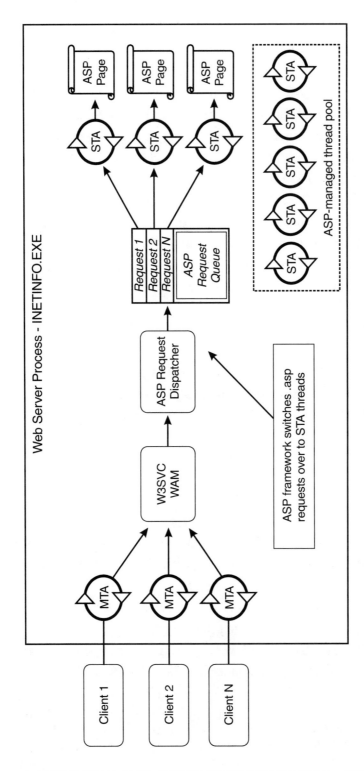

Figure 4.1 Inside INETINFO, a pool of MTA threads services the initial HTTP requests, and ASP manages its own pool of STA threads for ASP pages.

busy. Under Windows 2000, that thread pool is raised to 25, and the maximum queue size is 3,000.

Additionally, this entire architecture is built on top of MTS/COM+. This affects the way that the different objects that make up your application are deployed. When administering your Web site, the primary setting you can change to affect this deployment is the *isolation level* of your virtual application. Under Windows NT4, this property was represented by a checkbox that read, "Run in separate memory space." Under Windows 2000, you have a listbox with three selections for isolation level. Your choices are low, medium, and high. High isolation under Windows 2000 is the equivalent of checking the box under NT.

When your virtual application is configured in low isolation, ASP.dll and all page objects are loaded directly into the INETINFO process (Figure 4.2). Access between the WAM object and the individual page objects is relatively efficient, because all the objects are within the same process boundary. This scenario is the least stable, however, because poorly written pages or sub-objects that crash will bring down your entire Web server. That's why it is known as *low isolation:* You have not isolated the Web server itself from potentially unstable code.

The opposite end of the spectrum is high isolation. Your page objects (and any sub-objects) are created in a process external to INETINFO (Figure 4.3). On NT that process is MTX.exe, whereas on Windows 2000 it is DLLHOST.exe. The

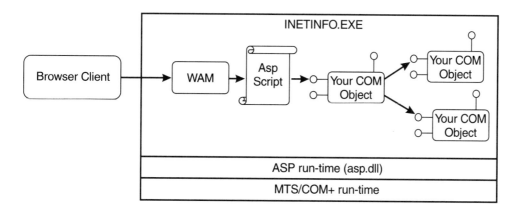

Figure 4.2 IIS virtual application, configured in low-isolation mode, calling COM objects in a COM DLL or MTS library package

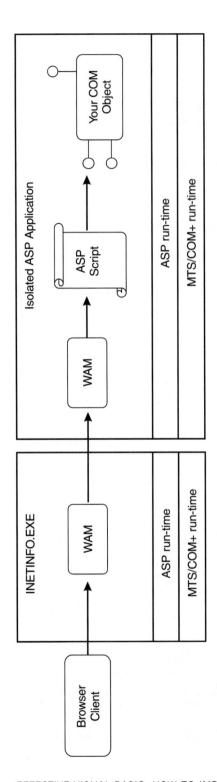

Figure 4.3 IIS virtual application configured in high-isolation mode, calling a COM object in a COM DLL or MTS library package

external process hosts not only your pages and custom objects, but also another WAM object local to that process. The WAM in INETINFO forwards requests to the external process WAM, which forwards them to the ASP queue. Performance is obviously negatively affected, because all requests have to make a process hop to generate a response. However, stability is improved because any crashes in your pages or objects only result in the external process being lost. The Web server can continue to function normally, and the next request for a page in the lost process will cause the creation of a replacement process and pages to service the request.

If you have configured more than one virtual application on the same Web server to run in high-isolation mode, you may also experience another performance problem. Each process running on a machine consumes valuable resources like clock cycles and memory. As more requests come in to different virtual directories, you lose more system resources to keep up with the slew of processes. Windows 2000 introduced a new isolation level, medium, to address this issue.

All virtual directories configured in medium isolation *share* a single external process, as shown in Figure 4.4. All page and custom objects created for these virtual directories live in the same instance of MTX.exe or DLLHOST.exe. This does nothing to overcome the request-by-request overhead of the external process; requests still have to be forwarded over a process boundary. However, this minimizes the impact of having multiple isolated applications because they all share the same system resources. If any one of your pages or objects crashes, all of your medium-isolation applications are lost; but again, the Web server continues to run and can immediately re-create the process and subsequent objects in response to the next incoming request.

Additionally, your choice of configuration options on your custom, configured components has an effect on overall deployment. If you choose to deploy your objects in library packages (MTS/COM+ library packages or standard COM DLLs), they will, of course, run inside the process in which the calling ASP pages reside. However, if you configure them as MTS/COM+ server packages, you introduce additional isolation into your architecture (Figure 4.5). Now, you have separated your custom object from the ASP pages that refer to it, which can in turn be separated from the INETINFO process. This has the

THE WEB AND VB

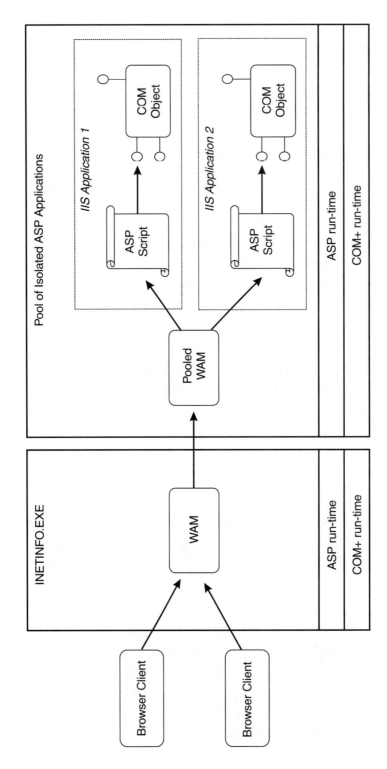

Figure 4.4 Several IIS virtual applications configured to run together in medium-isolation mode

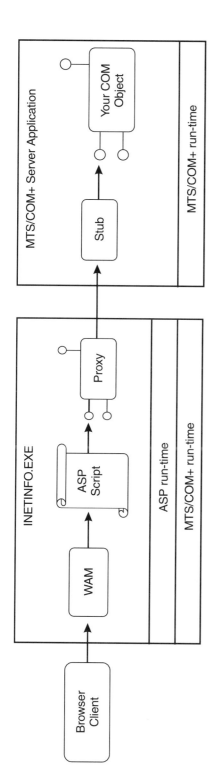

Figure 4.5 Low-isolation IIS virtual application calling a COM object in an MTS server package

highest overall stability because a crash inside a custom object does not even negatively impact the calling pages. Performance degrades accordingly, because requests for pages must hop to the first external process, and then to the second process to generate a single response.

Choosing among these different deployment scenarios can be difficult. You must take into account how many virtual applications your site is likely to host, how many custom COM objects they are likely to call, where those classes live in relation to each other, and how stable they are likely to be. It is very common for programmers to use high isolation during development because it is much faster and easier to debug and to rerelease your code. For example, if you need to recompile your DLL, it is much faster if it is deployed in high isolation and therefore in a separate MTS process. To release outstanding references to your DLL, you need only terminate that process. If your application was configured as low isolation you would have to shut down INETINFO, which involves terminating a host of services.

How you deploy your application for public use, however, should be based on providing maximum speed of access balanced against maximum availability of your application. Low isolation is certainly the fastest solution request by request, but if any single request causes a crash, your entire server crashes and availability is lost. To provide maximum stability, you would release with high isolation and all your COM DLLs in MTS server packages. However, your throughput will be dramatically reduced. You must evaluate your code against the needs of your users to make your design decision.

Scaling the Server

There will come a time when no amount of configuring your Web server will get you the throughput you need. As the number of users of your application grows, the amount of available resources to serve them shrinks in relation. You must think through the scalability issues of using multiple machines to serve your site. There are three basic architectures you can use to deploy your Web servers:

1. The single Web server
2. Multiple Web servers configured as a *session-based Web farm*
3. Multiple Web servers configured as a *method-based Web farm*

If you intend to serve your application on a single machine and never add a new machine, your only scalability option is to increase the clock speed of your machine. This process is both expensive and of limited scope. Chips can only go so fast, Moore's Law notwithstanding. The chips themselves can get to be quite expensive. So, to scale your Web site, you must add additional machines.

A multiple-machine server solution is known as a *Web farm*. Requests to a Web farm enter the system through a single point, *a load balancer*. The load balancer is often referred to as a *request broker*. A request for some resource is received, and the broker forwards that request to an available server. The Internet Protocol (IP) address used to send the HTTP request (whatever IP address results from the DNS lookup of the URL) actually maps to the broker, not to the IIS servers.

Web farms can be configured in one of two ways: session or method based. In a session-based Web farm, a user starts a conversation with your application through the load balancer. This initial request is forwarded to an available server through one of many possible algorithms (most likely, a round-robin placement). Once the session has been established, the user sends any subsequent requests to the application to that specifically assigned server. This means that you can use resources on the Web server, such as RAM or local disk space, to store information on behalf of your client. This type of farm, however, introduces what is known as a "single point of failure" into your application. If any one of your farm machines crashes, all users currently "pinned" to it will lose their connection and, more important, their session.

The other type of Web farm is method-based. In such an architecture, each incoming HTTP request is treated as a unique entity (as it was meant in the original HTTP specification) and is assigned to a server through the load-balancing algorithm. It doesn't matter if this is the first request from a given user, one of many from that user, or the last. Each request is forwarded to any available server. This means that you no longer have recourse to use Web server local resources on behalf of your users, but you also no longer have a single point of failure. If a user is midway through a conversation with your application and one of your servers goes down, the conversation is simply routed around on the next incoming request.

Of the three server configurations, the method-based Web farm will provide you maximum scalability and availability, but it requires you to spend more time planning for session state maintenance (this topic is addressed further in rule 4-3). The combination of server deployment and IIS configuration affects the overall stability and efficiency of your application. The choice to run your applications in or out of process with the server itself has a dramatic effect on performance and overall stability. Your architecture and the needs of your users should mandate which configuration to choose, but you cannot begin to make reasonable design decisions about the Web without understanding these choices. Once you have made decisions about how to install and use IIS, you can begin to make decisions about how to write the code to run in that architecture. One of the first problems you will face is how to maintain state in the face of your architecture decisions. The next two rules address this dilemma.

Rule 4-2: Manage Application State to Maximize Efficiency

Every application maintains state in one way or another. There are two fundamental types of state: *durable* and *transient*. Durable state is that set of information on which your software operates to provide value to the consumers of your application. This data exists independent of any given user interaction with the system, and is sometimes (although not always) used as read-only data. Examples could be an inventory of physical stock or a record of registered users. This rule deals with effective ways of managing durable state. The second kind of state, transient, is more commonly known as *session state*. This is the data collected *during* a given user interaction with your system, and is therefore a much more dynamic dataset. The next rule describes effective ways of managing this short-lived, read/write dataset.

Durable state is usually housed long term in a DBMS. Applications interact with the data on an as-needed basis. There are times when it makes sense to cache some or all of this data on the Web server in the same process as your application code. Many developers have found they can significantly improve their application's performance with caching techniques that share in-memory data across a set of ASP pages and COM objects. The increase in application performance is usually the result of a reduced number of round-trips to the

DBMS. It's much faster for a Web application to process a client's request using data that's close at hand as opposed to reading and writing data that lives across the network in a DBMS.

In this rule, we compare and contrast three common techniques to share in-memory data on the Web server. First, we'll look at using a BAS module. Next, we'll examine using the SPM. Finally, we'll look at using ASP `Application` variables to cache data. Each of these three techniques offers various advantages and drawbacks with respect to performance, synchronization, and concurrency. As you'll see, each technique has certain advantages over the other two. It's important to weigh quite a few factors when you're designing a data-caching strategy for a Web application built using VB components.

Using BAS Module Data

The first technique is done entirely with VB. You can share data across VB objects by defining constants and variables in a BAS module. For example, when you define a constant or variable in a BAS module, it can be seen by any component in the same ActiveX DLL project.

Keep in mind that BAS module variables are confined to a single thread. As discussed in rule 2-9, VB stores all BAS module data in *TLS*. Because a single running process can contain multiple threads, there can be multiple instances of a constant or a variable loaded in a single process.

Think back to the ASP architecture described in rule 4-1. ASP uses a pool of STA threads to service incoming requests. When ASP pages create objects from one of your components, these objects get distributed across the various threads in the pool. Whenever each specific thread creates an object from your ActiveX DLL for the first time, the DLL initializes all its BAS module data in TLS.

The primary advantage of this technique is speed. Using BAS modules can be as much as ten times faster than either of the other techniques described in this rule. It is quicker for an object to access TLS data than it is to access heap-based data (both the SPM and the ASP `Application` object rely on heap-based data). The performance of the SPM and the ASP `Application` object are also impacted by the need to perform a dictionary lookup based on a string value at run-time.

Another speed advantage of accessing BAS module data is that it never involves locking. Because all BAS module data is thread specific, there are no concurrency issues that require synchronization. There's no need to acquire and to release locks to maintain data consistency. Both the SPM and the ASP `Application`, on the other hand, must deal with concurrency issues. Therefore, they provide their own built-in locking schemes to prevent data from becoming inconsistent in the presence of multiple threads. Although locking and synchronization is often critical, the need to acquire and release locks is something that impacts performance.

There are two main drawbacks to using BAS module data. Both drawbacks are related to the fact that BAS module data requires one instance per thread. The first drawback is that having redundant copies of the same data in a process wastes memory. The second drawback to having multiple copies per process is that it's usually impractical to use the data in any way other than a read-only fashion. Let's concentrate on memory usage first and then we'll move on to discussing how multiple copies of a variable affect data consistency.

When you design a middle-tier application based on IIS, MTS, or COM+, you must consider that you're relying on a hosting process that runs lots of threads. For example, the process for an MTS server package can run up to 100 threads. The process for a COM+ application typically runs somewhere between 8 and 40 threads depending on how many processors you have. The ASP run-time in IIS4 runs an STA thread pool of 10 threads per process per processor by default, whereas the ASP run-time in IIS5 runs 25. As you can see, there are lots of threads per process in these middle-tier run-time environments, and each thread gets its own private instance of each constant and variable defined in a BAS module.

When you're using constants defined in BAS modules, you're giving away memory in exchange for better performance. You can easily determine how much memory is going to be used. Simply multiply the size of your BAS module data times the number of threads in the hosting process. This will tell you how much extra memory you need. Many developers are glad to give up memory for better performance.

To use this technique most effectively, it is important to build your ActiveX DLLs with the Retained in memory project option. Selecting this option prevents the DLL from unloading its BAS module data on any thread for the lifetime of an application. If you build a DLL without this option, BAS module data is continually unloaded and reloaded on a thread-by-thread basis. The Retained in memory option is important because it guarantees that BAS module data is initialized only once per thread. However, only use this option if you have upgraded to service pack 3 of VB6, because earlier versions contain known bugs with this option checked.

The second problem with BAS module data is one of consistency. Having multiple copies of a variable causes problems with regard to data consistency. The problem is that different objects in the same process see different instances of the same variable. You have absolutely no guarantees with respect to which objects share the same instance. This means that one object running in a multithread environment cannot reliably see changes written to the variable by another object. This makes it impossible (or at least very difficult) to use BAS module variables that are read/write as opposed to read-only.

Many programmers avoid declaring BAS module variables in ActiveX DLLs designed for the middle tier for the reasons we've just discussed. Others programmers have found that they can initialize BAS module variables when the DLL loads onto a thread. Things can work reliably if you have the discipline to use BAS module variables in a read-only fashion once they've been initialized. This provides the ability to load cached data dynamically with values that don't need to be compiled into your DLLs. The use of dynamic data makes such an approach more flexible than using constants. For example, you can load data you've retrieved from a DBMS.

The easiest way to initialize a BAS module variable is to supply a `Sub Main` procedure in your ActiveX DLL project. The `Sub Main` procedure must also be declared in a BAS module. As long as you set `Startup Object` to `Sub Main` in the Project >> Properties dialog, this procedure fires whenever your DLL is initialized on a thread. This means you can write an implementation of `Sub Main` that initializes your BAS module variables on a thread-by-thread basis. Again, make sure to use the Retain in memory option. You don't want to run the `Sub Main` procedure more than once on any specific thread.

There is one last thing to note about using BAS module variables. If you change your DLL project's threading model to single-thread, you force every object from the DLL to load onto a single-thread known as the *main* STA thread. Because all objects created inside the same process from a single-thread DLL always share the same thread, it means they all see the same instance of a BAS module variable. This allows you to read and write to a BAS module variable reliably from every object created from the same DLL.

Although a single-threaded DLL seems to solve certain problems with data consistency, it does far more damage to an application's concurrency. All clients' requests are bottlenecked through a single STA thread. For this reason, the use of single-threaded DLLs should be avoided when creating VB components for IIS, MTS, and COM+.

Using the SPM

The second important caching technique involves using the SPM. The SPM is a small component library that's built into both the MTS run-time and the COM+ run-time. The SPM is a name/value dictionary that allows you to read and write to named property values.

One of the big advantages to using the SPM is that it allows objects running on different threads within the same process to see a single instance of a named property value. This means that the SPM uses memory more efficiently than BAS module data because there is only one copy of each data item in existence. This also means that updates to the SPM by one object can reliably be seen by all the other objects inside the same process regardless of who's running on what thread.

Because shared properties in a property group are accessible from any thread, it's important to think through all relevant issues with regard to concurrency and synchronization. Fortunately, the SPM provides an easy-to-use scheme in which an object can acquire an exclusive lock while making a series of read and write operations to properties within the same group. In other words, the SPM makes it possible for an object to perform a sequence of read and/or write operations in isolation. This can prevent scenarios in which one object sees the partial, incomplete work of another.

Here's a sample of a component that updates two shared properties in isolation:

```
Dim rSPM As SharedPropertyGroupManager
Dim rSPG As SharedPropertyGroup
Dim rP1 As SharedProperty, rP2 As SharedProperty
Dim bAlreadyExists As Boolean

'** create and bind to two shared properties
Set rSPM = New SharedPropertyGroupManager
Set rSPG = rSPM.CreatePropertyGroup("MyGroup", _
                                    LockMethod, _
                                    Process, _
                                    bAlreadyExists)
Set rP1 = rSPG.CreateProperty("MyProp1", bAlreadyExists)
Set rP2 = rSPG.CreateProperty("MyProp2", bAlreadyExists)

'** read the value of MyProp1
Dim lTemp As Long
lTemp = rP1.Value

'** assign new values to MyProp1 and MyProp2
rP1.Value = lTemp + 10
rP2.Value = rP1.Value + 20

'** clean up
Set rP1 = Nothing
Set rP2 = Nothing
Set rSPG = Nothing
Set rSPM = Nothing
```

Notice the second parameter passed to the `CreatePropertyGroup` method. The parameter value of `LockMethod` sets the property group's isolation level. An isolation level of `LockMethod` informs the SPM to hold locks for the duration of the current method call. That is, once an object touches any property within a property group, it acquires an exclusive lock until the current method ends. The logic to release this lock is built into the MTS/COM+ interception scheme.

Locking is great for data consistency. However, locking also impacts concurrency in a negative way. You should avoid acquiring locks when and where they're not needed. It's not usually necessary to lump all your data together into a single property group. It's often better to split your data into multiple groups because each group handles locking independently. Although the ASP `Application` object also provides locking, it only provides a single application-wide lock. The SPM provides a more granular locking scheme that makes it possible to optimize concurrency while designing a synchronization scheme to prevent data inconsistency.

Some shared property groups don't need such drastic locking behavior. If you create a property group with an isolation level of `LockSetGet` instead of `LockMethod`, locks are not held for the duration of an object's method call. Instead, locks are acquired and released each time a property is accessed. This means `LockSetGet` has a lower impact on concurrency, but a higher risk of data corruption. With an isolation level of `LockSetGet`, it's possible to acquire and release a lock on the same property group several times inside a single method call. Because several locks can be acquired and released inside a single method, two components with identical methods may interweave their SPM operations given the right system conditions. `LockSetGet` has a smaller chance of causing a block on a piece of data, but a higher chance of corrupting it.

It is important to note that you cannot disable locking with the SPM. You have to create a property group with either `LockMethod` or `LockSetGet`. This is unnecessarily taxing, especially in situations in which shared properties are read-only once they've been initialized. Access would be noticeably faster if the SPM allowed you to read a shared property without acquiring and releasing a lock.

Another shortcoming of the SPM with respect to locking is that it always uses exclusive locks. The SPM is not as smart as a DBMS. A DBMS knows to use shared locks for read operations instead of exclusive locks. Shared locks prevent one reader from blocking another reader. With exclusive locking, one reader's locks block other readers. Shared locks, therefore, have a lower impact on concurrency and result in far less blocking.

Additionally, when you access the SPM, you're typically required to create and release three different COM objects (as shown in the previous coding example). The creation and destruction of objects requires processing cycles. This is yet another factor that widens the performance gap between accessing BAS module data and the SPM.

One last feature of the SPM is the ability to share data in ways that are not possible with BAS module data. You can share data across multiple ActiveX DLL projects as long as they run inside the same process. This is a very important point. If your Web server is configured as a Web farm (see rule 4-1), then shared properties are only shared on a single server in the farm, not across all servers. So, although you may treat SPM properties as read/write data repositories on a single machine, you should treat them as read-only when deploying a multiple-server solution.

You can also use the SPM to share data between components written in VB and components written in other languages such as C++. However, you should keep in mind that it is not practical for an ASP page to use the SPM directly. Although the SPM interfaces are exposed as "duals," the SPM components expose methods that cause enough problems that it's not worth trying to access them from an ASP page in which you're using VBScript or JavaScript.

Using an ASP `Application` Object

The final caching technique we are going to examine is using the ASP `Application` object. A VB object that's been created from an ASP page can create and access an ASP `Application` variable like this:

```
Dim rAppl As ASPTypeLibrary.Application
Set rAppl = GetObjectContext("Application")
rAppl.Value("MyProp") = "My quintessential value"
```

Your project must reference both the ASP TLB as well as the MTS/COM+ TLB to access the ASP `Application` object in this fashion. You should also note that with COM+, the `IISIntrinsics` attribute of your configured component must be set to `True`. This is the default value, so you usually don't have to adjust anything. Also note that this attribute is not accessible through the

COM+ Services administrative tool and is only accessible through the COM+ `Admin` objects.

The ASP `Application` object differs from the SPM in that the names of its variables do not have a process-wide scope. Instead, ASP `Application` variables are scoped within an IIS application (i.e., virtual directory). It's possible for two different IIS applications to run in the same process. The ASP `Application` variables of one IIS application are invisible and inaccessible to the other. This is a good thing because one IIS application cannot step on the ASP `Application` variables of another IIS application if there happens to be a naming conflict. However, it is limiting because you cannot share ASP `Application` variables across IIS applications.

When it comes to synchronization and locking, the ASP `Application` object doesn't provide any control over granularity. There is only one course-grained lock per application. This scheme is nowhere near as flexible as the SPM, because locking ASP `Application` variables is an all-or-nothing proposition. With the SPM you can lock shared properties in one group without locking the shared properties in other groups. On the contrary, whenever a VB object or an ASP page acquires the lock on the ASP `Application` object, all other requests attempting to access ASP `Application` variables are blocked until the lock is released. Like the SPM, the ASP `Application` object never uses shared locks. It always uses exclusive locking. As you can imagine, designs that frequently lock the ASP `Application` object can create quite a bottleneck in high-volume applications.

Unlike the SPM, the ASP `Application` object doesn't force you to use locks if you don't want them. Let's look at an example of when this is helpful. Imagine you're required to initialize a large set of environmental variables in the ASP `Application` object on application start-up. If you acquire a lock on the ASP `Application` object, you can guarantee that no client request sees your data until you've initialized everything into a valid state. Once you've completed the initialization, you can release the lock and use these variables in a read-only fashion for the rest of the application's lifetime. As long as the data is read-only, there's no reason to acquire and release locks. The lack of locking overhead incurred with `Application` variables also imparts a slight performance advantage over the SPM.

There's one last advantage that ASP `Application` variables have over the other two techniques. They can be accessed directly from ASP pages as well as VB components. This can be very convenient in projects in which the ASP developers and VB component developers are working side by side.

The same caveat applies to application objects as well as SPM objects: Technically speaking, an IIS *application* can span multiple Web servers when deployed on a Web farm. Each individual `Application` object resides on only one physical server. Use of the `Application` object should be avoided if you are deployed on a Web farm.

Weighing Your Options

This topic has examined three of the more common server-side data-caching techniques used by VB programmers. You now know to ask the right questions. Is achieving better performance more important than conserving memory? Can you use cached data in a read-only fashion or is it necessary to make updates over the lifetime of the application? Do you need locking to synchronize access and to maintain data consistency? If you don't need locking, how can you avoid it? If you do need locking, how can you minimize the amount of items you're locking at any one time? Hopefully, asking and answering these questions will help you the next time you need to design a data-caching scheme for a Web application.

You should also keep in mind that there is a fourth option. You may decide that none of the techniques presented in this topic are sufficient for your needs. For example, none of these three techniques offers any form of persistence or durability. In-memory data is fast to access, but it's easily lost in the case of a system failure or an application crash. None of these techniques provides transaction support for automatic rollback. None of these techniques provides a way to share data across processes or across machines. Lastly, neither the SPM nor the ASP `Application` object uses shared locks. They only use exclusive locks that have a much higher impact on concurrency.

Sometimes your data-handling requirements are too much for one of these three techniques. It's important to recognize the times when you should look elsewhere for assistance (see rule 3-6). The bottom line is that there are times when an in-memory caching scheme is the best thing to use, and there are other times when it's best to store your data in that old friend, the DBMS.

Rule 4-3: Manage Session State to Maximize Scalability

The previous item described three techniques for caching durable state on the Web server to maximize the efficiency of access to that data. Those techniques work because the data is largely treated as read-only. With a more dynamic dataset, one that is unique not only per user but often per request, those techniques will not work. Session state, therefore, requires a different strategy for storage and access.

During any interaction with your application, user identity and user activity combine to form session state. The typical example is a shopping cart: The session data consists of the current shopper, his credit card number, and all items currently in queue to be purchased. It is important to note that not all "users" are human: Your application may very well service requests from other software, and the sum total of their interaction can still be considered a session. Session state begins when a user (human or otherwise) first makes contact with your application. It is typically discarded when the session ends, through explicit termination or implicit time-out, although sometimes it is useful to make state semipermanent (by placing timestamped data in a temporary store on the client machine, such as timestamped cookies).

Session state is often managed in the middle tier, which seems to be logical. Because the middle tier is responsible for managing the business logic, the most efficient place to keep vital user information is as close to the code as possible. This would seem especially true in a Web-based application, given the potentially vast distances that may separate users from business code. In fact, this is the default state management technique for most developers just starting out in the Web space. ASP provides some commonly used tools for maintaining state this way. The ASP `Session` object is a COM object that resides in memory on the Web server and is available to any page in your application. It maintains a hash table of name/value pairs of data. Because it is memory resident on the same machine as the business code, accessing the data is extremely efficient. However, this rule explains why using the ASP `Session` object, or any in-memory solution on the Web server, can be limiting or disruptive to your application.

Pinning the Session to a Single Machine

Rule 4-1 described the three standard architectures for deploying a Web site:

1. Single Web server, where one physical machine services all incoming user requests
2. A session-based Web farm, where a logical gateway assigns requests to a given physical machine on a per-session basis
3. A request-based Web farm, where a logical gateway assigns requests to a given physical machine on a per-request basis

These are summarized in Figure 4.6. To maintain session state on the server itself, you would have to deploy one of the first two configurations. With both, you can guarantee that all incoming user requests from a given session are serviced by the same machine every time, and you can store state information in memory on the server. However, because both of these methods *pin* a user to

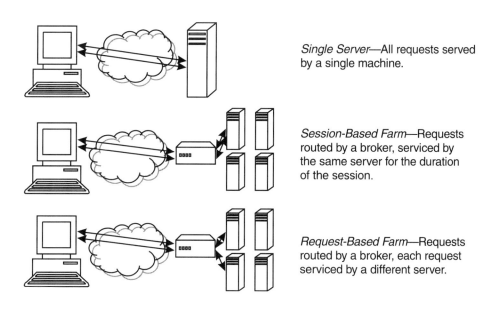

Single Server—All requests served by a single machine.

Session-Based Farm—Requests routed by a broker, serviced by the same server for the duration of the session.

Request-Based Farm—Requests routed by a broker, each request serviced by a different server.

Figure 4.6 Standard architectures for deploying a Web site

a specific server (once the user makes a request to your application, all subsequent requests are targeted to the same server), if that server fails, all users pinned to that machine lose any session data stored so far and are forced to log back into your application.

Because request-based farms offer the best scalability and availability, they are the best choice for your application. However, because you can now expect that several machines will service each user's requests over the course of the session, you can no longer use middle-tier memory as a storage device for state information.[1] As users hop around your Web farm, they are interacting with different globs of physical memory. There is no such thing as shared memory across your multiple servers that can be used to store the information. Therefore, you can no longer use the ASP `Session` object or like techniques to keep track of the user session. If we rule out the middle tier, that leaves only two other locations for maintaining state: on the client machine itself, or on a database server on your network.

Storing Session Information on the Client
Remember that in a multitier architecture, all (or at least most) of the logic that makes use of state information "lives" on the middle tier. If the client is now going to maintain important state information, this implies that everything the client knows has to be shipped to the server on *every request*. Otherwise, the server would be unable to maintain a continuous session. Remember also that requests and responses between Web clients and Web servers are just HTTP messages: They are simple packets with a well-defined header and a free-form body. There are three basic ways to get this information embedded in the request: in the header, via cookies or `QueryString` variables; or in the body, via hidden form fields. ASP provides some great tools for dealing with all three. Keep in mind that if you want to program against the ASP object model, you have to reference the Microsoft ASP Object Library (*asp.dll*) as well as the MTS or COM+ Services library, depending on whether you are deployed on NT or

---

[1] There is another drawback to the method-based Web farm, and it is that each individual user request has to be re-authenticated by the new server. This will have an obvious effect on the efficiency and complexity of your application, but has little to do with session data.

Windows 2000. The ASP objects are now supplied to your components via the `ObjectContext` interface of those two libraries.[2]

Using Cookies

Cookies are pieces of named data stored by the client's browser and associated with a given Web server. Once set on the client machine, every subsequent request sent to that server will have each associated cookie embedded in the header. Let's say you wanted to store a piece of information about the user (`FavoriteMovie=Time_Bandits`). The raw response that sets a temporary cookie on the client machine could look like

```
HTTP/1.1 200 OK
Server:Microsoft-IIS/5.0
Date: Fri, 23 Jun 2000 19:58:53 GMT
Content-Length: 115
Content-Type: text/html
Set-Cookie: FavoriteMovie=Time_Bandits ...
```

A subsequent request might look like

```
GET /DreamTheater.asp HTTP/1.1
...
Cookie: FavoriteMovie=Time_Bandits
```

You are, of course, free to manipulate the headers directly in your application, but ASP provides you a shortcut to reading and writing cookies: the `Cookies` collection of the ASP `Request` and `Response` objects. Using these handy collections, the previous headers can now be generated or read with the following code:

```
'** Set cookie to browser
Dim rResponse As ASPTypeLibrary.Response
Set rResponse = GetObjectContext.Item("Response")
rResponse.Cookies("FavoriteMovie") = "Time_Bandits"
```

---

[2] There exist third-party products that you can either purchase or download that help hide the complexity of each of these three methods. Many take the form of ISAPI filters, which can transparently add cookies or HTML text to your outgoing responses, without making you write all this complicated code. We urge you, however, to understand the three methods before choosing such a product, to understand better what it's doing to your data.

```
'** Read cookie from browser
Dim sFavMovie As String
Dim rRequest As ASPTypeLibrary.Request
Set rRequest = GetObjectContext.Item("Request")
sFavMovie = rRequest.Cookies("FavoriteMovie")
```

The practical effect of these methods is to generate or read the previous headers, but in a more object-oriented style.

Generally, cookies are scoped to the session. When the session times out or the user closes the browser or reboots the machine, all cookies are lost. You can explicitly extend their lifetime by setting an expiration date. If you use the `Expires` property of the cookie, it will be written to disk on the client's machine and will be sent back to the server on every subsequent request until the expiration date is passed. For example, if you want to make sure that you can read the user's favorite movie until January 2002, you would use

```
rResponse.Cookies("FavoriteMovie").Expires = _
                                  "January 1, 2002"
```

This is the only widely available method of storing semi-permanent state on the client machine.[3]

There are a few reasons not to use cookies. The first is size limitation. To prevent lazy, sloppy, or malicious Web developers from easily filling an entire hard drive with cookies, most browsers set a maximum size limit on each cookie (you can expect it to be around 4KB). This doesn't sound like much of a limitation, but, depending on the complexity of your application, this can be a significant determining factor. Second, the ability of the browser to accept cookies is *optional.* Users have the choice, usually through the "security" settings of the browser, to disable cookies. If you are certain of your target audience, and can ensure that they will allow cookies on their browsers, cookies are the cleanest way to store data on the client machine. If conditions are not so ideal, however, you should consider one of the following two alternatives: `QueryString` variables or hidden form fields.

---

[3] There are more narrow-focus methods, including custom ActiveX objects and controls, as well as built-in behaviors in IE5, such as `saveSnapshot` and `UserData`. However, these techniques have limited availability because of required software as well as special security requirements.

QueryString *Variables*

Your second choice may be `QueryString` variables. Remember that every hyperlink contains a mandatory target and then optional data values. Once the target page or object has been contacted, the rest of the data, stored as name/value pairs, can be parsed by the receiver. To embed the state information in a `QueryString`, you have to hand-roll your output HTML. For instance, if you have a page that needs the user's favorite movie, say MyDreamTheater.asp, you might use the following code to write the page that links to it:

```
'** Generate an HTML page
rResponse.Write "<HTML><HEAD><TITLE>" & _
                "Where do you want to go now?" & _
                " </TITLE></HEAD>"
rResponse.Write "<BODY>"
rResponse.Write "<A HREF = " & _
                "'MyDreamTheater.asp?FavoriteMovie" & _
                "=Time_Bandits'>" & _
                "The Perfect Theater</A>"
rResponse.Write "</BODY></HTML>"
rResponse.Flush
```

The raw header of the request, when the user clicks on the `The Perfect Theater` link, would look something like this:

```
GET /DreamTheater.asp?FavoriteMovie=Time_Bandits HTTP/1.1
```

To read information out of the request, you use the ASP `Request` object's `QueryString` collection. Because every item has to have a name, you could read the data as such:

```
Dim sFavMovie as String
sFavMovie = rRequest.QueryString("FavoriteMovie")
```

The drawbacks to this technique are, again, size limitation (IE gives you 4,000 characters per `QueryString`) and the complexity of writing out the HTML dynamically for every page. Also, you may note that the data being passed is visible not only in the View Source window of the browser, but also in the address bar after the user has clicked on the link. Although none of the three client-side techniques is particularly well suited for sensitive information, `QueryString` values are the least appropriate because they will be visible to users by default, without them having to do any peeking under the hood.

Hidden Form Fields

Lastly, on the client side, you can write hidden form fields into the output HTML. A hidden form field has two distinct advantages over `QueryStrings`: there is no inherent size limitation (other than actual page size, which is a function of your design, not preexisting technologies), and, if you use the `POST` method, the data is not visible to users unless they explicitly view the source of the page. Hidden form fields share one drawback with `QueryStrings`: the tedium of writing a lot of conditional Response.Write("SOME HTML HERE") statements to generate the page.

In general, an HTML form is a series of name/value pairs embedded right into the HTML that must be explicitly submitted to a target. You specify the target with the attribute `ACTION`, then specify the protocol with the `Method` attribute. `METHOD=GET` will embed all the form information into the `QueryString`, whereas `METHOD=POST` packages them all into the body of the request. Choosing `POST` is what hides all the data from the user (unless, of course, they choose to view the source—the sneaks).

So the hidden form fields equivalent to the previous `QueryString` example would look like this:

```
<!--Hidden form fields in HTML page-->
<FORM NAME="GoToTheMovies"
      ACTION="MyDreamTheater.asp" METHOD="POST">
<INPUT TYPE="HIDDEN"
       NAME="FavoriteMovie" VALUE="Time_Bandits">
</FORM>
```

Form elements can take many types: buttons, textboxes, select boxes, and so forth. In this example, we use `TYPE="HIDDEN"`, which is just a data value invisible on the Web page that is packaged and sent with the form's requests. You can also choose either to place a standard Submit button in the form or use scripting code to fire the request. This example uses the latter approach. For instance, you may generate this function:

```
<!—Script embedded in HTML page-->
<SCRIPT LANGUAGE="JavaScript">
    Function GoToMovies {
        Document.GoToTheMovies.Submit();
    }
</SCRIPT>
```

Lastly, there has to be some event that triggers the function. In this instance, it will be an HTML hyperlink almost identical to the `QueryString` example:

```
<A HREF="javascript:GoToMovies()">Go To the Movies</A>
```

Now, when the user chooses the `GoToTheMovies` link, your client-side function will submit the form to the appropriate target page, which will unpack all the values as necessary from the body of the request. The other normal option for submitting forms is the use of the Submit button (`<INPUT TYPE="SUBMIT"></INPUT>`), but in the case of hidden form fields, making your user interact with a visual form button seems to defeat the purpose.

To read data from hidden form fields, you must take advantage of another collection hanging off the ASP `Request` object, the `Forms` collection. To find out what cinematic experience most excites your user, you could use the following code:

```
sFavMovie = rRequest.Forms("FavoriteMovie")
```

Storing State in a Database

Even if you decide you would rather store your session information in a database, you still have to use one of these three techniques to maintain a session ID on the client. Using this technique, the bulk of your data is stored in a table in the database, keyed by a session ID field. Your server code stores this session ID on the client using one of the three previous methods. Each incoming request contains the associated session ID, which the server uses to correlate the message with any stored data. This technique provides a lot more security for the session data itself, but does not eliminate your need to store information on the client. It just reduces the information stored there to the bare minimum. For more information about the details of SQL Server and ADO coding, see Chapter 5.

To restate the problem: If your Web site outgrows the single-server model, you have to make a decision about how to track user session state. A single server, by definition, does not scale with user load, and a session-based Web farm that mimics a single server solution does not provide the best stability or uptime. Switching to the most stable and scalable solution—a request-based Web farm—prohibits you from using in-memory solutions to store client state. Therefore, you must choose between using cookies (which are the easiest to use but can be disabled by the client), `QueryString` variables (which cannot be disabled, but are more complex to maintain and are not very pretty), or hidden form fields (which are complex to maintain, cannot be disabled, and don't interfere with the user interface experience). Each of these methods may be used alone or in conjunction with a database to store the bulk of data, while using one of these methods to track a session ID.

Your primary responsibility in the middle tier is to provide the greatest accessibility, usability, and stability to your users. Note that the previous sentence didn't include the phrase "and to take the easy way out." Stability and scalability in the middle tier directly translate into the number of servers available and how easily a user can move around among them. Storing state information somewhere other than the Web server makes sense because it allows users to be served by any machine on your network without losing data, and that means your users will think better of your application.

After you have solved the problem of user state, your next task is to determine what logic to write in an ASP page, and what to store in a COM DLL. Writing COM components that can be used by ASP pages is simple in VB; writing them well, and understanding how they work, is a little more complex. The next several rules describe the nature of scriptable COM components, and how they interact with the plumbing inside ASP.

Rule 4-4: Understand the Differences Between DCOM and HTTP

Learning how to set up a Web site is an important step. Learning why you need to is critical. Just because your application can be configured as a Web-enabled product does not mean that it must be. Although a Web-based solution is generally a good idea, a lot of people who are in favor of it can't tell you why it is a better way to deploy than a standard LAN solution. Aside from the obvious Internet arguments about availability to the world, there are several architectural reasons that a Web-based solution may be a preferred design.

Ultimately, your client must somehow communicate its work requests to your server. This agreed way of communicating is called a *protocol.* In many cases HTTP, which is currently the most popular Web-based protocol, has advantages over Distributed COM (DCOM) with Remote Procedure Call (RPC) (the protocol most frequently used in LAN-based COM deployments). This rule compares the two forms of communication and shows some of the advantages of using HTTP over DCOM.

In its purest form, a distributed Web application consists of one or more clients, one or more servers, and usually some kind of data store. Additionally there is a set of requests that the clients make to the servers. HTTP and DCOM represent two different ways to submit this set of requests.

Communicating Using RPC and DCOM

When using DCOM, your clients must know some things up front. They must know the GUIDs for the components and interfaces you are going to use when issuing requests. They must be able to see the TLB for the interfaces, so they can marshal information. They must also know the server where the components live. Much of this information must reside in the client's registry. Configuring a client machine for a DCOM deployment can be cumbersome, particularly when new server components are going to be added, or information about them changes. In many cases, changes to the system require revisiting the client machine to update the configuration. It is often not enough to locate the client binary on a file server and to perform updates there. DCOM by nature requires registry configuration on the client for communication.

Communicating Using HTTP

When using HTTP, there is no required client configuration, beyond the presence of a browser. Actually, there is not even a client install required.[4] The user interface is prepared on the fly and sent to the client on a request-by-request basis. A Web server generates documents and passes them as a response to requests from the client. For this to work, a client must first know how to send and receive HTTP requests. HTTP is most commonly used to deliver HTML documents, so clients would also have to be able to parse HTML. Of course, Web browsers facilitate both of these requirements. Communication with server-side components can occur at the server prior to streaming HTML, so configuration can be centralized. This usually means that the client only needs to be able to render HTML and to understand HTTP, and does not need any additional configuration. Of course, this is highly beneficial, because evolving a deployed system will no longer require a visit to any client machines. You could think of a Web server as a kind of virtual centralized client. As the user base grows, centralized configuration becomes more important, and the HTTP configuration advantage over DCOM becomes more realized.

Because HTTP is not tied to any platform, another advantage is the ability to make the client platform independent. Any machine that can understand HTML and communicate with HTTP can play the role of a client, provided it can connect to the desired application. With DCOM, clients must be configurable, and must be able to communicate via RPC. DCOM is realistically a Windows-only solution, and attempting to use it across platforms is prohibitive. In the case of HTTP, as long as a machine's platform supports a browser, it can participate as a client to your Web server. When it is time to add new clients to the system, all the new client needs is a browser and your URL. There may be some server-side configuration such as adding a new username and password, but all the new client needs to know is simply where to point his or her browser. It's hard to imagine a more open-ended solution for managing your client base.

---

[4] This may or may not be literally true. Although most new computers ship with a browser already installed, there still exist situations in which installing a browser is a required step. Additionally, it is also possible that your Web site uses technologies like custom plug-ins that also require installation. However, a fairly robust and powerful Web site can be developed that requires no special client-side configuration or install.

An HTTP solution can also be ported from an intranet to the Internet simply by moving it to the correct Web server. In addition to the client configuration requirements mentioned earlier, attempting to use DCOM through firewalls is problematic, particularly with respect to security issues like authentication. DCOM is just not designed for clients across the Internet. It is aimed more directly at LAN solutions.

Another advantage of HTTP is its inherent statelessness. Connections between machines participating in an HTTP conversation are *short-lived*. HTTP is a request/response protocol, meaning the clients issue a statement, and the server responds with a document. Any physical connection between the two machines is built up just before issuing a request and is torn down just after the response is received. DCOM, while still a request/response protocol, requires an open connection prior to clients making requests. This means that for DCOM clients to issue a work statement, they must first connect, then make the request, then at some later time disconnect. With VB components, the process of connecting can be quite a chore. HTTP is connectionless, in that the request for processing and the connection occur in the same call, and when the response is sent, the conversation is completed.

When using HTTP, the server does not have to worry about connected clients disappearing over time. With DCOM, the connection must be validated periodically. To achieve this, a pinging mechanism is used by clients to say to the server "I'm not dead yet." This generates additional network traffic. The HTTP solution is much more optimized for concurrency, because system resources are not consumed between calls, as with DCOM. It does, however, introduce a state management problem when a client needs to make a set of related calls. Details of how to manage state with HTTP are covered in rule 4-3. DCOM-based clients have an obvious place to manage their state; namely, the object to which they are connected can store it between calls. However, the connection-oriented protocol consumes many more resources, which is a high price to pay for state management, particularly in larger systems.

We have stated that adding new clients to a system is trivial with HTTP, but what happens as these new clients begin to consume more and more server resources? Additional clients will mean additional concurrent users, and a higher workload on the server. Regardless of your protocol, a processor can only do so much work. At the most physical level, scalability is achieved by processing more cycles per second, which means more processors. More processors either means more machines, or a single, very expensive machine. Ultimately, though, a single machine will still only scale so far, so only a multiple-machine solution has the capability to continue growing.

Web-based solutions are better prepared to address this, in part because the problem has occurred repeatedly to ill-prepared sites on the Internet. There are many load-balancing solutions for Web architectures. The connectionless protocol allows each request to be routed to and serviced by the least busy machine in a Web farm. Because DCOM clients require a connection, a client must be tied to one machine throughout the connection lifetime. If the connected client's machine goes down between calls, the client is out of luck. With HTTP, if a machine in a Web farm goes down, calls are simply routed elsewhere, with no service interruption. This makes it much easier for HTTP-based solutions to provide fault tolerance as well (see rule 4-1 for further details on Web farm architecture).

Eliminating ASP from the Distributed Application

One item that has been missing from Web solutions is the ability to invoke methods from client code on server-side objects. There have been vendor-specific solutions in the past like Remote Data Services (RDS), but there has not been an industry standard specification for HTTP-based method invocation.

With the emergence of XML, a new standard for requesting services over HTTP has come on the scene. The Simple Object Access Protocol (SOAP) is a specification for executing method calls over HTTP using XML to deliver state to and from the server. Because SOAP is not tied to anything except HTTP and XML, it is possible for a client on one platform to invoke methods on a server that runs on a different platform, using a different component technology. As long as both parties understand XML and can use HTTP to communicate, there are no dependences on the operating system or the hardware. Technologies like SOAP will drastically change how HTTP-based solutions are implemented.

Essentially, a SOAP method is an HTTP request with a specially formatted XML body. Inside the HTTP headers, you must include a new custom header,

`SOAPMethodName`. This header's value represents the name of the interface, and the method on that interface, that is being invoked.

The body must contain a named XML element, `soap:Envelope`, with an optional `soap:Header` and a mandatory `soap:Body`. The body element does the bulk of the work. It identifies the name of the method and contains all parameter information. The receiving layer on the server parses the SOAP method, either finds or creates an object capable of rendering a response to the method invocation, invokes the method, and passes the parameter information onto the object. In this respect, SOAP operates much like the `IDispatch` interface in COM: It takes a named method and a list of parameter values, and invokes that method on behalf of the calling client.

The underlying SOAP layer then takes the output from the method and creates a SOAP response, which is an HTTP response with a specialized XML payload (just like the request). Here is an example of a SOAP request for the method `GetNameFromSSN`, which takes a social security number and returns the full name of the person.

```
POST /people.pl HTTP/1.1
Content-Type: text/xml
SOAPMethodName: interface#GetNameFromSSN

<soap:Envelope xmlns:soap="uri for SOAP">
   <soap:Body>
      <GetNameFromSSN xmlns="interface">
         <ssn>111-11-1111</ssn>
      </GetNameFromSSN>
   </soap:Body>
</soap:Envelope>
```

The resulting response would look like this:

```
200 Ok
Content-Type: text/xml

<soap:Envelope xmlns:soap="uri for SOAP">
   <soap:Body>
      <GetNameFromSSNResponse xmlns="interface">
         <name>John F. Doe</name>
```

```
            </GetNameFromSSNResponse>
        </soap:Body>
</soap:Envelope>
```

This specification does not imply any specific API for processing the call, nor does it require any specific operating system or object model on the client or server side of the conversation. It merely requires the ability to parse and create XML, understand HTTP, and have a layer in place (either created on your own or downloaded from a third party) that can handle the specific SOAP elements. Essentially, with HTTP, TCP/IP, and XML (all open, universally accepted standards) you can replace RPC, DCOM, and NDR, which are proprietary and not firewall friendly.

Using SOAP, clients can invoke methods on an object given a known server that exposes the object. SOAP invocations are packaged in standard HTTP messages, and are serviced by the SOAP listening service on the server. Objects are invoked transparently to the client, methods are called, and the results are packaged and shipped back to the client. The client can either deal directly with the creation and reception of SOAP methods, or use a client-side service called the Remote Object Proxy Engine (ROPE) to do that grungy work for them. In either case, not only has your application achieved location transparency in object method calls, but operating system and object model transparency as well, and all without a single *Web page* to speak of.

The Downside of Using HTTP

As with most technologies, there are always trade-offs. The HTTP solution is limiting in terms of state management as well as client complexity. With VB, you can build feature-rich front ends that are simply not available with HTML. Internal controlled user bases are excellent candidates for DCOM-based deployments, as well as back-end solutions sitting behind a Web server/farm. Also, in some cases, mandatory client configuration could be viewed as a positive thing, particularly when you want to limit client access to specific machines.

Another thing to consider with DCOM is that it has a mature and well-tested implementation. Although HTTP works fine in its current form, it is part of an emerging suite of technologies. Exciting new implementations like SOAP are impacting how HTTP will be used in new solutions, but these technologies are still in their infancy. DCOM is battle tested and solid.

You must consider your target deployment and decide which protocol is best for you. But if you are looking at larger deployments, and scalability and extensibility are important to the system, consider using HTTP as the protocol instead of DCOM. It is generally a more open-ended solution for enterprise development. However, if your user base is guaranteed to live entirely inside your firewall and requires a customized front-end, DCOM may be the correct path. HTTP opens up the doors to a wider, heterogeneous audience by sacrificing the benefits of a stateful protocol.

Most of the hesitation developers have about moving to the Web model is based on the fear of losing the use of previously developed components and previously learned techniques. Much money and time has been spent at many companies building libraries of VB/COM components that contain the bulk of your business logic. You need not fear: Microsoft has provided a simple migration path for these components to be used over the Web. The next two rules describe how to write components for use with the ASP model, as well as how those objects interact with the underlying ASP plumbing.

Rule 4-5: Write COM Components for Scripting Environments (Like ASP)

ASP is just one of many available scripting environments in Windows. IE and the WSH are other examples, and all have become important consumers of your COM objects. However, scripting environments place three important restrictions on our COM objects: (1) Only the object's default interface is accessible, (2) this interface must support `IDispatch` (late-binding), and (3) some forms of parameters are incompatible. These restrictions have an important impact on how you design and build your COM-compatible classes in VB. (If you're new to COM, rules 2-3 and 2-5 provide some important background.)

Building the Default Interface

An interface is simply a list of method signatures. COM objects must implement one or more interfaces, and these interfaces represent the sole access mechanism for clients. By default, the interface-based nature of COM is hidden from

VB programmers. (See rules 2-1 and 2-2 for more information on interfaces, and a class's default interface.) In particular, when you develop a class in VB, the set of public properties and methods form its default interface. This makes your VB class available to other COM programmers without any explicit effort on your part. For example, consider the following VB class `CVideo`, part of a set of library-related classes:

```
'** class module: CVideo
Option Explicit

Public CallNumber As String

Public Sub CheckOut(ByVal iDuration As Integer)
    '** implementation...
End Sub

Public Sub Returned()
    '** implementation...
End Sub
```

The default interface for this class actually consists of four methods: a `Get` property method for reading the value of `CallNumber`, a `Let` property method for writing the value of `CallNumber`, and the obvious methods `CheckOut` and `Return`. These methods are accessible to other VB programmers by using a class-based reference:

```
Dim rObj As TypeLibName.CVideo       '** class-based object reference
Set rObj = New TypeLibName.CVideo
rObj.CallNumber = "45.19362891b3"
rObj.CheckOut 14    '** two weeks
```

Likewise, these methods are also accessible to scripting clients (e.g., VBScript):

```
Dim rObj2       '** variant implies IDispatch-based object reference
Set rObj2 = CreateObject("TypeLibName.CVideo")
rObj2.CallNumber = "45.19362891b3"
rObj2.CheckOut 14
```

This is made possible by the additional fact that all interfaces in a VB class automatically support `IDispatch`, the only interface scripting clients truly understand. Thus, not only are VB classes automatically COM compatible, but they are scripting compatible as well.

Passing Parameters to Your "Scriptable" Objects

At this point the only limitations to keep in mind are those related to parameter passing. First, your parameters cannot involve UDTs. And second, all `ByRef` parameters—the default in VB—must be declared as `Variant` to be compatible with VBScript (and must be eliminated altogether when used with JavaScript because Java does not support pass by reference). For example, consider the following method, which is passed a string by reference:

```
Public Sub SomeTask(s As String)     '** ByRef by default
   '** implementation...
End Sub
```

This leads to a run-time-type error in VBScript:

```
Dim v                                '** v is a variant
v = "hello world"
obj.SomeTask v                       '** error: "Type Mismatch"
```

For compatibility, the parameter `s` must be of type `Variant`. Note that you could, instead, rewrite the VBScript to typecast the parameter explicitly:

```
Dim v
v = "hello world"
obj.SomeTask CStr(v)     '** this executes without error
```

However, you lose pass-by-reference semantics: Any changes to `s` within `SomeTask` are not reflected back in `v`. As such, this really isn't a good technique. It is better simply to remember to define your methods with the acceptable `Variant` parameter type.

What About Custom Interfaces?

So what's the big issue with scripting environments? Problems arise when your classes implement *custom interfaces:* These interfaces are inaccessible. For example, a better way to build a set of library-related classes is first to design a common interface that all such classes will implement. Let's call this interface `ICheckable`:

```
'** class module: ICheckable
Public CallNumber As String

Public Sub CheckOut(ByVal iDuration As Integer)
End Sub

Public Sub Returned()
End Sub
```

Each class then implements this interface (e.g., `CVideo`):

```
'** class module: CVideo (revised)
Option Explicit

Implements ICheckable

Private Property Get ICheckable_CallNumber() As String
    '** implementation...
End Property

Private Property Let ICheckable_CallNumber( _
                                ByVal RHS As String)
    '** implementation...
End Property

Private Sub ICheckable_CheckOut( _
                                ByVal iDuration As Integer)
    '** implementation...
End Sub

Private Sub ICheckable_Returned()
    '** implementation...
End Sub
```

In this case, notice that the class contains *no* public members. This implies that its default interface is empty, and hence the class is not scriptable. This is true even though `ICheckable` does indeed support `IDispatch`.

Because interfaces form the basis of all COM programming, and thus COM objects typically implement a multitude of interfaces, lack of support for custom interfaces is a serious limitation of scripting environments. What solutions are available to the COM programmer?

Solutions
First, you can ignore the benefits of interface-based programming and use only default interfaces. The primary disadvantage to this approach is that when you try to "version" your classes, you will be unable to change the interface (e.g., correct an error in a method signature) without breaking existing client code. Obviously, this approach is applicable only when you are building your classes from scratch.

A second approach is to add the necessary public methods to your classes and recompile. Once again, there is the problem of how to version, and also how to deal with conflicting custom interfaces (e.g., suppose the class has two interfaces, both with a method called `CheckOut`). A third, similar approach is simply to change all the private interface-based implementations to public:

```
Option Explicit

Implements ICheckable

Public Property Get ICheckable_CallNumber() As String
    '** implementation...
End Property
    .
    .
    .
```

This actually works, with each method becoming a member of both the default interface and the custom interface. However, it requires access to the source code and, more important, requires that your interfaces are already script

THE WEB AND VB

compliant (i.e., with regard to parameter passing, as discussed earlier). This approach also forces your scripting clients into a somewhat cumbersome naming scheme:

```
Dim obj
Set obj = CreateObject("TypeLibName.CVideo")
obj.ICheckable_CallNumber = "45.19362891b3"
obj.ICheckable_CheckOut 14
```

On the other hand, versioning is less of a problem with this naming scheme.

But suppose you are working, or plan to work, with custom interfaces, or you simply don't want to modify your classes' default interfaces. Custom interfaces provide distinct advantages (in design, implementation, and maintenance), and the reasons not to modify an existing class are many: It may already be in production use, its interfaces may be immutable, or you don't have access to the source code. In these cases you need a more elegant solution to support scripting environments.

This leads us to a fourth and final approach, based on *wrapper* classes. The idea is to provide a separate wrapper object—with a default interface—that simply forwards calls along the custom interface to the original object. For example, recall that an instance of the revised `CVideo` class contains both a default interface (empty) and the custom interface `ICheckable` (Figure 4.7). To make `ICheckable` available to scripting clients, a wrapper object is instantiated and then hooked up to this interface, as shown in Figure 4.8.

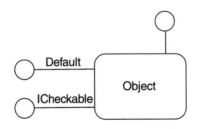

Figure 4.7 A COM object with a default and a custom interface

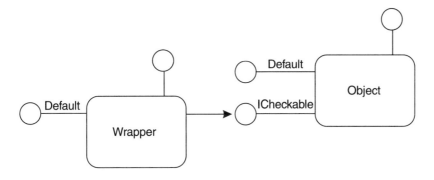

Figure 4.8 A scriptable wrapper object around a nonscriptable custom interface

As long as the wrapper's default interface is a one-to-one mapping to the custom interface, scripting clients now have complete access to all methods. Note that no changes whatsoever are required to the original class; in this case, CVideo. Thus, class design and development can proceed as before based on sound object-oriented principles, compiled clients are not impacted in any way, yet scripting environments with their important limitations are cleanly supported. For example, suppose ICheckable defines the following UDT and method:

```
Public Type TMemberInfo
    sName As String
    lCardNumber As Long
End Type

Public Sub DonatedBy(uMember As TMemberInfo)
End Sub
```

CVideo implements this as normal:

```
Private Sub ICheckable_DonatedBy(uMember As TMemberInfo)
    '** implementation...
End Sub
```

However, the wrapper class would define a public method of the same name that takes each UDT field as a distinct parameter and then packages them up for the underlying call:

```
Public Sub DonatedBy(ByVal sName As String, _
                    ByVal lCardNumber As Long)
   Dim uMember As TMemberInfo

   uMember.sName = sName
   uMember.lCardNumber = sCardNumber
   Call rObj.DonatedBy(uMember)    '** forward call to CVideo instance
End Sub
```

This assumes `rObj` is a reference to the wrapped object (discussed later).

There are at least two different implementation strategies you should consider when taking this approach. The first is a simpler design that is less error prone for clients, but requires as many as *N* wrapper classes, where *N* = number of classes ´ number of custom interfaces. As an example, let's wrap `CVideo`'s `ICheckable` interface. First, we create a class named `CwICheckable_CVideo` with a private object reference variable and the following `Class_Initialize/Class_Terminate` events:

```
'** class module: CwICheckable_CVideo
Option Explicit

Private rObj As ICheckable

Private Sub Class_Initialize()
   Set rObj = New TypeLibName.CVideo
End Sub

Private Sub Class_Terminate()
   Set rObj = Nothing
End Sub
```

When the wrapper class is instantiated, it automatically creates an instance of `CVideo` and hooks it up. Likewise, when the wrapper object is about to be destroyed, it automatically destroys the underlying `CVideo` object as well. Then we simply provide one public method for each method in the custom interface, forwarding each of the calls:

```
Public Property Get CallNumber() As String
    CallNumber = rObj.CallNumber
End Property

    .
    .
    .

Public Sub Returned()
    rObj.Returned
End Sub
```

Finally, the scripting client now accesses `ICheckable` of `CVideo` as follows:

```
Dim rObj
Set rObj = CreateObject("TypeLibName.CwICheckable_Video")
rObj.CallNumber = "45.19362891b3"
rObj.CheckOut 14
```

That's it!

The disadvantages to this approach are two-fold: the development overhead of having to create *N* wrapper classes, and the run-time overhead of creating extra objects and forwarding calls. Although there is nothing you can do about the latter, there is a simple technique you can apply that may dramatically reduce the number of wrapper classes you must develop. The idea is to use a *one-to-many design* whenever different classes implement the same interface. For example, suppose that `CVideo`, `CBook`, and `CAlbum` all implement the `ICheckable` interface. In this case, you can define a single wrapper class named `CwICheckable` much like before, except delete the `Class_Initialize` subroutine and provide an explicit `Init` method in its place:

THE WEB AND VB

```
'** class module: CwICheckable
Option Explicit

   .
   .
   .

Public Sub Init(ByVal sProgID As String)
    Set rObj = CreateObject(sProgID)
End Sub

   .
   .
   .
```

The idea is to leverage polymorphism—different types of objects implementing the same methods—and the flexibility of `CreateObject` to reduce the number of wrapper classes. The only drawback is that the scripting client is now responsible for calling the `Init` method and triggering the instantiation of the underlying object:

```
Dim rObj
Set rObj = CreateObject("TypeLibName.CwICheckable")
rObj.Init "TypeLibName.CVideo"
rObj.CallNumber = "45.19362891b3"
rObj.CheckOut 14
```

Designing your component to be script compatible is only half your task. The architecture in which your object will live, the ASP model, has specific services you can use within your code and certain pitfalls of which to beware. The next rule introduces some of the most important of each.

Rule 4-6: Understand How Your COM Objects Interact with ASP

Rule 4-5 details how to write COM components in VB that can be used with a scripting language. Once you understand `IDispatch` and the default interface, you can write objects that can be used by an ASP page. Writing objects that can be used by a script page is only a part of understanding the interaction between COM components and ASP. You must also understand the physical interaction between the ASP model and your custom objects. The first part of this rule gives you a better idea of how the ASP model makes use of your custom objects; the second part explains how your objects can make use of the ASP model. Specifically, this item describes

- Why you shouldn't use the ASP `Session` or the `Application` objects to store references to your custom objects
- The pros and cons of storing references to the ASP intrinsic objects in your custom objects

Understanding these issues will help you design a Web application that uses the power of VB without compromising the ASP model or your ability to reuse your code in other systems.

The ASP Intrinsic Objects

ASP provides a good deal of functionality through five objects collectively known as the *ASP intrinsic objects.* Through them, your server-side logic can interact with the Web server on which your pages live, as well as the actual HTTP messages that make up a user's interaction with your application. The model provides two objects for manipulating the HTTP messages (the `Request` and `Response` objects), two objects for managing the different types of application state (`Session` and `Application`), and one for interacting with services provided by your server (the `Server` object).

The `Request` object is a read-only representation of the HTTP request that caused your page to be initialized and to run. Your code uses it to determine details about the nature of the request. To formulate an answer to the request, your page can manipulate the read/write properties of the `Response` object. This allows you more granular control over the actual return message to the client.

The `Session` object provides a simple interface for storing and accessing session state. Its use is straightforward: Simply add a value to the `Session` object by providing a name and a value. For example,

```
Session("myValue") = "my value"
```

The `Application` object provides a semantically identical service, except that instead of storing per-user state, it stores information across all the pages on a given server. The `Server` object provides access to the COM activation sequence, special character encoding methods, and other features provided by the Web server itself. Understanding how these objects make use of your custom COM objects, and vice versa, is the purpose of the rest of this rule.

VB COM Objects and the STA

VB makes it easy to create apartment-threaded components that run under the STA model (see rules 2-9 and 3-1). When you write the code for this type of component, you never have to worry about locking to prevent concurrency from causing data inconsistencies or data corruption. This is a great advantage because you can write your components from a single-threaded perspective and yet still load and run your objects in multithreaded environments such as COM+, MTS, and IIS.

It's important that you understand the two primary benefits that are provided by the STA threading model. First, the STA threading model offers system-provided synchronization. Programmers never need to write custom synchronization code for objects that run exclusively on STA threads. Second, the STA threading model guarantees that no object will ever be accessed by any thread except for the thread that created it. This means that objects that exhibit thread affinity can safely run in the STA. However, you should also note that objects that exhibit thread affinity cannot run under the more sophisticated threading models such as the MTA or the TNA.

All components built with VB6 (and earlier versions) exhibit thread affinity. This means that every VB object must run under the STA model. One of the main reasons for this constraint is the VB team's use of TLS. The VB team uses TLS when building support into a VB component for things like the implementation for `IUnknown` and `IDispatch`. A VB object will more than likely crash if any other thread than the thread that created it ever accesses it. This leads to an important observation. Component builders and Web developers who use VB must understand the limitations of the STA threading model.

Making the Most of the STA Threading Model

When you create a VB DLL for an IIS/ASP application, make sure you leave your project's threading model set to the default setting of *apartment threaded*. Don't change it to *single-threaded,* because that will force your objects to be loaded into the main STA. Because the creating ASP page is running on an STA thread that is not the main STA, this causes an unnecessary thread-switching proxy/stub layer. This results in some fairly significant performance degradation and can also lead to some strange and harmful blocking behavior.

As you know, VB makes it easy to create apartment-threaded components that run under the STA model. However VB makes it impossible to create more sophisticated components that run under the MTA or TNA threading models. The good news for VB programmers is that this doesn't impose much of a limitation in an IIS/ASP application because each ASP worker thread is an STA thread. This is true under IIS5 with the Windows 2000 Server as well as under IIS4 with the Windows NT Server.

When you create a VB object from an ASP page, you can do it in such a way that the two run on the same STA thread. This is a big performance win because the COM run-time doesn't need to place a thread-switching proxy/stub layer between the ASP page and a VB object. All you need to do is set up your components in a COM+ library application (or MTS library package) or run them as nonconfigured components. In either case, objects created from your components load onto the same STA thread as the ASP page that creates them.

When you design an application in which ASP pages are creating VB objects, you must follow an important rule. Every VB object must be released at the end of the request in which it was created. Another way to say this is that VB objects must be defined at page scope. It is unacceptable to hold on to a VB object across requests. Let's discuss why this is such an important issue.

Remember that VB objects exhibit thread affinity. This means that only the thread that created it can access a VB object. This isn't a problem when you create and release an object within the scope of a single client request. But, if you attempt to hold on to a VB object across multiple requests by assigning it to an ASP `Session` variable, you end up pinning the client to a specific worker thread in the ASP thread pool.

To explain why this situation is undesirable, let's look at an example that highlights the issues that the IIS/ASP team had to work through when they designed the ASP run-time (i.e., the code in ASP.dll). Once you see the relevant issues caused by objects with thread affinity, you'll have a better appreciation why the ASP run-time treats apartment-threaded objects the way it does.

Imagine a scenario in which a client's request runs some code that creates a VB object and assigns it to an ASP Session variable. This VB object gets created on whichever STA thread from the ASP thread pool processes the request; let's say thread 9. What if the next request from the same client is processed by thread 3? A problem occurs because thread 3 can't access a VB object that has affinity to thread 9. If this second request requires access to the VB object, it would have to switch from thread 3 to thread 9 (and back) to complete its work.

To make things worse, what if the second request being processed on thread 3 created a second object? This object would have affinity to thread 3. Now imagine what would happen if a third request for the same client came in on thread 4 and needed to access the two VB objects that had been created in the first two requests. The third request would have to switch from thread 4 to thread 3 back to thread 4 then to thread 9 and finally back to thread 4.

You can see this situation is only going to get worse if the client continues to create more VB objects across additional threads in the ASP thread pool. If this situation actually occurred (and fortunately it doesn't), your application performance would go downhill pretty quickly because of all the thread switching and blocking. Fortunately, the scenario described in this paragraph never happens because of design decisions made by the IIS/ASP team.

The IIS/ASP team had to choose between the lesser of two evils. They decided that pinning clients to threads was preferable to having a situation in which a single request requires access across multiple threads. They added code to the ASP run-time to determine when an apartment-threaded object is assigned to an ASP Session variable. When the ASP run-time sees that a client session is assigned an apartment-threaded object, it routes all futures requests for that session through the same STA worker thread. Although this prevents the undesirable scenario described in the previous paragraph, it also has an unfortunate side effect. The ASP thread-pooling scheme cannot work at its best because it cannot use the first available thread in the pool to process each incoming request.

The thread-pooling architecture of the ASP run-time was designed to dispatch the first available worker thread from the STA thread pool to service any incoming requests. However, as you can see, when you assign a VB object to an ASP Session variable, the ASP run-time must locate (and possibly block) the one thread that created the object. Although ASP is capable of serializing all future requests over the same thread, you can see that this situation doesn't allow ASP to make the most of its thread-pooling scheme. An incoming request can be blocked waiting for its session's thread to free up, whereas there are several other ASP worker threads sitting around idly with nothing to do.

The most important point to understand is that the threading model of an IIS/ASP application is severely compromised when an application allows apartment-threaded objects to live beyond the scope of a single client request. This means you should always create and destroy your VB objects inside the scope of a single ASP request. Don't assign a VB object (or any other apartment-threaded object) to an ASP Session variable. The bottom line is that your Web application will not scale if you don't follow this rule.

Now that you know about the problems with apartment-threaded objects and ASP Session variables, it's time to think through the same issues with regard to ASP Application variables. Assigning a VB object to an ASP Application variable would create another problem that is even more severe. If you assign an apartment-threaded object to an ASP Application variable, the requests from many different clients have to be routed through one STA thread. This would result in even more severe blocking behavior, not to mention additional thread switches.

Fortunately, the ASP run-time (ASP.dll) of IIS4 doesn't even allow you to assign an apartment-threaded object to an ASP Application object. If you attempt to do this, your code will fail with the error message "Cannot add object with apartment model behavior to the application intrinsic object." You can, unfortunately, make an end run around this error by creating your object using the HTML "<OBJECT>" tag:

```
<OBJECT ID="appObject" SCOPE="Application"
        RUNAT="server" PROGID="myLibrary.myClass">
</OBJECT>
```

Even if your object is apartment-threaded, this line will not cause a run-time error when executed. Worse, you can then, in script, assign this reference to an `Application` variable. You will experience crashes as a result, so be careful to avoid this situation.

The ASP run-time exhibits the same behavior in IIS5 as long as the ASP `AspTrackThreadingModel` property is set to `True`. Note that the default setting for this property is `False`, but it can be reconfigured for an IIS application or an entire site. However, you should see that IIS turns off these checks by default, which means you have the extra responsibility of making sure you do the right thing. Never assign a VB object to an ASP `Application` object.

How Do You Access These Objects from VB?

The relationship between the ASP objects and your COM objects is two-way. So far, we have examined the relationship between ASP pages and the custom COM objects to which they refer. Just as it is possible to store references to custom objects inside the ASP intrinsic objects (namely, `Session` and `Application`), so too is it possible to store references to those ASP intrinsic objects in your custom objects. To do so, you can reference the Microsoft Active Server Pages Object Library from your VB project. To use the objects, however, you need more than just a reference to ASP.dll. Your components have to be *configured components.* This means that your project must have a reference to either the Microsoft Transaction Server library under Windows NT or the COM+ Services Library under Windows 2000.

As it turns out, since IIS4.0, Microsoft's IIS has been built on top of MTS (and now COM+). The WAM component, a vital piece of the IIS plumbing, resides in WAM.dll, which is installed as a configured component under both systems. Every virtual directory or site you create in IIS gets mapped to either a shared MTS package (COM+ application) or its own unique package/application.

Both of these frameworks provide a COM object called `ObjectContext` to configured components. `ObjectContext` is a configured component's view of the world in which it lives. It so happens that, because ASP pages are built on top of IIS, which in turn is built on top of MTS/COM+, it is this `ObjectContext` object that contains the references to the intrinsic ASP objects. To access them from your compiled code, you may do something like the following:

```
Dim rRequest as ASPTypeLibrary.Request
Set rRequest = GetObjectContext().Item("Request")

'** use Request object somehow
If rRequest.Cookies("myCookie") = "myStringValue" then
    '** do something
End If
```

Benefits of Accessing ASP Intrinsic Objects Directly

Many developers tap directly into the `Request` and `Response` objects to avoid having complex interfaces on their components. If the components can read and write the HTTP packets directly, you can avoid having a bunch of extra parameters on your method calls (or worse yet, a bunch of extra method calls) to pass vital information to the component. As an example, imagine a custom object that exposes a method, `Foo`, which takes two input parameters in addition to the value of a cookie associated with the user. Without the ASP intrinsic objects, your code might look like this:

```
    '** compiled method inside your object...
Public Sub Foo(sFirstParam As String, _
               sSecondParam As String, _
               sCookie As String)
    '** use sFirstParam, sSecondParam, and sCookie to find something in the DB
End Sub

'** and now the ASP code...
Dim rMyObj
```

THE WEB AND VB

```
Set rMyObj = Server.CreateObject("myLib.myObj")
rMyObj.Foo Request.Form("fParam"), _
           Request.Form("sParam"), _
              Request.Cookies("myCookieValue")
```

However, with the intrinsic objects, things look cleaner:

```
'** compiled method inside object (revised)...
Public Sub Foo()
    Dim rRequest As ASPTypeLibrary.Request
    Set rRequest = GetObjectContext().Item("Request")

    Dim sFirstParam As String, sSecondParam As String
    Dim sCookie As String
    sFirstParam = rRequest.Form("fParam")
    ssecondParam = rRequest.Form("sParam")
    sCookie = rRequest.Cookies("myCookieValue")

        '** use sFirstParam, sSecondParam, and sCookie to find something in the DB
End Sub

'** resulting ASP code...
Dim rMyObj
Set rMyObj = Server.CreateObject("myLib.myObj")

'** notice cleaner call to Foo...
rMyObj.Foo
```

As you can see, the interface on your method calls is considerably cleaner, and your ASP code is much more succinct. The custom object is entirely responsible for managing the full response to the client as well.

What Are the Disadvantages of Using the ASP Intrinsic Objects?

Any method call that makes use of the ASP intrinsic objects is limited to being called by ASP pages. When activated by any other kind of client, say a COM executable, your code cannot take advantage of the ASP library. Therefore, you must take pains not to call those methods from non-ASP clients.

Do not take this to mean that you should never reference the ASP TLB in your DLLs. Using the ASP intrinsic objects can provide power and simplicity to your code. You must merely take pains to separate carefully calls that require the ASP library from those that do not. One way to do so is to create all the ASP-reliant methods on the public interface of your classes (so as to be visible from scripting clients), and then to create a custom interface with parallel versions of the methods that do not use ASP. In this way, only your script-ready interface can call on those objects, whereas the custom interface for your COM components and applications uses a different technique.

This solution is somewhat unwieldy, creating two interfaces with similar method calls but entirely different implementations. However, it provides the best possible combination of strategies for both ease of development and ease of reuse.

There is a lot to think about when creating COM objects to be used in an ASP application. The different ways that the underlying ASP model makes use of your object and vice versa have a large impact on both the performance of your application and your ability to reuse your code in other applications. Understanding the possibilities and limitations inherent in the system will help you better design and implement your components and ASP pages.

The rest of this chapter will help you design ways to move data out of a database, through your middle-tier objects, and onto a Web browser while maintaining a clean separation between the different layers of your application. Because there is no longer a preconfigured front-end (such as a VB executable), your user interface is created in the middle tier and is then passed to the client. This leads to confusion of the boundaries between different responsibilities in your application. The next several rules use XML, the Extensible Stylesheet Language: Transformation (XSLT) specification, and some best practice patterns to help you keep your application streamlined.

Rule 4-7: Use XML Instead of Proprietary Data Transfer Formats

You have by now been exposed to the phenomenon called XML. You have buckled under enormous peer pressure and surfed the Web for a tutorial. You have probably learned a lot of (sometimes conflicting) ideas about what XML is and what it can do for you. You have probably learned that XML is (1) a text file with a bunch of angle brackets, (2) a self-describing abstract data format, (3) a group of tools for navigating and transforming data, (4) the next HTML/ASCII, (5) the next SQL, or (6) all of the above. Although all these things are true to greater and lesser extents, there is a single definition that sums up the spirit and intent of this technology (with thanks to the many who have popularized this definition):

$$XML = Esperanto[5]$$

Esperanto was invented so that people from all over the world could communicate with each other. It is a simple, standardized universal language that was meant to be easy to learn and to use. If a Japanese woman met a Brazilian man on a London bus, they would at least be able to carry on a polite conversation while they waited for the next stop. XML is exactly the same thing. XML is a great way for code to talk to other code, regardless of where the code lives or what language it speaks. If your VB component met a Java bean on www.aLondonBus.com, they should be able to have a polite discussion. This is the promise of XML. XML is for interoperability: communicating structured information between two programmatic entities.

What makes XML so good for this purpose? The first reason is that the most common way of transferring XML is as plain old text. This simple fact means that XML is easily transportable to any operating system and any language. "Sure," you say, "text is great. Why don't I just write my own spec?" The answer is that XML is the product of years of research by the World Wide Web Consortium (W3C) and others to create a simple architecture that is flexible enough to be applied to any structured data problem, but standardized enough to be used between two problem domains.

The XML Infoset describes all the common abstractions that make up a valid XML document, without limiting the specific vocabulary you use to convey the data. The XML 1.0 syntax rules provide a common physical representation of these abstractions as well as the rules for creating your own vocabulary

---

[5] Some have pointed out that this is a dangerous analogy, because Esperanto has been, by and large, a dismal failure. We are only implying a similarity of intent. XML has been, in its short life, infinitely more successful than Esperanto is ever likely to be. In fact, we would be much less surprised to overhear a Japanese woman talking to a Brazilian man in XML than we would to hear them chatting in Esperanto.

(with specifications for different physical serialization formats, like UTF-8 and UCS-2), and the Namespaces recommendation provides a method for ensuring that your application's XML vocabulary is unique across all XML documents. Taken together, these three specifications mean that you can model data in an application-specific way (XML 1.0 syntax vocabulary) guaranteed to not have vocabulary conflicts with another application (XML Namespaces) but sharing a standard base of data abstractions for easy parsing by any XML-aware system (XML Infoset). In addition to these three core specifications, there also exist a wide array of other tools and specifications for addressing more specific problems in XML. For example, XSLT for converting between vocabularies, XLink for connecting two XML documents, the Simple API to XML (SAX) and Document Object Model (DOM) APIs for manipulating a dataset, and so forth. The wide industry support for this standard should be enough to convince you of its value.

What this means to you is that you can design the public interfaces of your components that need to communicate structured data to accept XML as input and to write it back as output. What you do *inside* the privacy of your own code is, as always, your own business. Let's see what this means to you by starting with a simple example. Imagine you are writing a component that manages a video store. One function it may provide would be to list all videos more than a year overdue. You might have written this function to return an array of titles:

```
Public Function ReallyLateTapes() As String()
    Dim saReturnArray() As String

    '** gather names of late tapes, append tapes to array...
    ReDim saReturnArray(...)
    .
    .
    .
    saReturnArray(i) = "Army of Darkness"
    .
    .
    .

    '** return the array
    ReallyLateTapes = saReturnArray
End Function
```

This is a fairly straightforward technique if your end client is another piece of VB code. The consumer code may just assign the result set to a `Variant` and then manipulate the values. Of course, it gets a little more complex if your client is written in C++: now, the client has to deal with the grunge that is the `SAFEARRAY` in C++, which is never fun. In both cases, though, you are assuming two things: (1) The client is running on a Windows box, and (2) it fully understands the format of the return data. Because an array is just an opaque list of values (in this case, strings), there is nothing built into the return data to describe it to the consumer code. The client already has to know what to expect and how to deal with it.

You may use XML to return this data instead. To build and manipulate XML documents, add a reference to the Microsoft XML DLL (the latest version is msxml3.dll, although when you actually create objects from it, the library name will appear as MSXML2) to your VB project. The primary class you will need from this DLL is `DOMDocument`. `DOMDocument` represents a full XML value set. You may choose to use this as your return type. Now, your function would look like this:

```
Public Function ReallyLateTapes() As MSXML2.DOMDocument
    '** create a new XML document
    Dim rDoc As MSXML2.DOMDocument
    Set rDoc = New MSXML2.DOMDocument

    '** create a root element node and append it to the document
    Dim rRoot As IXMLDOMNode
    Set rRoot = rDoc.createElement("LateTapes")
    rDoc.appendChild rRoot

    '** create subnodes to add to root node, like:
    Dim rNode As IXMLDOMNode
    Set rNode = rDoc.createElement("LateTape")
    rNode.Text = "Army of Darkness"
    rRoot.appendChild rNode

    '** repeat for all tapes...
    .
    .
    .
```

```
'** return document!
    Set ReallyLateTapes = rDoc
End Function
```

The DOMDocument object is an in-memory representation of an XML document. It can be randomly accessed using the navigation methods built into the Node object of MSXML3.dll. Your client can now use the data values, the same as it could in the array example, but can also discover information about the data at run-time. Client code could look like this:

```
'** the client
Dim rObject As New MyLibrary.TapeManager
Dim rDoc As DOMDocument

'** get the XML document
Set rDoc = rObject.ReallyLateTapes()

'** get the document root element and first data element
Dim rRoot As IXMLDOMNode, rNode As IXMLDOMNode
Set rRoot = rDoc.firstChild
Set rNode = rRoot.firstChild

'** you can discover metadata at run-time
Dim sRootName As String, sElemName As String
Dim sTapeTitle As String
sRootName  = rRoot.nodeName    '== "LateTapes"
sElemName  = rNode.nodeName    '== "LateTape"
sTapeTitle = rNode.text        '== "Army of Darkness"
```

Your consumers are no longer *required* to know the structure of your data to get value from it. They can discover properties like name, data type, number of child elements, and so forth, by examining the document itself. However, the DOMDocument object is a COM object. By passing this object as the return value of your function, you are making the assumption that your client is running Windows *and* that it is using the same version of MSXML.dll *and* that it is COM aware.

Also note that you could get the exact same functionality from a disconnected ADO Recordset. Look at the similarities: Both have built-in metadata

(`Node.nodeName` versus `Recordset.Fields(1).Name`), both are in-memory COM objects, both allow for random access of data, and both require the end user to be a Windows machine with a specific DLL registered (MSXML3 versus MSADO15). A lot of code is written with this type of signature for all-VB environments:

```
Public Function ReallyLateTapes() As ADODB.Recordset
```

In this way, you get to tap into the long and storied history of ADO as well as the power of SQL statements for using datasets. The big drawback is that interoperability with other systems is almost nil.

The most generic way to return the data would be as a serialized XML document. The XML specification defines an abstract data format and description language without specifying a specific serialization format. This means that almost any encoding scheme is acceptable as long as there is a parser that can read it. The plain ASCII format is the most widely accepted format today, because any operating system can read this encoding.

Therefore, a better method signature for your `ReallyLateTapes()` function would be

```
Public Function ReallyLateTapes() As String
    '** create an XML document
    Dim rDoc As DOMDocument

    '** generate DOMDocument as before
    .
    .
    .

    '** serialize the document to UTF-8
    ReallyLateTapes = rDoc.xml
End Function
```

Subsequent client code could rehydrate the XML like this:

```
'** revised client code
Dim rObject As New MyLibrary.CVideoManager
```

```
Dim sXML As String
sXML = rObject.ReallyLateTapes()

Dim rDoc As DOMDocument
Set rDoc = New DOMDocument

rDoc.LoadXML sXML
```

Now, the client has received a plain string and turned it back into a fully functional XML `DOMDocument` model.

What does this function do? It generates the same data structure as the last function, but returns a string instead of a COM XML document object. Now, your function is much more universally accessible. ASCII text can be read on any platform anywhere. If your object is interacting with other server-side components, this is a much better way to return your data.

What if you are writing your component to run on a Web server? You may want to return data directly to the client layer. Most browsers now have built-in support for XML data with default parsing of the data. In addition, there are tools in use today for converting a pure XML dataset into more human readable formats. The process of converting an XML document into some other format programmatically is called *transformation*. This can be accomplished with a language called XSLT.

To bypass server-side components and return XML directly to the browser, use the ASP `Response` object (see rules 4-1 and 4-6 for more information on using the `Response` object). The `MSXML2.DOMDocument` object has a method, `Save`. `Save` takes a single variable of type `Variant`. You can specify a filename as a string for this parameter, and your XML will be written to disk at that file location. This is not particularly useful for a server-side component. More important, if you pass in a COM object that supports the `IStream` or `IPersistStream` interfaces, the document will write itself out to your object. The ASP `Response` object happens to implement `IStream`, so you can send XML straight down to the browser by saving to the `Response`. Now, your function would look like this:

```
Public Sub ReallyLateTapes()
    '** create a new XML document
```

```
        Dim rDoc As MSXML2.DOMDocument
        Set rDoc = New MSXML2.DOMDocument

        '** do stuff to create and fill the document
          .
          .
          .

        '** get a reference to the Response object
        Dim rResponse As ASPTypeLibrary.Response
        Set rResponse = GetObjectContext().Item("Response")

        '** return XML to browser
        rDoc.save rResponse
     End Sub
```

You have now bypassed any server-side components (you are not returning a value from a function) and have passed an XML document straight across the wire to the browser. If you do nothing else, you will invoke the default parser for XML in the target browser. In IE4.x, this means you generate a default Dynamic HTML (DHTML) page of collapsible data nodes for the user to play with. If you want to have more granular control over the *display* of your XML, pick up a book on XSLT. In brief, you can affiliate a template rule file (XSLT program) with your XML by including a directive in your XML file itself. When it is loaded, the parser will recognize the directive, download the XSLT file from your server, and apply it to your XML before displaying it.

All of the techniques listed here are about how to *communicate* your data. Don't fall all the way down the XML hole: You still need SQL and ADO and all your other tools and code to maintain and to access your data on the server side. Think back to the Esperanto analogy: Esperanto was not meant to replace native languages. That same Japanese woman would go back to Japan and speak Japanese. Why? Because there are 2,500 years of infrastructure built up in Japan that depend on the Japanese language, and is optimized to use it. Switching everything over to Esperanto would slow down society and throw away a lot of useful stuff.

When your video store manager class wants to search your whole tape library to find out which tapes are overdue, who rented them, who the manufacturer was, and where to order more copies, this data should still be stored in a relational database on the server side. You should still use SQL statements to interrogate the database, probably through a set of ADO objects. These technologies provide power and efficiency that cannot be matched by XML and its current tool set. However, once you have gathered the data, analyzed it, sorted it, and are ready to report the results of your actions, XML is the method for returning data to the client.

The simplest way, currently, to achieve this is through the `ADO Recordset` object's `Save` method. This method also takes an object as its first parameter, which can either be a string denoting a file path or a COM object that exposes the `IStream` interface. Before version 2.1, ADO has only a single serialization format: the Advanced Data Tablegram (ADTG) format. This is a proprietary binary language for persisting ADO objects to disk. Now, however, you have a second choice, which is XML. Therefore, to take maximum advantage of the power of relational (databases) while still providing maximum interoperability with other code, your function might look something like this:

```
Public Sub ReallyLateTapes()
    '** create an XML document
    Dim rDoc As New DOMDocument

    '** create some ADO objects
    Dim rRS As New ADODB.Recordset
    Dim rCN As New ADODB.Connection

    '** use the recordset and connection to access and manipulate a database
    '** make sure the recordset isn't the default type (forward-only, read-only)
    '**     because this style of recordset does not support the .Save method
    .
    .
    .

    '** get a reference to the Response object
    Dim rResponse As Response
    Set rResponse = GetObjectContext().Item("Response")

    '** serialize the recordset back to the client
    rRS.Save rResponse, adPersistXML
End Function
```

What you need to keep in mind is that your components, to provide maximum interoperability, should be able to accept XML as input and emit XML as output whenever structured data is required. Other than that simple rule, what you do inside your objects should not depend on the latest industry buzz words. XML is for communication; SQL and ADO are for heavy lifting.

Rule 4-8: Be Deliberate About Presentation versus Business Logic

Developing well-designed, maintainable Web applications requires a tremendous amount of planning and effort. Many Web development tools available today promote rapid development of poorly designed, spaghetti code applications. It's not to say that the tools are bad, nor that the tools are the problem. Rather, the tools have made the task so easy that anyone can build a Web application with very little programming experience or training. ASP applications are no exception to this exploding problem. Consider the following code snippet from an ASP page:

```
<%@ Language=VBScript %>
<HTML><HEAD></HEAD><BODY>
<%
    Dim sConn, sText, sTHead, sTClose
    Dim rConn, rRS
    sConn = "Provider=sqloledb;Server=(local);" & _
            "Database=Pubs;UID=sa;Pwd="
    Set rConn = Server.CreateObject("ADODB.Connection")

    rConn.Open sConn

    Set rRS = Server.CreateObject("ADODB.Recordset")
    rRS.Open "Select au_lname from authors", rConn

    sTHead = "<Table>"
    Do Until rRS.EOF
        sText = sText & "<TR><TD>" & _
                rRS("au_lname") & "</TD></TR>"
        rRS.MoveNext
    Loop
```

```
        sTClose = "</Table>"

    Response.Write sTHead & sText & sTClose
%>
</BODY></HTML>
```

This is not a very complex page, yet it has something in it of which many ASP programmers are guilty. This page mixes presentation-tier and middle-tier code. Essentially, this creates a two-tier application on top of an inherently three-tier architecture. This style of programming makes it hard to maintain or upgrade your user interface without affecting your business logic, and vice versa.

Keep in mind that, in the world of the Internet, the logical presentation tier is different from the physical presentation tier. The physical layer is the Web browser that a client uses to access your Web server. The browser contains no built-in ability to interact with your proprietary server-side information and logic. It is simply a generic rendering engine for HTML. Therefore, although the user interface is physically constructed on the client machine, it must be logically generated on the server. One physical layer, the Web server, is responsible for two logical layers: presentation and business logic.

To produce truly scalable and maintainable applications, Web applications need to create a finer distinction between these two layers of code. There are plenty of issues that result if you don't make this distinction:

1. Mixing presentation layer and data access code is fundamentally bad design (data access code should be very low impact, using a get-in-late/get-out-early style, entirely unlike most user interface code).

2. Any programmer tasked with maintaining this code needs to be proficient in both user interface and business logic techniques.

3. Changes to one tier will necessitate changes to the other—precisely what having three tiers is supposed to avoid.

Clearly, this coding style violates the both the letter and spirit of the *N*-tier architecture. This rule demonstrates some alternatives to this brittle programming style.

Use MTS Components

MTS components running in the middle tier are one alternative. Using this approach we can move the data access code and business logic out of our ASP page and into a component that gets invoked from the ASP page. This is the most widely used approach today. MTS components leverage context information provided by MTS and ASP. They allow your COM components direct access to the underlying ASP architecture to interact directly with the HTTP requests and responses (see rule 4-5). For example, consider the following ASP code:

```
<%@ Language=VBScript %>
<HTML><HEAD></HEAD>
<BODY>
<%
    Dim rRef
    Set rRef = Server.CreateObject("BusObj.CFoo")
    rRef.ShowAuthors
%>
</BODY></HTML>
```

This small piece of ASP code generates the same results as the original example. However, you'll notice that the amount of business logic has been minimized. All we are doing in this code is calling a business object that is running in MTS. The component being called knows how to access the database and how to display the authors in a table format. The code in the component is as follows:

```
Public Sub ShowAuthors()
    Dim rCtx As ObjectContext
    Dim rRsp As Response
    Dim sConn As String, sText As String
    Dim sTHead As String, sTClose As String
    Dim rConn As ADODB.Connection
    Dim rRS As ADODB.Recordset

    Set rCtx = GetObjectContext()
    Set rRsp = rCtx.Item("Response")
```

```
    sConn = "Provider=sqloledb;Server=(local);" & _
            "Database=Pubs;UID=sa;Pwd="
    Set rConn = New ADODB.Connection
    rConn.Open sConn

    Set rRS = New ADODB.Recordset
    rRS.Open "Select au_lname from authors", rConn

    sTHead = "<Table>"
    Do Until rRS.EOF
    sText = sText & "<TR><TD>" & _
            rRS("au_lname") & "</TD></TR>"
    rRS.MoveNext
    Loop
    sTClose = "</Table>"

    rRsp.Write sTHead & sText & sTClose
End Sub
```

Note that this code looks very similar to the original ASP code. It performs all the data access but it also has some more interesting pieces to it. Mainly, the references to `ObjectContext` and the `Response` object. These objects are provided to us by the MTS run-time and the ASP run-time. If you have done any ASP programming, you should be familiar with the `Response` object and its methods that allow you to write information out to the browser. `ObjectContext` in MTS gives you, the developer, a way to reach up into the available context information provided by ASP and snatch a reference to the `Response` object. This contextual information is passed along to you when your object is created from the ASP code.

Although this example proves that all the logic need not exist inside an ASP page, it suffers from an identical flaw: Both the business logic and the presentation logic are maintained in this same piece of code. The only advantage to this second method is having access to the development environment VB provides, with a real debugger, compile-time type checking, and working IntelliSense. So, although the code may be easier to write the first time, it is no easier to maintain in the long run.

Use WebClasses

`WebClasses` are a framework first provided in VB6. The entire purpose of `WebClasses` is to provide a cleaner way of maintaining your presentation and business logic inside a COM component while still keeping the two layers separate. You create one by choosing the IIS `Application` project type when creating a new project. It is important to keep in mind that this technology will not be supported in VB7, so you are committing yourself to a VB6 solution for as long as you wish to maintain it. For that reason, you may want to examine the long-term solution offered in rule 4-9.

In simplest terms, a `WebClass` project provides a generic ASP entry point into our COM component. The ASP page launches an object called the `WebClassManager`, which brokers communication between the user and your business components. All output is generated in terms of HTML *templates* that can be created by designers and then imported into the `WebClass` project. This template is responsible for incorporating any dynamic output from the `WebClass` into the final response. For this to work, and to keep from having to place table generation code in the `WebClass`, the business object is going to save the results in an XML format that the HTML template can render.

Let's first look at the code in the ASP file generated by the `WebClass`:

```
<%
    Server.ScriptTimeout=600
    Response.Buffer=True
    Response.Expires=0
    If (VarType(Application("~WC~WebClassManager"))=0) _
    Then
        Application.Lock
        If (VarType(Application("~WC~WebClassManager"))=0) _
        Then
            Set Application("~WC~WebClassManager") = _
                    Server.CreateObject( _
                        "WebClassRun-time.WebClassManager")
        End If
        Application.UnLock
    End If
```

```
        Application("~WC~WebClassManager")._
            ProcessNoStateWebClass "Project1.WebClass1", _
                            Server, _
                            Application, _
                            Session, _
                            Request, _
                            Response
    %>
```

The first interesting piece of code is the line that creates the `WebClass-Run-time.WebClassManager` object and stores it in the application variable `~WC~WebClassManager`:

```
    Set Application("~WC~WebClassManager") = _
            Server.CreateObject( _
                "WebClassRun-time.WebClassManager")
```

The `WebClassManager` lives in a file called MSWCRUN.dll. When we created our IIS `Application` project, VB set a reference to this library for our application. If you go to the object browser in VB you can see the `WebClassManager` class listed under the `WebClassLibrary`. Note that you will not be able to see the `WebClassManager` class unless you select the Show Hidden Members option in the object browser. MSCWRUN.dll is the run-time for our `WebClass`. The run-time will serve as an entry point to our `WebClass`.

The next real interesting piece of code in the ASP file is the call to the `ProcessNoStateWebClass` method on the `WebClassManager`. You can see that the parameters passed into the `ProcessNoStateWebClass` method include all the ASP objects as well as the ProgID for your `WebClass` component (`Project1.WebClass1`, in this example). The only real purpose of the ASP page is to serve as the entry point to our `WebClass`. Each `WebClass` gets its own ASP file. This is the only file a client needs to call to access the `WebClass`.

A running `WebClass` has a global property called `NextItem`. To generate a response to the client, you set the `NextItem` property to one of the predefined HTML templates. A `WebClass` never interferes with the rendering of HTML in a template; it can merely provide dynamic information to the template for its own use. Each template is treated as a separate COM object by the `WebClass`, and to render it to the user, the `WebClass` calls the `WriteTemplate` method on the appropriate template. For example,

```vb
Private Sub ShowAuthors_Respond()
    Dim rObj As BusObj.CFoo
    Set rObj = New BusObj.CFoo

    rObj.ShowAuthorsXML

    ShowAuthors.WriteTemplate
End Sub

Private Sub WebClass_Start()
    Set NextItem = ShowAuthors
End Sub
```

When the `rObj.ShowAuthorsXML` method is called, the following code executes:

```vb
Public Sub ShowAuthorsXML()
    Dim sConn As String
    Dim rConn As ADODB.Connection
    Dim rRS As ADODB.Recordset

    sConn = "Provider=sqloledb;Server=(local);" & _
            "Database=Pubs;UID=sa;Pwd="
    Set rConn = New ADODB.Connection
    rConn.Open sConn

    Set rRS = New ADODB.Recordset
    rRS.Open "Select au_lname from authors", rConn

    rRS.Save sLocation, adPersistXML
End Sub
```

This code in the business object creates a recordset and then saves it in an XML format using the `Save` method with the `adPersistXML` format tag. This is a new feature in ADO 2.1. Once this method is done executing, the

WebClass regains control and simply calls ShowAuthors.WriteTemplate. The following code below is what appears in the ShowAuthors template:

```
<HTML><HEAD><TITLE>2 Tier Problem</TITLE></HEAD><BODY >
<XML ID="dsoAuthors" SRC="authors.xml"></XML>
<TABLE DATASRC="#dsoAuthors" DATAFLD="rs:data">
    <TR><TD>
         <TABLE DATASRC="#dsoAuthors" DATAFLD="z:row">
         <TR><TD>
             <INPUT TYPE="text" DATAFLD="au_lname">
         </TD></TR>
         </TABLE>
    </TD></TR>
</TABLE>
</BODY>
</HTML>
```

This technique solves the problem of separating presentation and business logic. However, it introduces a complex framework into your application that may cause it to be buggier and harder to debug (a tragic double whammy). Additionally, it is a technology not supported in future releases of VB. Although moving you in the right direction, it will be better, in the long term, to use more generic technologies like XML and XSLT to do this work for you. That is the focus of the next and last rule in this chapter.

Rule 4-9: Use XSLT to Move from Data to Presentation

XML and XSLT provide the best pathway for moving data from the database to the presentation tier. The previous rule described several ways to move complex logic out of the ASP page and into your compiled components. This rule introduces a third party to the dialog: the stand-alone XSLT program. Your compiled components can retrieve data from the database as XML, and instead of having built-in logic for turning that data into presentation-level HTML, it can call this third-party XSLT program to do that work on its behalf. This provides the perfect separation of tiers: database code in the database and ADO objects, business code in your compiled COM+/MTS components, and an XSLT program to generate the user interface.

What Is XSLT?

XSLT is a transformation language specified by the W3C. One of its primary purposes is to provide programmers with a language for transforming raw data into consumable information. Although the original idea was to facilitate the translation of an XML dataset from its native vocabulary to someone else's proprietary vocabulary, it can just as easily output any textual format: HTML, comma-delimited text, and so forth.

Part of the beauty of XSLT is that it is written in XML. Every valid XSLT program is also valid XML. This is also one of the drawbacks of XSLT. Because it has to be written as XML, the syntax of the language is a bit awkward. Once you get used to it, though, it becomes a very logical way to program.

XSLT is defined by its three major characteristics. First, any XSLT program is a combination of static and dynamic information. Think of an ASP page. Typically, in an ASP page, you combine straight HTML output with code that has to be executed to generate a response. For example,

```
<!--Here is the static output -->
<HTML>
    <HEAD><TITLE>My Page</TITLE></HEAD>
    <BODY>

    <%
       '** here is the dynamic part
       Dim sCookieVal
       sCookieVal = Request.Cookies("username")
       Response.Write "Hello, " & sCookieVal & "!"
    %>

    <!--The rest of the static output-->
    </BODY>
</HTML>
```

In this example, you express some static output, meaning it never changes from execution to execution. This is the straight HTML in the listing. Also included is a piece of script that retrieves the user's name from a cookie and then greets him by name. Obviously, this content must be dynamic to respond personally to each user. XSLT works the same way: You combine text that will never vary from call to call with XSLT functions that perform operations to generate other text. We'll look at an example in just a minute.

Second, XSLT is a declarative, rule-based language. The rules are organized into what is called a *transformation tree* prior to being executed. The rules as stated in code can be arranged in any order in the source file, and they can be rearranged into another arbitrary order during compilation. XSLT rules describe patterns to be matched in the source document, and a new pattern with which to replace it in the output document. This is drastically different from the standard procedural style of programming you are used to in VB, in which a program consists of a series of lines of code that operate in order, first to last.[6]

Finally, XSLT is a side effect-free language. This means that you cannot change the state or the context of your environment through standard means as the program is executing. Therefore, no single executing XSLT statement can alter the way another XSLT statement has performed or will perform. A good way of thinking about this in VB terms is that you no longer have global variables. Where you might, in VB, declare a variable in a public module, called `giNumTimesCalled`, and use it like this:

```
Public Sub Foo()
    '** do some work
    '** increment global tracking variable
    giNumTimesCalled = giNumTimesCalled + 1
End Sub
```

you may not do this in XSLT. The reason is that functions that have side effects cause your program to be executed in a given order. If several functions were accessing the same global variable, and their execution was based on the value stored there, the order in which those statements are executed becomes very important. In XSLT, order of execution isn't important at all.

This inability to modify global state is what allows the declarative rules of your program to be arbitrarily arranged in the transformation tree. It also allows you to mix and match rules from several sources to create a new program.

---

[6] This is obviously an oversimplification. Procedural programs have all kinds of branching involved and are not merely linear. However, the effect is the same: Procedural programs are about executing code in a specific order. In declarative languages, execution order is generally arbitrary.

Because no rule will ever modify the executing context, you can arbitrarily combine them as necessary to accomplish your tasks.

Why Is the XSLT Methodology Helpful?

Let's take a simple dataset example, and work it through a standard procedural transformation, then through XSLT. This will demonstrate the two main benefits of using this method:

1. Avoiding brittle middle-tier code that does not adapt well to changing data structures.

2. Creating code that is reusable not just across applications, but also *across application tiers*

Here is the dataset on which we will operate. Let's start with the base assumption that your component receives its data as XML:

```
<?xml version="1.0"?>
<books>
<category cattype="Geek Books">
    <book>
        <title>Don't Go Into the Light: Why Computer
                Programmers are All Cave Trolls</title>
        <author>Wispy N. Pale</author>
        <summary>Peer into the dark and humid psyche of
                the computer programmer.</summary>
    </book>
</category>
<category cattype="Non-Geek Books">
    <book>
        <title>Breathing for Dummies</title>
        <author>Anne Out</author>
        <summary>How to get the most out of your daily
                breathing.</summary>
    </book>
</category>
</books>
```

First, let's look at the procedural way to transform this data into HTML output, then we'll look at XSLT.

Transforming the Dataset Procedurally

To process XML in a COM component, you need a reference to Microsoft's XML parser, MSXML3.dll. Assume that you have received the XML in the previous section from your data source, and have stored it in an `MSXML2.DOMDocument` object called `xData`. Your program needs to navigate the entire structure of the XML document, checking for node names and converting the values to HTML output. Here is a sample program that does this:

```
'** declare a string to hold the eventual output HTML
Dim sOut As String
sOut = "<HTML><BODY>"

'** get a reference to the root node of the document
Dim rRoot As IXMLDOMNode
Set rRoot = xData.firstChild.nextSibling

sOut = sOut & "<H1>Here's my " & rRoot.nodeName & _
       "</H1>" & vbCrLf

Dim rCatNode As IXMLDOMNode
Dim rBookNode As IXMLDOMNode

'** loop through the immediate children of the root, which
'**    are elements of type "category"
For Each rCatNode In rRoot.childNodes
    sOut = sOut & "<H3>These are " & _

    '** get the value of the "cattype" attribute of the current "Category" element
    rCatNode.Attributes.getNamedItem("cattype").Text & _
                                      ".</H3>" & vbCrLf
    sOut = sOut & "<UL>" & vbCrLf

    Dim sTitle As String, sAuthor As String
    Dim sSummary As String

    '** loop through the immediate children of the category, which
    '** are book nodes
    For Each rBookNode In rCatNode.childNodes
      '** pull out the title, author, and summary from the current book node
      sTitle = rBookNode.selectSingleNode("title").Text
```

```
        sAuthor = rBookNode.selectSingleNode("author").Text
        sSummary = rBookNode.selectSingleNode("summary").Text
        sOut = sOut & "<LI><U>" & sTitle & "</U> by <I>" & _
            sAuthor & "</I>..." & sSummary & "</LI>" & vbCrLf
    Next rBookNode

    sOut = sOut & "</UL>" & vbCrLf
Next rCatNode

sOut = sOut & "</BODY></HTML>"
```

The output looks like this (as rendered by a browser):

Here's my books

These Are Geek Books.

- <u>Don't Go into the Light: Why Computer Programmers Are All Cave Trolls</u> by *Wispy N. Pale*...Peer into the dark and humid psyche of the computer programmer.

These Are Non-Geek Books.

- <u>Breathing for Dummies</u> by *Anne Out*...How to get the most out of your daily breathing.

The previous code is fairly ugly. The first major problem is the continual use of the `sOut = sOut & ...` syntax, which can be extraordinarily slow given VB's known problems dealing with string manipulation. Because you have to keep track of the output of the program as it progresses, however, there is not really a better way to do this, unless you had a reference to the ASP intrinsic `Response` object, and used `Response.Write` to output each individual addition to the page.

Second, this code has dependences on a particular scheme. It assumes that elements of type `book` exist with elements of type `category` and contain a `title`, `author`, and `summary` element; otherwise, the navigation fails to work correctly and your output is either garbage or nothing. This is the brittle-code problem. If there are relatively minor changes to the XML structure (nesting `book` within a subcategory under category, for instance), this entire program is ruined. It is possible to design the program to be flexible in the face of changes to the input data, but such a program would be dramatically more complex and very hard to maintain.

Lastly, not much of this code is reusable. Even on other documents with similar vocabularies to the one just described, there is no guarantee of the structure of those documents. Therefore, this code, with its structural dependences, is too specific to be reapplied. The code is far too concerned with the underlying details of document structure and navigation to get the bird's-eye view of what is really important—namely, matching specific patterns in the source document *as and wherever they occur.*

Transforming the Dataset with XSLT

As mentioned earlier, an XSLT program is a syntactically valid XML document. Therefore, an XSLT program should start with the following line:

```
<?xml version="1.0"?>
```

and should optionally include an encoding scheme in the declaration. The root node should be a stylesheet, and it must be defined as follows:

```
<xsl:stylesheet
  xmlns:xsl="http://www.w3.org/1999/XSL/Transform"
  version="1.0">
```

The namespace defined and prefixed as `xsl` is required for XSLT programs to be executed. XML elements belonging to this namespace are understood by the parser to be XSLT commands or statements, and are fed to the XSLT processor.

Most XSLT programs contain at least one template element. Templates are the rules that make up an executable transform. Each template is associated with a pattern to be matched in the source document, and every match to the pattern in the source will have the template applied to it. The pattern is defined as an `XPath` statement. `XPath` is a specification for navigating around an XML tree and selecting nodes from the overall set. `XPath` statements look, in their simple form, remarkably like file paths in Windows. So, to apply a template to any node of type `book` that is a child of a node of type `category`, you could define a template like this:

```
<xsl:template match="category/book">
    <!--Some transformation work here-->
</xsl:template>
```

The full vocabulary of XSLT statements contains commands for retrieving values, comparing values conditionally, controlling flow (looping constructs, case statements), and defining variables. (Remember that in the context of XSLT, "variable" can be read to mean "constant".) We could use this vocabulary to write an XSLT program that operates much the same as our previous procedural example:

```
1   <?xml version="1.0"?>
    <xsl:stylesheet
      xmlns:xsl="http://www.w3.org/1999/XSL/Transform"
      version="1.0">
3       <xsl:template match="/">
4         <html><body><h1>Here's my books</h1>
5         <xsl:for-each select="/books/category">
6           <h3>These are <xsl:value-of
                select="@cattype"/></h3>
7           <ul>
8           <xsl:for-each select="book">
9            <li><u><xsl:value-of select="title"/></u> by
10             <i><xsl:value-of select="author"/></i>...
11             <xsl:value-of select="summary"/></li>
12          </xsl:for-each>
13          </ul>
14        </xsl:for-each>
15        </body></html>
16      </xsl:template>
17  </xsl:stylesheet>
```

Note: Line numbers have been added at the left for convenience. They are not to be construed as part of the actual program. Line numbers would be meaningless in a language for which execution order is arbitrary.

This XSLT stylesheet has a single template that matches the document's root node ("/"). Line 4 is the first static content we are adding, some simple HTML text. Line 5 should look very familiar, even with the strange markup. Notice the XSLT statement (prefixed by the `xsl` notation): `<xsl:for-each select="/books/category">`. This statement does exactly the same thing in XSLT that the `For Each rCatNode in rRoot.ChildNodes` line did in our first VB example. It loops through all the children of the root node (`books`) of type `category` and executes some code for each iteration.

On each loop, the program will output the static/dynamic content mix defined on line 6. The `<xsl:value-of>` command is the heart of XSLT: It selects a single node, given an `XPath` statement, and places its value in line in the output. In this particular case, we introduce a new notation in `XPath`: the `@`. Prefacing a pattern in `XPath` with this symbol implies that the value being sought is an attribute, not an element. So this specific example (`<xsl:value-of select="@cattype"/>`) means to take the value of an attribute named `cattype` of the current element (which will be of type `category` because of the pattern match in the parent `<xsl:for-each>` statement) and place it in line.

Nested in this loop is a second `<xsl:for-each>`, this time matching any elements of type `book` contained in the current `category`. Finally, for each book, the program selects the value of the subelements `title`, `author`, and `summary`, and outputs them in the context of an unordered list in HTML.

To use the stylesheet to process the source instead of VB, your VB code would change to look like this (remember, your source is in a `DOMDocument` object called `xData`):

```
Dim xXSL As MSXML2.DOMDocument
XXSL.Load "myStylesheet.xsl"

Dim sOutputHTML As String
OutputHTML = xData.TransformNode(xXSL)
'** returns OutputHTML to client
```

As noted, this program has output identical to that of the VB example, and accomplishes it in the same way: by presupposing the original source document's structure, and operating within that framework. The looping constructs expect elements of type `category` to contain elements of type `book`, which will contain a `title`, `author`, and `summary`. If the structure of the source is not identical to these assumptions, the output of the program will be wrong. This stylesheet is just as brittle as the VB example.

To avoid this problem, we have to add another XSLT command: `<xsl:apply-templates/>`. This statement forces the parser to apply the template rule with the best match to the elements contained in the current execution context. (More simply, it tries to apply templates to the children of the current node.) So a second XSLT stylesheet, which also produces identical output to the two previous examples, is as follows:

```
<?xml version="1.0"?>
<xsl:stylesheet
  xmlns:xsl="http://www.w3.org/1999/XSL/Transform"
            version="1.0">

    <xsl:template match="/">
        <html><body><h1>Here's my books</h1>
           <xsl:apply-templates/>
        </body></html>
    </xsl:template>

    <xsl:template match="/books/category">
        <h3>These are <xsl:value-of
            select="@cattype"/>.</h3>
         <ul>
            <xsl:apply-templates/>
         </ul>
    </xsl:template>

    <xsl:template match="book">
       <li><xsl:apply-templates/></li>
    </xsl:template>

    <xsl:template match="title">
       <u><xsl:value-of select="."/></u> ,
    </xsl:template>
```

```
    <xsl:template match="author">
        by <i><xsl:value-of select="."/></i>
    </xsl:template>

    <xsl:template match="summary">
        ...<xsl:value-of select="."/>
    </xsl:template>
</xsl:stylesheet>
```

The first big change you'll note is that there are a lot more template elements in this program than in the previous example. Each template, you'll remember, is a rule that can be applied anywhere in the source document, *in arbitrary order*. There is still a template that matches the root element (the first template), but all it does is spit out the generic HTML framework, then call our friend `<xsl:apply-templates/>`. What actually happens is that, as the XSLT is being parsed with the source, this template is applied to the root node, which then asks the parser/processor to attempt to apply templates to its children. In this model, each rule invokes the processor to apply additional rules until there are no elements left to process, or none that match the pattern of any rule.

Also note that the last four templates match a *relative* pattern instead of an *absolute* pattern. Instead of drilling all the way down into the document by saying `match="/books/category/book/title`, it simply matches to any node of type `title` *in the current context*. This is how template rules become reusable in an arbitrary order. If you can avoid specifying the full path to the element in question in the match, you can then use the same template rule regardless of where the element itself lives in the source.

Now, applying this program is very different from using the procedural method and its fraternal twin (the first XSLT example). Instead of forcing a structure on the source document (and failing if the structure is wrong), this third example simply matches the defined rules to any part of the source where the pattern matches. A `title` element in this example does not have to live inside a `book` element to have its value output as underlined text in HTML. This could allow you to have `title` elements of both books and categories, and the same template could be used to output its value. However, if the relative context of a `title` element is important, you may still differentiate between them by writing two separate templates: one that matches `book/title` and the other that matches `category/title`. Part of the power of XSLT is to allow you, the programmer, to decide when the structure of the input document is important, and when it can be ignored.

In fact, you could separate the final four templates into their own stylesheet document and reference it from the main stylesheet. If those four templates were saved in a fully formed XSLT document called `bookDetails.xsl`, then your revamped main XSLT would look like this:

```
<?xml version="1.0"?>
<xsl:stylesheet
  xmlns:xsl="http://www.w3.org/1999/XSL/Transform"
            version="1.0">
   <xsl:import href="bookDetails.xsl"/><!--Note new statement-->
   <xsl:template match="/">
      <html><body><h1>Here's my books</h1>
         <xsl:apply-templates/>
      </body></html>
   </xsl:template>
   <xsl:template match="/books/category">
      <h3>These are <xsl:value-of
         select="@cattype"/>.</h3>
       <ul>
          <xsl:apply-templates/>
       </ul>
   </xsl:template>
</xsl:stylesheet>
```

The new line `<xsl:import href="bookDetails.xsl"/>` specifies that the contents of the specified file should be included as part of this stylesheet. Therefore, the output details of `book`, `title`, `author`, and `summary` elements can be reused by multiple stylesheets, acting on multiple different source formats, without reprogramming them.

You can see how this style of transforming the data eliminates most of the brittle-code problem, but you were promised a second benefit: being able to reuse your code across application tiers. With XSLT, if your clients have the right kind of configuration, you can actually foist the grunt work of processing the source document onto the client machine. Currently, those clients would have to have MSXML 3.0 or later, and IE5 or later.

To do so, simply add a line to the source XML document that looks like this:

```
<?xml-stylesheet type="text/xsl"
                 href="http://www.a.com/myxsl.xsl"?>
```

(where the `href` parameter points to a valid stylesheet document) and then ship the XML straight down to the browser. The browser will trigger MSXML to parse the XML, which will recognize the stylesheet directive. It will download the stylesheet from the given URL and use it to process the XML file. Only the final output will be rendered in the browser. Now you can write code for transforming data straight into presentation format, and either run it on your server when unsure about the client's environment or use the client machine when conditions are right.

Are There Drawbacks?

Of course, there are drawbacks. The first and foremost is that you have to learn a new syntax and style of programming. Declarative programming is different from procedural programming, and it can sometimes take time to achieve the correct mind-set (and avoid writing XSLT like the first example). Another problem is compliance with the specification: Microsoft has announced its intentions to comply fully with the W3C recommendations for XSLT, but their implementations to date are incomplete. However, they release a technology preview of MSXML approximately every two months, with each release getting closer to full compliance.

Additionally, you have, to a certain extent, broken the rules of *N*-tier application modeling: You have coupled your business logic to a specific output format. However, it is trivial to redeploy an XSL file once an application is in production: Simply copy the new file over the old. If your output format changes, or the presentation layer is replaced, you can replace the XSL file without replacing compiled components. The problems of having broken the model are, therefore, easily overcome.

XSLT is a new and powerful tool for transforming XML into other XML vocabularies or other textual output formats. It is useful for much more than simply presentation-level formatting: As business-to-business systems begin exchanging an ever-greater amount of data with each other, something is going to have to live in the in-between spaces to facilitate communication. XSLT is poised to be that tool, and knowing it and its uses will be a major benefit to any programmer.

This brief introduction to the material cannot do it nearly the justice it deserves. For more information, see the Microsoft Web site (msdn.Microsoft.com/xml) or the W3C Web site (www.w3c.org), as well as some fine books currently in print that devote hundreds and hundreds of pages to this language. For example, consider *Essential XML* by Box, Skonnard, and Lam (Addison-Wesley, 2000).

Chapter 5
Effective Data Access from VB

5-1 Efficiency basics: round-trips, SQL statements, and providers.

5-2 Don't over-encapsulate data access.

5-3 Never hold database connections as data members.

5-4 Deadlock is common—develop defensively.

5-5 Use firehose cursors whenever possible.

5-6 Make the right data searching decision (avoid `SelectSingleNode` abuse).

VB and databases go together like bees and honey. Every professional VB programmer has, at one time or another, written an application that interacts with a database. The tools available to the VB programmer make this interaction easy to create, but they also make it easy to create *poorly*. This chapter gives you some concrete examples of how to make the most out of your database access code. It describes proper application design techniques (rule 5-2), tells you the proper object-oriented techniques and warns you of some object-oriented pitfalls (rules 5-2 through 5-4), and lays out some of the specifics of interacting directly with the data (rules 5-5 and 5-6). The chapter begins, though, with first principles: Rule 5-1 describes some common efficiency tips that will help you get started with your data access code.

Rule 5-1: Efficiency Basics: Round-Trips, SQL Statements, and Providers

One thing programmers must always worry about when developing an application is efficiency. Users like their applications to work fast. Nobody likes to stare at the hourglass cursor for more than a few seconds. Considering that most applications communicate with a database at some point, understanding how to gain efficiency in that process can provide dramatic efficiency improvements to all of your applications. This rule seeks to define some of the basics, specifically:

- Minimizing round-trips, and understanding why they are so expensive
- Planning the best way to communicate your SQL query to the database
- Choosing the appropriate data provider for your application

The concepts will give you a good foundation for efficient data access. The rest of this chapter builds from this foundation to give you a tool set for creating fast, reliable, easily maintained data access code.

Minimize Your Round-Trips

You have certainly heard this advice before. Either in discussions about databases, remote DCOM objects, or HTTP traffic, you have seen this commandment. The advice is equally true for all these situations. Essentially, a round-trip is any message (generally thought of as a request) sent from one piece of code to another, and the sender waits until the receiver performs some function and returns a result back (generally, the response).

In the abstract, you can think about any request/response pair taking part in the following series of steps.

1. *Create the request.* The client code must decide what message to send, and then format it correctly for shipment.

2. *Send the message.* The client must invoke whatever protocol is necessary to send the message to the client, whether that is NDR packets over RPC (DCOM), HTTP messages over TCP/IP (the Internet), or what have you. It usually involves invoking some kind of system service.

3. *Receive the message.* The targeted receiving service recognizes the inbound message and turns it over to the appropriate piece of code for handling.

4. *Process the request.* Server code interprets the request and performs some activity based on that message.

5. *Repeat steps 1 through 4 for sending the response back to the requester.* The server code must now create a response and send it over the wire, where it will be received and handled.

Each one of these steps *may* involve considerable expense in the form of processing cycles, RAM, disk space, network bandwidth, and so forth. Even in the abstract, it is reasonable to conclude that a reduction of round-trips between pieces of code should provide a dramatic increase in program efficiency.

In the specific case of your VB code interacting with a database, these steps normally look like this:

1. *Formulate SQL query.* Your VB code must, in some way, generate a request to the database as a SQL statement.

2. *Use ADO to send the query to database through the `Connection` object.* You will have created an ADO `Connection` object and called its Open method. Now, you can use the Execute command to send the request.

3. *The database receives the message through its established connection.*

4. *The database processes the SQL command.* SQL statements require a two-step processing algorithm: First, they are compiled into a binary form. Second, they are optimized for maximum performance. The optimized binary code is then executed.

5. *The database returns a result to you as a recordset.* Your results are streamed back as Tabular Data Stream (TDS) results, which are received by ADO and converted into a `Recordset` object. Technically speaking, this is actually four more steps (see step 5 in the previous abstract example): Formulate the TDS response, ship it over the wire, receive it at the client, and process it into an ADO recordset.

The processing step (step 4) is usually a very expensive step. For the database itself, compiling and optimizing the SQL request can be quite resource intensive (see rule 5-3 for more details on how SQL can optimize some of this expense).

More often than not, however, it is the actual transit time of the message across the wire (step 2) that is the biggest drain on your application's performance.

To gain efficiency in your application, then, you must design it in such a way that the number of requests to the database is minimized. This could mean caching a large amount of data on the client side for examination, which would incur one large method call early in the application but would considerably speed up any subsequent operations (see rule 5-6 for an example of this approach). It could mean buffering outbound database requests until you can send a series of them in a single batch. Whatever path you take, you should recognize that each and every time you invoke the `Execute` command on an open `Connection` object, you are causing these eight steps to be incurred. Find a way to limit these conversations and you will notice dramatic results.

Determine the Best Method to Send SQL Queries

Once you have designed your application to minimize the number of times you send a SQL query, you must then decide how best to formulate and send the query itself. In essence, you have three primary choices:

1. Individual SQL statements
2. A batch SQL statement
3. A SQL stored procedure

Simple SQL queries, with only a single statement and no parameters, are easily sent as an individual statement. You could use the `Connection` object's `Execute` method like this:

```
Dim rConn As ADODB.Connection, rRS As ADODB.Recordset
    .
    .
    .
Set rRS = rConn.Execute "SELECT * FROM authors"
```

Simple requests like these are easy to execute in this manner. They are notable because they either return no results or a single result set.

Most SQL queries are considerably more complex than this. They may include a variety of logical instructions, and may return more than one result.

Such a SQL query is referred to as a *batch*. In some cases, you could choose to execute the entire batch as individual statements like the previous example, but other times there may be conditional logic in the batch that requires a single execution context to work correctly. In this scenario, you are forced to create your batch command in a single script and send it to the database in one fell swoop. For example, imagine that you need to update 100 separate records. You may execute 100 individual statements, or collect them all into a single batch statement (one long `String` variable) to be executed together. For example, consider the following subroutine to update a database:

```
Public Sub UpdateProductCustomer(iProductID As Integer, _
                                 iCustomerID As Integer)
    Dim sSQLBatch As String
    Dim rConn As ADODB.Connection
    Set rConn = New ADODB.Connection
    sSQLBatch = "UPDATE Inventory SET Amount=Amount-1 "&_
                "WHERE ProductID=" & CStr(iProductID) &_
                vbCrLf

    sSQLBatch = sSQLBatch & _
                "UPDATE Accounts SET balance=" & _
                "balance-59.99 WHERE CustomerID=" & _
                CStr(iCustomerID) & vbCrLf

    sSQLBatch = sSQLBatch & _
                "INSERT Orders(CustomerID, ProductID) " &_
                "VALUES(" & CStr(iCustomerID) & ", " & _
                CStr(iProductID) & ")"

    rConn.Open "<proper connection string>"
    rConn.Execute sSQLBatch
    rConn.Close
    Set rConn = Nothing
End Sub
```

With this particular example, three separate SQL statements are concatenated into a single message to be sent to the database. Using a batch drastically reduces the number of round-trips needed, as mentioned in the previous section, and also allows SQL to optimize further the way those statements are executed. If sent individually, they cannot be optimized as a whole, only as unique statements.

The final option is to take advantage of stored procedures. Stored procedures are identical syntactically to batch SQL statements, but they are stored in the database itself. They are precompiled and preoptimized so that, when invoked, these two steps are already complete and therefore the overhead of execution is drastically reduced. Even when the procedure requires parameters from the calling client, this holds true. Thus, a stored procedure is even more efficient than a batch statement sent by the client (for more details, see rule 5-2).

Choose the Appropriate Provider

Now your application has a minimal number of calls to the database, mostly using stored procedures and batch SQL commands. Your final task is to determine which provider your ADO `Connection` object will use to do the communicating.

There has been a change recently in the technology used as the communication layer between custom code and the data layer. ODBC has historically served this purpose. Your custom code need only interact with an abstract data manipulation interface, which then uses a database-specific driver to translate the generic request into specific commands. Thus, your code could write data access statements against the ODBC layer, which would invoke the driver for your specific database (SQL Server, Oracle Server, DB2, and so on). Figure 5.1

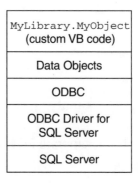

Figure 5.1 Using ODBC to communicate with SQL Server

illustrates the layers connecting a VB component using ODBC to talk to SQL Server.

The problem with ODBC is that it was a technology written before the full advent of object-orientation mania. It consists of a series of flat, procedural interfaces that resemble the Win32 API. Additionally, the ODBC driver pool was limited to interacting with relational DBMS. These two problems combined to make ODBC a dated technology that didn't adapt well to new programming techniques or alternative data sources.

The OLE DB layer was introduced as a solution to both of these problems. Built on top of the COM specification, this new communication layer provides a set of services identical to those of ODBC, but in an object-oriented approach more in line with today's programming practices. Additionally, OLE DB is not limited in the kinds of data sources with which its providers can communicate. Therefore, OLE DB is a much more flexible technology.

To make sure you use the native OLE DB provider for SQL Server, for instance, you would create your connection string like this:

```
rConn.Open "provider=sqloledb;data source=(local);" & _
           "User ID=sa;Password=;Catalog=pubs"
```

In addition to specifying the provider, this connection string points ADO to the desired database and table, as well as specifies the username and password of an authenticated account with permissions to access the data. Figure 5.2 shows the layers of access through which this connection travels.

One major downside to OLE DB is the lack of an extensive library of providers on the market. Because the technology is much newer than ODBC, there hasn't been enough time to develop a highly evolved library of stable, efficient providers for the wide array of data sources available. The stopgap solution was the use of the ODBC provider for OLE DB. By using this provider, OLE DB programmers can take advantage of existing ODBC drivers through the OLE DB architecture. However, this approach is much slower, because both the OLE DB *and* the ODBC layers must come into play, and each carries a significant amount of overhead (Figure 5.3).

Although this method was great for taking advantage of OLE DB while the provider library was still catching up, there are enough native OLE DB providers

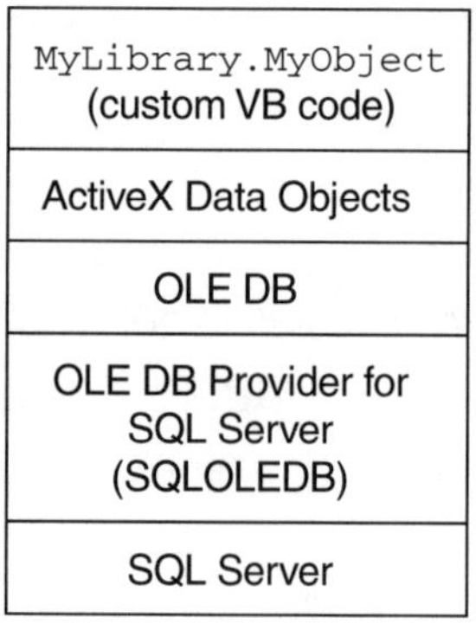

Figure 5.2 Using SQL Server's native data provider

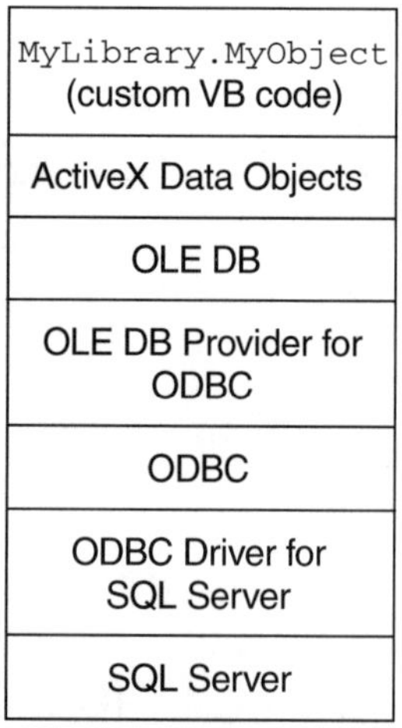

Figure 5.3 Using ODBC as your data provider

available now that you should be able to avoid the extra overhead. For ADO users, the ODBC provider for OLE DB (MSDASQL) is the default provider. To specify ODBC explicitly as your data access technology, your connection string would be formatted like this:

```
rConn.Open "provider=MSDASQL;data source=(local);" & _
           "User ID=sa;Password=;Catalog=pubs"
```

Unfortunately, unless you specifically choose the correct native provider in your connection string, you will end up incurring the extra cost of the ODBC layer. Therefore, take pains to create your connection string with the correct native provider specified. You can always look up the list of available providers in the help files for ADO. The three most common are the providers for SQL Server (SQLOLEDB), Oracle Server (MSDAORA), and the Microsoft Jet database engine (Microsoft.Jet.OLEDB.3.51 and Microsoft.Jet.OLEDB.4.0).

These tips should give you three techniques for immediately improving the performance of your data code. In general, you should be examining your logic to make sure that you make the minimum number of round-trips to the database as possible, that each round-trip uses the most efficient kind of SQL query, and that each query is sent via the most efficient data provider for your database. The rest of this chapter delves deeper into the details of your database code. The next rule describes some of the OOD decisions you will face when making data access classes for your application.

Rule 5-2: Don't Overencapsulate Data Access

You are convinced by now. VB really is an object-oriented development tool. As such, you are now busily applying all the OOD rules to your VB applications. You have learned what you can and can't do with inheritance (interfaces only), you've written polymorphic classes, and you have learned the arts of encapsulation and abstraction.

These last two points you have really taken to heart. Instead of creating monolithic forms and global BAS modules to hold all your procedures, you have now created a pantheon of classes to model your business objects. To create a pure OOD, you create a class for every abstract concept in your application. For example, imagine an application that helps manage inventory at a video rental store. Your application has modeled such entities as `CVideoStore`, `CStoreManager`, `CTapes` (a collection of `CTape` objects), and so forth.

The Object-Oriented Purist

What happens when you get around to modeling your database access code? If you extend this object-oriented style to its extreme, you may want to encapsulate access to each individual table into a separate class. For this video store application, assume that the database is stored in SQL Server and has three main tables: `tbl_Customers`, `tbl_Videos`, and `tbl_Rentals`. The `Customers` table is a list of all registered customers of the store, each with a unique identifier. The `Videos` table contains a list of all titles in the store, including the total number of tapes owned and the total number currently in stock. The `Rentals` table keeps track of which customers have which tapes checked out. To process any rental, your code must make sure the tape is in stock, verify that the customer's account is in good standing, and then decrement the number in stock while creating a new record in the `Rentals` table.

If you took the object-oriented tack, you might model one class for each table in the database. Each of these classes would contain logic for establishing and relinquishing a connection to the database, as well as for reading and modifying the data in the tables. For example, you might have a `CCustomers`, `CVideos`, and `CRentals` class (Figure 5.4). Each would expose methods to your other objects that would allow the user to check out a video.

Let's assume that *each* class also exposes identical `Connect` and `Disconnect` methods for database connection management. Given this, the rest of the exposed methods could be

```
'** class module: CCustomers
Public Function Standing(sCustID As String) As Boolean
    '** access the customer's record via a SQL query and see if the
    '**    account is in good standing
    '** Ex:   SELECT cus_GoodStanding FROM tbl_Customers WHERE
    '**               id_Customer = sCustID
End Function

'** class module: CVideos
Public Function InStock(sVidID As String) As Boolean
     '** check the given video to see if the InStock column is greater than zero
End Function
```

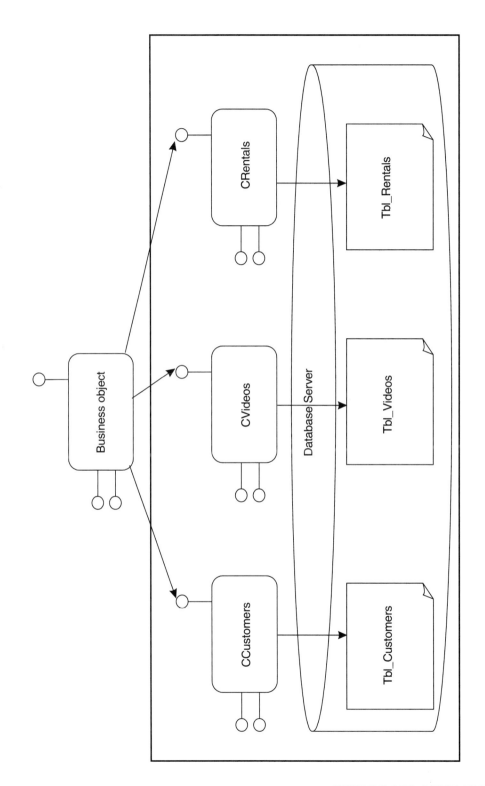

Figure 5.4 Standard OOD of one class per table

EFFECTIVE DATA ACCESS FROM VB

```
Public Sub DecrementStock(sVidID As String, _
                          Optional iAmount As Integer = 1)
    '** decrement the InStock column for the video by the given number of copies
End Sub

'** class module:  CRentals
Public Sub AddRental(sCustID As String, _
                     sVidID As String, _
                     Optional iRentalTerms As Integer=3)
    '** insert a new record with the customer ID, video ID, date rented & date due
End Sub
```

The client (i.e., business object) that uses these three objects might look something like this:

```
'** business object
Public Sub RentVideo(sCustID As String, _
                     sVideoID As String)
    Dim rCustomers As New CCustomers
    Dim rRentals As New CRentals
    Dim rVideos As New CVideos
    Dim bSuccess As Boolean

    '** connect to customers, check standing, and disconnect
    rCustomers.Connect
    bSuccess = rCustomers.Standing(sCustID)
    If Not bSuccess Then
    Err.Raise vbObjectError + 2049, _
              "RentVideo.Check Standing", _
              "Customer not in good standing"
    End If
    rCustomers.Disconnect

    '** connect to videos, check stock, decrement stock, disconnect
    rVideos.Connect
    bSuccess = rVideos.InStock(sVideoID)
    If Not bSuccess Then
    Err.Raise vbObjectError + 2050, _
              "RentVideo.Check Stock", _
              "Video currently not in stock."
```

```
        End If
        rVideos.DecrementStock sVideoID
        rVideos.Disconnect

        '** connect to rentals, add new record, disconnect
        rRentals.Connect
        rRentals.AddRental sCustID, sVideoID
        rRentals.Disconnect
    End Sub
```

By doing this, you may have achieved object-oriented purity (and, therefore, some level of code maintainability). In your design, you have each idea (collection of customers, collection of tapes, list of orders) modeled as a class. You have encapsulated the gory details of database connection management behind two public methods, `Connect` and `Diconnect`. You have also hidden the SQL statements that do all the work inside the `Standing`, `InStock`, `DecrementStock`, and `AddRental` methods.

Drawbacks of Being So Pure

By creating a class for each table, you have lost more in performance than you have gained in maintainability, and it is guaranteed that the application's success or failure will be judged more on efficiency and scalability than on purity of design. In particular, this design is deficient in three major respects: (1) It doesn't take advantage of optimizations in the database engine itself, (2) it uses too many scarce resources, and (3) it makes too many round-trips to the database.

First of all, you are passing dynamic SQL queries with each object. Whenever SQL Server attempts to execute a query, two things happen: The query is compiled, and then an optimized execution plan is created. Both of these steps take time. Recent versions of SQL Server have implemented an optimization that allows the database to create and cache a temporary stored procedure for simple queries (like a simple `Select` or `Insert` statement) to avoid reoptimizing on every call. However, if your queries are more complex, each reexecution requires the compilation and optimization steps. Each of your objects is then tying up valuable server-side processing cycles recompiling and reoptimizing identical SQL statements on every call.

Second, this design is tying up too many scarce resources—namely, database connections. Connections are expensive resources on the server side, and you have (potentially) created three distinct connections using this design. If the previous client code forgets to call `Disconnect` on each object, these connections remain open until the object maintaining the connection is released (probably by the object reference going out of scope). This design trusts the client code to remember to call each method correctly. It is quite acceptable to open and close numerous connections in your application, but you should open them as late as possible and release them as soon as the operation is complete (see rule 5-3).

Lastly, in any distributed application, round-trips over the network are the most common reason for sluggish performance. With this pure OOD, you are guaranteeing that no matter what code exists inside your three classes, at least four round-trips will be incurred to accomplish your task: one for the `CCustomers` object to verify the account status, one for the `CVideos` object to check the quantity in stock, one for `CVideos` to decrement the stock quantity, and one for `CRentals` to add a new record. Four round-trips may not sound like much, but imagine that your system is processing video rentals for hundreds or thousands of customers simultaneously. Suddenly, that network traffic can become overwhelming.

Solution: The Stored Procedure

The answer is to take advantage of *stored procedures.* A stored procedure is just business logic that runs in the database written using the Transact-SQL language. The first big advantage this gives you is that stored procedures are compiled and optimized the first time they are called. The compiled commands and the execution plan are then cached on the server in the procedure cache, and are reused on each successive call to the procedure. Now you only incur the overhead of compiling and optimization once, instead of on every call.

The other major benefit is that you can combine all your business logic (pertinent, of course, to a single server) into a single Transact-SQL batch. This means that not only do you require fewer connections (one instead of three); you require fewer round-trips to the server (one instead of four). A single stored procedure that accomplishes all the tasks of the rental process might look like this:

```sql
/* Procedure is called CheckOutVideo, and takes two parameters */
CREATE PROCEDURE CheckOutVideo @ID_Cus varchar(10),
                @ID_Vid varchar(10)
AS

/* Set nocount attribute to allow for immediate error trapping */
Set nocount on

/* Set a local variable equal to the number of a given video currently in stock */
DECLARE @Quantity int
SELECT @Quantity = vid_InStock FROM tbl_Videos
       WHERE id_Video = @ID_Vid

/* Set a local variable equal to the account standing of the given customer */
DECLARE @Standing bit
SELECT @Standing = cus_GoodStanding FROM tbl_Customers
       WHERE id_Customer = @ID_Cus

/* If the account is in good standing */
IF @Standing=1
BEGIN
    /* If there are videos in stock */
    IF @Quantity>0
    BEGIN
        /* Decrement stock */
        UPDATE tbl_Videos SET vid_InStock =
              @Quantity - 1 WHERE id_Video = @ID_Vid
        /* Insert new rental record */
        INSERT INTO tbl_Rentals (id_Rental,
              id_Customer, id_Video, ren_RentedOn,
              ren_DueBack) VALUES (NEWID(), @ID_Cus,
              @ID_Vid, GetDate(), DateAdd(dayofyear, 3,
              GetDate()))
    END
    ELSE
        /* Alert caller that there weren't enough tapes */
        /* NOTE: You may choose, instead of using RAISEERROR, simply to
           return a value that your application will understand to be a failure
           condition, thus avoiding having exceptions over the network*/
        RAISERROR('Video currently not in stock.', 11, 1)
END
ELSE
```

```
/* Alert caller that customer is not in good standing */
    RAISERROR('Customer not in good standing.', 11, 1)
GO
```

This batch combines the functionality of all three of our classes. It takes in a customer ID and a video ID, checks the customer's standing, checks the number of tapes in stock, and takes care of updating the information in the database. It does this using one connection and a single method call. The result is a single data access class called `CDataAccess`:

```
'** class module: CDataAccess
Public Sub RentVideo(sCustID As String, _
                    sVideoID As String)
    On Error GoTo errHandler

    Dim rConn As New ADODB.Connection
    rConn.Open "<proper connection string>"

    '** call stored procedure, passing in customer ID and video ID
    rConn.Execute "EXEC CheckOutVideo '" & _
                  sCustID & "', '" & sVideoID & "'"
    rConn.Close
    Exit Sub

errHandler:
    '** close connection on failure condition
    rConn.close
    '** report error to user
    Err.Raise vbObjectError + 2049, _
              "CDataAccess.RentVideo", Err.Description
End Sub
```

As you can see, now you only incur the single connection to the database, and all of the logic of renting a video can be achieved in a single round-trip (a single `Exec` statement in SQL). The resulting business object is now very simple:

```
'** business object
Public Sub RentVideo(sCustID As String, _
                    sVideoID As String)
```

```
    On Error Goto errHandler

    Dim rDAObj As New CDataAccess
    rDAObj.RentVideo sCustID, sVideoID
    Exit Sub

errHandler:
    Err.Raise vbObjectError + 2050, _
              "CBusiness.RentVideo:" & Err.Source, _
              Err.Description
End Sub
```

The resulting architecture is shown in Figure 5.5.

You should make special note of the `Set nocount on` statement in the stored procedure. Its use enables the error traps in your VB code to operate as expected. If you use the ODBC provider for ADO (MSDASQL), errors raised from the stored procedure are trapped normally, even without this statement. However, if you switch to the newer, OLE DB native provider (SQLOLEDB), you will run into problems. This provider defaults to provide multiple result sets for each stored procedure, and errors are not raised explicitly to the client but are passed implicitly along with the result sets. To trap for them, you would have to loop through each physical recordset contained in your logical recordset, using the recordset's `NextRecordset` method. To avoid this ungainly code, simply add the `nocount` statement to your stored procedure, which will override this default behavior and cause your errors to be raised explicitly in the client.

Stored procedures can also be used to return values through output parameters or recordsets. You can access the output parameters by using an `ADO Command` object and its `Parameters` collection to build manually a list of both input and output parameter objects that can be fed to the procedure. Then, after executing the stored procuedure, you can query the output parameter objects for their value. Likewise, you can cause the procedure to return a result set, which can be read into an `ADO Recordset` object. Given these two facts, there should be very few instances when a truly dynamic SQL query (one generated inside your compiled code) is necessary. Most of the actual SQL logic can, and should, reside in the database itself.

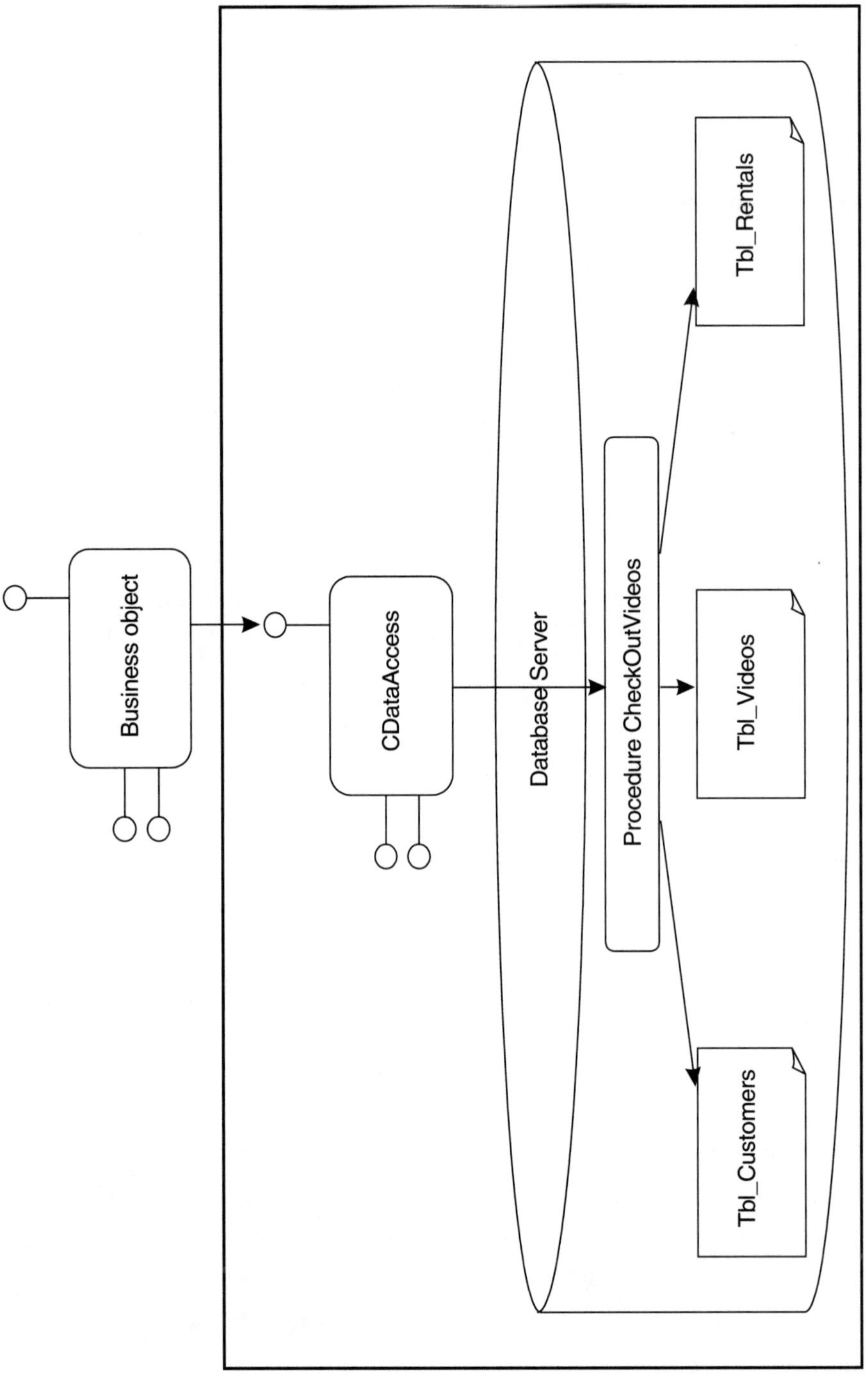

Figure 5.5   Design to reduce round-trips, based on stored procedures

There are downsides to everything in life, and stored procedures are no exception. If you choose to use stored procedures, you lose some of the encapsulation of your code. Some logic is stored in DLLs, some inside your databases. This creates a somewhat arbitrary separation between two parts of your business logic. In addition, the development tools for writing and maintaining stored procedure logic are not quite as advanced as those for writing VB, and you lose some of the features on which you depend as a VB programmer (IntelliSense, integrated debugger, and so on).

What If You Require Multiple Database Servers?
If your application's data resides on more than one physical database server, this changes the rules somewhat. A standard stored procedure technically only works against the database in which it is stored. There are extensions to the Transact-SQL language that allow one database to make calls on another database, but in doing so you lose some of the benefits of the stored procedure on the second server (precompilation, fast execution). More dangerous, you have hardwired two distinct databases together, which can impact your flexibility in migrating data.

The actual advice of this rule is to model your data access code as one object *per database connection* instead of one *per database entity.* Therefore, for each physical server on which you will operate, create stored procedures that take care of related operations. Then, create objects that manage the connection to that specific server and the calls to those local stored procedures. As shown in Figure 5.6, this keeps the object-oriented encapsulation and abstraction rules as pure as possible (you are modeling entities at the lowest granularity that is reasonable) while still using the power and efficiency of the stored procedure.

Stored procedures are more efficient than anything you could compile into your code. A lot more efficient. OODs are great and there is no reason not to pursue them in your VB projects. It is simply important to recognize when other solutions, such as stored procedures, provide a better solution to a given problem. Always evaluate your design for how well it solves the problem at hand, and not for how well it matches someone else's notion of "good" design.

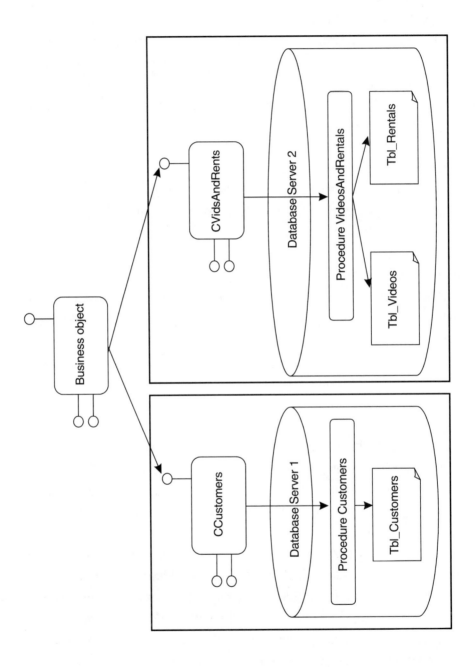

Figure 5.6 An efficient design in the presence of multiple databases

How you design your object-oriented application is very important. Equally important is understanding how to use other object-oriented technologies within that application. The ADO model can sometimes make it tempting to write bad code. The next rule illuminates some of the problems of which to be beware when designing around the `ADO Connection` object.

Rule 5-3: Never Hold Database Connections as Data Members

In the early days of VB (circa 1993), database programming was a simple and explicit part of development. You opened the database connection in your main form's `Load` event, and you closed it in your main form's `Unload` event. During the day your users issued all database calls on this connection. Everything was straightforward. This solution is still reasonable for small deployments with just a few users. However, times are changing. Gone are the salad days of Data Access Objects (DAO) and five-user systems. VB is now frequently used in distributed solutions with hundreds and even thousands of concurrent users.

With large numbers of users, holding a database connection open for each user is simply unreasonable. However, creating and tearing down connections on each call is also an inefficient data access strategy. Many users are not actually using a connection at any given moment, so it would be great if users could share connections during their idle times. This would require some centralized code to pool unused connections and to distribute them on request. It would take a lot of time for a developer to write all this code, if that were necessary. Fortunately, just such a technology is already available for both ODBC and OLE DB.

There are many benefits associated with a business tier, and most are associated with the centralization of services for a distributed set of users. When services are moved to a server machine, their associated resources can be pooled across the user base. Database connections can be expensive to create and tear down, particularly when the data source is deployed on a separate machine. Database connection pooling works by temporarily storing a physical connection in a centralized area rather than actually disconnecting from the source. The code that manages the connection storage is often called a *dispenser*. It must also listen for new connection requests. When a new connection request arrives, the dispenser first looks through the available connections being pooled.

If it finds a connection with the same attributes (including such values as user ID, password, and perhaps transaction ID), it returns a reference for the existing connection to the requesting code. If an appropriate match is not found within the pooled connections, a new connection is opened for the requesting client.

By sharing connections across clients, a system can become more scalable because requests can be serviced more quickly. The cycles associated with creating a connection can be greatly reduced (*provided a matching connection is already pooled and available*), and the associated round-trips are eliminated as well. Additionally, users that use pooled connections will not always be consuming (during idle time) their own dedicated pipeline to the database, so resources are saved. Pooled connections that are unused over time are slowly and incrementally closed, further optimizing resource allocation in the system.

So who is doing this connection pooling for us? It is performed by code in DLLs provided with OLE DB (as of version 2.0) and ODBC (as of version 3.0). For ODBC, the connection pooling code lives in ODBC.dll, which is the driver manager DLL. For OLE DB, the connection pooling code lives in MTXDM.dll (the dispenser manager). In either case, the code for connection pooling is already in place.

Today's VB developer commonly uses ADO as a wrapper to OLE DB, and interacts with database connections through ADO's `Connection` object as shown here:

```
Dim sCONN As String
Dim rConn As ADODB.Connection

'** some DB connect string
sCONN = "Provider=SQLOLEDB;" & _
        "Persist Security Info=False;" & _
        "User ID=sa;" & _
        "Initial Catalog=pubs;" & _
        "Data Source=(local)"

'** instantiate proxy and make connection
Set rConn = New ADODB.Connection
rConn.Open sCONN
```

```
'** use the connection to perform an action query...
rConn.Execute "<some kind of action query>"

'** close connection and destroy connection object
rConn.close
Set rConn = Nothing
```

This `Connection` object is really more of a proxy for the actual connection that lives underneath it. The physical connection is not created until the `Open` keyword is used. Notice the usage follows an "allocate-late/release-early" strategy. That means that the connection is not opened until it is about to be used, and then it is closed as soon as possible. This is different from the days when connections were held as long as possible.

Most seasoned VB developers recognize the need for pooling resources, and attempt to do so by hanging on to an ADO `Connection` instance, then passing it around as needed. They remember the days of maintaining one database connection for the life of a process, and may be tempted to repeat the technique in a distributed system. This could be achieved in the middle tier by declaring an ADO `Connection` reference at the top of a BAS or class module and using it for multiple calls, or even multiple clients. It could be declared publicly, or simply passed in the argument list to methods that needed it. Although this does function correctly, it is not a good programming practice, because this sharing of connections is already happening down in the data access DLLs.

The issue of retaining database connections as data members really stems from the intermingling of business state and an actual pipeline to data. Although state is, by definition, maintained between calls, database connections are usually only maintained for performance reasons. There is no need to maintain a connection physically between calls. The only state that is required between calls to reestablish a database connection is the connection string information, such as server name and user ID. The technique of sharing an ADO `Connection` between calls and/or users is really an attempt to mimic database connection pooling for performance. Because both OLE DB and ODBC already do this, any attempts to share an ADO `Connection` object in VB code would be duplicating code that already exists. Furthermore, the duplicated code written in VB would be far inferior, both in performance and functionality, to the existing code in OLE DB and ODBC.

Developers should adopt the policy of "get in, get done, and get out" when it comes to their database interaction, as illustrated in the previous code example. Unless specifically needed for some other purpose, ADO connections should be declared locally, opened just before the data-specific work is requested, then closed as soon as possible after the work is finished. This "allocate-late/release-early" strategy releases the database connection to the pooling mechanism, which is exactly how things are designed to work. When the next `Open` method is invoked on an `ADO Connection` object, the connection that was released into the pool (or an equivalent one) will be returned. However, in between database calls, the "idle" connection can be used to service other requests.

OLE DB and ODBC are designed to pool database connections for us. Because they already manage our connections, it does not make sense to store database connections in our data members. You could actually think of the connection pooling as a set of implicit data members that is shared between users. Your explicit storage of the `ADO Connection` object is really just duplicated work, and would be inefficient compared with the built-in connection-pooling code. For better performance, avoid keeping database connection references as data members in your systems. Let the connection-pooling mechanisms do their job.

Rule 5-4: Deadlock Is Common; Develop Defensively

Rule 5-1 laid out some ground rules for designing efficient data access code in a VB application. This rule explores a more complex topic: *lock management*. Developers who fail to take the time to understand locking usually write applications that perform poorly and incur deadlock more than normal. Understanding the different locking issues that occur in a multiuser system is important. You should know how to design and develop defensively to avoid the common pitfalls of poorly designed systems.

Locking

Locking is used to hold resources during the life of a transaction. The idea of a lock is to prevent changes to data that would adversely affect a running piece of code. There are two basic types of locks: *read* and *write*. Read locks are acquired before reading some data, whereas write locks are acquired before writing some data. A read lock on a piece of data prevents other users from acquiring a write lock on the same data, but those users may acquire their own read locks. For this reason, read locks are sometimes referred to as *shared locks*. A write lock is exclusive. In effect, no other write or read locks may be acquired on the locked data. Table 5.1 summarizes this discussion.

The performance of your system is dramatically affected by locking. As more and more locks are held, the probability of one transaction needing something locked by another transaction increases. When this happens, blocking occurs and overall concurrency decreases. This has a negative impact on application efficiency.

Serialized Transactions and the Lock Manager

Lock managers are responsible for acquiring the locks in the system. Because the lock manager is implemented differently on various platforms, its behavior varies as well. It is important to understand the lock manager for the systems with which you work.

Serialized transactions are transactions that run one after the other; no code for any transaction is running concurrently with any other transaction in a serially executed world. The benefit of this approach is that no two transactions run simultaneously, and therefore there can be no blocking. The drawback is that all transactions would queue up into a first-in/first-out line, and your ability to access data in a timely fashion would be severely impaired.

Lock managers have the ability to make the system "feel" as if it is serialized while still allowing other users/transactions to be running at the same time.

Table 5.1   Algorithm to grant or deny requests for a DB lock

Type of Lock Held	Ask for Read Lock	Ask for Write Lock
None	*Granted*	*Granted*
Read	*Granted*	***Denied***
Write	***Denied***	***Denied***

To make a transaction run in a serialized mode requires that anything the transaction touches, either with read or write access, be locked for the life of the transaction. In this scenario, some transactions can cause adverse affects on other transactions for no good reason. For instance, a long-running transaction that acquires a lot of read locks, with no intention of ever updating the data, still holds those locks for the entire lifetime of the transaction. Short-running transactions that wish to update the same data must wait for the original transaction to terminate.

SQL Server's lock manager can implement other, different locking modes by setting the isolation level. The default mode is `Read Committed`. This means that when a transaction begins, any records that are updated or added may not be seen by other transactions until the transaction commits. However, if a read is performed in a transaction (T1) running at `Read Committed`, the lock is only held for the life of the read, not the life of the transaction. This allows a separate transaction (T2) to update the record read by of the first transaction T1, even though T1 has not committed. Imagine the following scenario:

1. T1 reads a record and makes a decision based on the values it discovers.
2. T2 modifies the record because T1's read lock was terminated just after the read.
3. T1 returns to the original record, discovers a new value, and cannot continue.

T1 has been negatively affected by T2 running concurrently because the two transactions did not run serialized. You can change the isolation level of SQL Server from `Read Committed` to `Serializable` to solve this problem. By running at an isolation level of serializable, T2 would not be able to modify the record read by T1.

MTS and COM+ provide a transaction infrastructure for developers. To protect us from hurting ourselves, MTS and COM+ promote our isolation level from `Read Committed` to `Serializable` when we call from a transactional configured component to SQL Server. This is good because we don't run into problems similar to the previously described issue, but it also lowers concurrency in the system and may cause more transactions to end up deadlocked. Even though MTS and COM+ provide valuable services to us as we develop our transactional code, we should be wary of the decisions made on our behalf under the hood.

Deadlock

Deadlock occurs when all of the following conditions are true, in this order:

1. Transaction T1 begins and acquires some data locks.
2. Transaction T2 begins and acquires its own data locks.
3. Transaction T1 requires a lock on data already locked by T2 in order to complete.
4. Transaction T2 requires a lock on data already locked by T1 in order to complete.

An example is shown in Figure 5.7. In such a situation, system intervention is required to break the stalemate. Both T1 and T2 are waiting for a lock to be released. This will never happen, though, because each is waiting for the other. Only an outside force can recognize the problem and step in to solve it.

All database lock managers have the ability to perform this type of intervention. Some are better than others. The simplest scenario is when both transactions involved in the deadlock are trying to access records under the control of a single lock manager. This allows for a single lock manager to determine that a deadlock has occurred and to take the appropriate steps to alleviate it. If, however, the deadlocked records belong to two different lock managers, some data must be exchanged back and forth between the lock managers involved in order for the problem to be noticed and addressed.

There are solutions to prevent the deadlock problem. One approach is to have the transactions run serially.[1] This is obviously not a real solution for a concurrent system because the wait time for each transaction would be unacceptable. Another approach is to obtain all locks before the transaction runs to

---

[1] This does not mean run them in `Serializable` mode, but rather, physically run them one after the other.

EFFECTIVE DATA ACCESS FROM VB

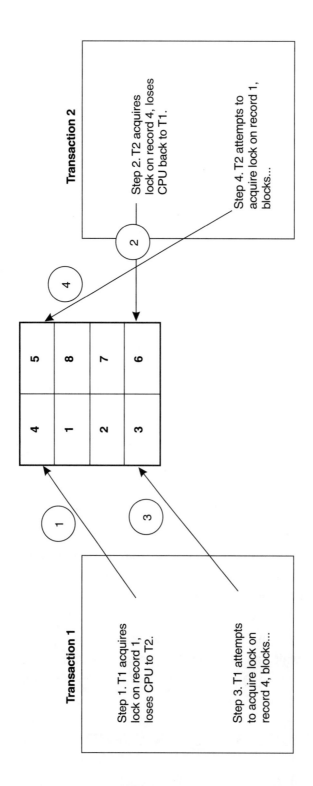

Figure 5.7 An example of deadlock

ensure all locks could be obtained.[2] This approach is too expensive for any but the simplest systems. Therefore, it is generally accepted that deadlocks are a distinct possibility. Lock managers must have the ability to detect deadlock, and developers should design their applications to minimize the likelihood of deadlock occurring.

MTS and COM+ use a time-out method for deadlock detection. The approach is rather simple to implement and thus is very common. When a transaction begins, a timer starts. If a transaction runs for too long, the system assumes it to be in a deadlock situation, and the transaction is aborted and rolled back. This method has its faults because some transactions may take longer than the allowed time and will be rolled back even though no deadlock has occurred. How long the transaction can run is a configurable setting in MTS and COM+. Under MTS the transaction time-out can be set only at a global level. In COM+, on the other hand, it can be configured globally to the whole computer, or on a component-by-component basis. Using the Component Services tool, you can set the global time-out by pulling up the properties dialog for your computer, then choosing the Options tab. You may override the global setting by explicitly setting a time-out on the properties of a particular component.

The default transaction timeout value for both MTS and COM+ is 60 seconds. Under MTS the transaction clock starts ticking as soon as the first object of a transaction begins a method call. Even if the method requires no locks or data access, the transaction time has started its countdown. If you don't finish in the allowed time, your work will be aborted. Under COM+ the transaction clock starts when a transactional object actually does something that requires a lock. This is a better approach because it delays the start of the clock until the last possible moment.

The time-out approach for deadlock detection by both MTS and COM+ works well in a distributed environment. Because our MTS/COM+ objects may perform transactional work against multiple resource managers, and those

---

[2] See *Principles of Transaction Processing for the Systems Professional,* by Phillip Bernstein and Eric Newcomer (Morgan Kaufmann Publishing, 1997), p. 204.

resource managers do not have the ability to detect a distributed deadlock, the time-out method makes the most sense.

Minimizing Deadlock Opportunities in Your Application Design

An overriding principal to minimizing deadlocks and blocking is to acquire locks as late as possible and to hold locks for as short a time as possible. The less time a lock is held, the less likely it is to block another user. The way to do this is to minimize the amount of time it takes your transaction to run. Your goal is to do your work as quickly as possible while acquiring locks as late as possible and letting them go as soon as possible. As the number of active transactions in a system increases, the probability of one transaction blocking another transaction increases.

There are two primary ways to minimize deadlock potential in your application. The first technique is to reduce the length of time a transaction runs; the second technique is to minimize the amount of time a transaction holds locks.[3]

Minimizing Transaction Length

One surefire way to decrease the length of time it takes your transaction to run is to eliminate as many round-trips to the server as you can. You can do this through batch SQL statements or stored procedures (see rules 5-1 and 5-2 for more information on this topic). The more round-trips you eliminate, the better your chances for avoiding deadlocks.

Another thing to do is make sure you are not performing the same reads over and over but rather are storing the data in memory after the first read. Because the data is locked, it is not going to change. For instance, if your SQL logic must continually refer back to a value taken from the database, cache that value from the first read into a local variable. Use the variable for comparison later in the statement instead of reexecuting the read. Your lock is still in effect, but using the cached value is much quicker than reading it from the database again.

---

[3] See *Principles of Transaction Processing for the Systems Professional* by Phillip Bernstein and Eric Newcomer (Morgan Kaufmann Publishing, 1997), p. 207.

Minimizing Lock Time

Minimizing how long locks are held may not be as straightforward as you may like. Recall that when you place a transactional object in MTS or COM+, any database calls will go out with an isolation level of serializable. This includes method calls that you do not need or intend to run at an isolation level of serializable. With MTS and COM+ the transaction setting is placed on the component, not the method. This means that if a component is marked as transactional and it has a set of methods for reading data and a set of methods for writing data, all methods will run at serializable even though the reads might not need to.

To avoid this problem you can redesign your object into two separate objects: one with the transactional methods that need to be serialized and one that is not transactional. In MTS and COM+, the first object is configured to require transactions, while the second object is configured with transactions not supported. You can execute the nontransactional methods at any point in the transaction without incurring extra locks.

Another, simpler, approach is to look for ways of structuring your code so that you grab the locks as late as possible. Don't do a series of reads at the beginning of a method and then do a bunch of data validation that you could have done before the database reads. Structuring your code well is critical to minimizing the length of time a lock is held. The closer to the end of the transaction you acquire locks, the sooner they will be released. Remember this motto: "Get in, do your work, and get out!"

Rule 5-5: Use Firehose Cursors Whenever Possible

When designing any software system, shared resource usage is (or, at least, should be) one of the primary development concerns. Your software should take a low-impact approach to shared resources as much as possible: Get in late, finish early, leave no trace. These resources can be the usual suspects, like memory, disk space, or clock cycles, but they can also be more esoteric, like open database connections and network connections. Not surprisingly, when designing a distributed application that accesses a central database, all of these resources come into play.

When you access a database in your application, there are two things you can do: read (or analyze) the data or update it. All operations on the data fall into one category or the other. The first and biggest trap into which most programmers fall when starting out with database programming is to write code that tries to do both at once. The typical vehicle for this (usually) mistaken notion is the `ADO Recordset` object. The Microsoft SQL Server Programmer's Toolkit says that an ADO recordset "allows you to add, update, delete, and scroll through records in the recordset." A recordset gives you this ability through the use of *cursors*.

A cursor is often referred to as a *pointer to a row in a database*. In reality, it is an object that caches some information about the results of your query. In most cases this information is just a set of *keys* that uniquely identify those records in the database that satisfy your query, but in some instances it is a full copy of the information in those records. A cursor is just a mechanism that lets you access your set-based data in a record-based way.

You can specify what kind of cursor to use through the `CursorType` and `CursorLocation` properties of your `Recordset` object. You have four choices for type: `Forward only`, `Static`, `Keyset`, and `Dynamic`. You have two for location: `Client` and `Server`. The valid combinations are summarized in Table 5.2. For example, only the static cursor can exist on the client side. The actual types available to your application depend on the OLE DB provider you are using to access the data. All of these are provided by SQLOLEDB, the native OLE DB provider for SQL Server. You should check the documentation for the provider you are using.

When you execute a query, some rows from the database are deemed appropriate to be in the result set. In the case of a static cursor, a duplicate of each field requested from each row returned is cached in the cursor. Each of the

Table 5.2 Recordset cursor availability

Side	Forward Only	Static	Keyset	Dynamic
Server	Yes	Yes	Yes	Yes
Client	No	Yes	No	No

other cursors just cache keys that identify rows in the live database, not the data itself. This is the essence of the difference between static cursors and the rest: As the underlying (live) data changes, a static cursor will not reflect those changes, whereas the rest will. As your client code uses the data returned from the query, with a static cursor they simply retrieve the cached information; with the others, they use the cached key to look up the live data.

A forward-only cursor is a server-side cache of keys that only allows forward navigation through the result set. The only standard exception is that you may still use the MoveFirst method, which simply reexecutes the entire query and repopulates the cursor. A keyset cursor will execute the query once, and will populate with all the keys to those rows that match the query. From that point on, the number of rows and keys to those rows remain static while the cursor is open, although the underlying data may change. With a dynamic cursor, each time the cursor is accessed through *any* method, the query is in effect re-executed and the keyset is repopulated. The actual number of rows in the result set may be increased or decreased depending on the requery.

Here is a typical (and bad) way to use a dynamic cursor to analyze and make changes to data:

```
'** declare a connection string and SQL query
sSQL = "SELECT * from Antiquities"
sCONN = "<proper connection string>"

'** declare a new recordset and connection
Dim rRS As ADODB.Recordset
Dim rCN As ADODB.Connection

'** open the connection
Set rCN = New Connection
rCN.ConnectionString = sCONN
rCN.Open

'** open the recordset with a server-side, dynamic cursor
Set rRS = New ADODB.Recordset
rRS.CursorLocation = adUseServer
rRS.CursorType = adOpenDynamic
rRS.LockType = adLockPessimistic
```

```
Set rRS.ActiveConnection = rCN
rRS.Open sSQL

'** do something interesting
rRS.MoveFirst
Do While Not rRS.EOF
    If rRS.Fields("City") = "Constantinople" Then
        rRS.Fields("City") = "Istanbul"
        rRS.Update
    End If
    rRS.MoveNext
Loop
```

Notice that this example uses a dynamic server-side cursor with locking set to pessimistic locking. This means that when the query is run, a cursor is built in memory on the server. It is populated with the keys to every row in the `Antiquities` table (due to the `Select *` without a `Where` clause). Now, as we loop through the recordset, we are actually using cached row keys to look up individual rows and are then making updates based on a conditional (`"City = 'Constantinople' "`). Because the application specified pessimistic locking, a write lock is applied to each row as it is read into the buffer, meaning that any `Update` method against that row will always succeed. Had the code specified optimistic locking (`LockType = adLockOptimistic`), the lock would only be applied during the actual call to update the record, and therefore might fail if another user or application had changed the underlying values after we read the record into the buffer.

One problem with using cursors is that overhead can be pretty high. Cursors take up space in the database (in SQL Server, in tempdb) and take up space in memory. Depending on the size and complexity of the query, this could add up to a lot of overhead. They also increase the network traffic between your application and the database because each time your code accesses a row, the actual row data has to be refetched from the server.[4] Lastly, while you have one of these recordsets open, you are also keeping the *connection* open, and data-

---

[4] In point of fact, even firehose cursors suffer this same problem. However, a firehose cursor permits only forward-only movement, and thus encourages you to scroll through the data once, as quickly as possible. The only type of cursor that efficiently allows for scrolling around the data is a client-side, static cursor, because you would be scrolling through a local cache.

base connections are valuable resources that should be closed as quickly as possible.

In addition, if you are using a cursor to update data, you have to write fairly complex code to make sure that each update succeeds. This code will differ depending on your locking scheme. With optimistic locking, you have to verify on each write that another user has not changed the data. With pessimistic locking, you merely have to verify that you are physically able to make the update, because you are guaranteed a write lock on the row.

Some programmers have begun using *disconnected recordsets* to solve the concurrency problem. A disconnected recordset is just a normal recordset with an `ActiveConnection` property that has been set to `Nothing`. To create one, the recordset's `CursorLocation` must be `adUseClient`, and therefore its `CursorType` must be `adOpenStatic`. In addition, `LockType` must be set to `adLockBatchOptimistic` (if updating). What actually happens is that a client-side cursor is created and filled with duplicates of all the data returned from the query. Now, there are no locks held on the underlying data while your application uses the recordset, and the connection can be closed and returned to the connection pool (if one exists).

The problem comes when you try to reconnect to the server and post updates. The underlying live values may have changed while your application did its work. As the updates are posted, you have no way of knowing which are still valid. After calling the `UpdateBatch` method, you have to filter your recordset using the `adFilterConflictingRecords` constant. You have to loop through each of these records and attempt to fix the problem or notify the user that those updates could not be processed at the time. Managing this scenario is complex and error prone.

The solution to all these issues is to avoid cursors as much as possible. SQL Server was designed to be set based, not record based. You should separate the acts of reading and analyzing data from the act of updating it. You should limit yourself as much as possible to using action queries in SQL when you want to make changes to the data, and use what's called a *firehose cursor* for reading data out of the database. A firehose cursor is misnamed: It isn't really a cursor at all. It is the default mechanism for SQL Server to return data. When a firehose cursor is specified, the database server does not create a cursor or incur any of the overhead associated with it. It simply fires back the result set in default format. It will fill its output buffer, wait for the client application to clear that buffer, and then it will fill it again. In this way, the server returns the data as fast as the client can suck it down (hence, *firehose*). This method also places minimal locks on the data. Data is only locked long enough to be fired into the output buffer, then it is released, so there is very little chance of having a concurrency problem while retrieving the data.

One nice thing about ADO is that the default setting for a recordset object is the firehose cursor. To choose one manually, you have to set `CursorType = adForwardOnly`, `CursorLocation = adUseServer`, `LockType = adLockReadOnly`, and `CacheSize = 1`. Now, you can only move forward through the recordset (if you use the `MoveFirst` method, you will reexecute the query). You can read the data into a local structure or analyze it in code. For example, you could loop through the `Antiquities` results and display a list of all the cities included. The important thing is to treat the recordset as a way to read data, not to update it.

If you wanted to make the changes that were made in the first code sample, but without using an updatable cursor, execute a simple SQL statement through the `Connection` object:

```
rCN.Execute "UPDATE Antiquities WHERE City=" & _
            "'Constantinople' SET City='Istanbul'"
```

Because this is a pure SQL action query, the entire set is operated on simultaneously by the query, and lock times on individual rows are held to an absolute minimum.[5] There is much less of a chance to have a lock collision during execution of a command like this, and you don't incur any of the disk, RAM, or network traffic overhead that you would by looping through a cursor one row at a time looking for a match. If you are not expecting any records to be returned as a result of your query, you can optimize this statement by adding the `adExecuteNoRecords` option as the third parameter. Additionally, for more complex manipulations of your data, you may want to rely on stored procedures

---

[5] This is only true if your SQL query does not take part in a transaction.

instead of dynamically issued SQL statements. This can reduce network traffic and improve efficiency (see rule 5-1 for more information).

Two general exceptions to this rather broad rule are if you need to update the contents of either a memo field or a binary field. These types of fields can be rather complex to access through standard SQL statements, whereas ADO recordsets make them much easier to accommodate. Therefore, if your application must update either of these kinds of fields, you may wish to pursue an updatable recordset solution.

If you absolutely must provide a scrollable recordset of data to your users, use a disconnected recordset (client side, read-only, no active connection). ADO disconnected recordsets actually use a firehose cursor to retrieve the data values and populate the client-side cursor. Once you disconnect the connection, you have placed minimal burden on the server and still provide a full-feature cursor to the application. Just remember, to minimize your shared resource usage (memory, disk space, network connections, database connections), do your reading and updating separately. Use a firehose cursor to read data, and use direct SQL action queries to make changes.

Rule 5-6: Make the Right Data Searching Decision (Avoid `SelectSingleNode` Abuse)

This point has been reiterated many times in this book: A large percentage of good application design is picking the right tool for the task at hand. It is very easy to get caught up in the hype about a new technology without really understanding where it fits in the grand scheme of things. XML (and, specifically, Microsoft's XML parser) is a great example. Now that SQL Server and ADO can trade information in XML, it may seem like a smart idea to eliminate the layers between your code and the data, and work straight with XML itself. It turns out that in some cases this would be a very poor decision.

The Seek-and-Find Component

Imagine that you are writing a search component for a distributed application. Your component will live in the middle tier, and the data is stored on another machine in SQL Server. A user will be requesting a single row/element from the dataset at a time. Fast response times are an absolute must for your application.

There are three different ways you can go about searching for a single record in the dataset:

1. Import the data into a local XML file and use XML's `SelectSingleNode` function to find the specified element.
2. Leave the data in SQL Server and select rows using Transact-SQL.
3. Import the data into a local ADO recordset and use `Recordset.Find`.

Let's take a look at the code and results for each of these methods. We will examine the most optimized code for each method, and compare response times.[6]

The XML Way

You've heard all about the great things that XML can do for you. You know that SQL Server can now return datasets to you as XML documents, and you decide to cache the entire dataset in memory on the local machine as an XML DOMDocument. Your component keeps a reference to this dataset, and uses it to respond to queries from the user.

Assuming that the user has requested a given record based on its `OrderID`, which is passed to your function as a parameter called `iInOrderID`, and your full DOMDocument is called `xOrderDetails`, your code would look like this:

```
Dim rReturnNode As IXMLDOMNode
Set rReturnNode = xmldoc.selectSingleNode _
    ("/xml/rs:data/z:row[@OrderID='" & iInOrderID & "']")

If (rReturnNode is Nothing) Then
    '** report no match found
Else
    '** report match
End If
```

---

[6] For these examples, we used a Pentium III, 500 MHz with 128MB RAM, SQL Server 2000, VB6, ADO 2.6, and the July 2000 XML Technology Preview. The recordset contains 2,155 records that describe the details of product orders, with an index in SQL Server on the `OrderID` column.

When this code is run on the test machine, the response time of the `SelectSingleNode` call is, on average, 0.0127 seconds.[7]

Bear in mind that XML does not optimize for searching for a node in a document. Nodes can be arbitrarily ordered in the document tree. Nodes cannot be indexed, although they can be sorted. Additionally, your code has to suffer the initial hit of loading the document over from the database, which itself takes time, especially if the database lives far away on the network.

One other major benefit you get from XML is cross-platform interoperability. If your component lives not only on a different machine from your database, but on an entirely different operating system, then XML is the perfect choice for delivering your data. There are numerous protocols springing up based entirely on this notion, such as SOAP, which defines a firewall-friendly way of calling methods on an object via XML.[8] If, however, both your component server and the data server are Windows-based machines, you should examine the next two solution possibilities.

The SQL Server Way

The second option is to leave the data in the database on the remote machine and use Transact-SQL `Select` statements to find specific rows. You would probably use ADO as the front-end to this code. It would look like this:

```
Dim rCN As New ADODB.Connection
Dim rRS As New ADODB.Recordset
Dim sCONN As String

sCONN = "<proper connection string>"
rCN.Open sCONN

rRS.CursorLocation = adUseServer
rRS.CursorType = adOpenStatic
Set rRS.ActiveConnection = rCN
rRS.Open "Select * from OrderDetails WHERE " & _
         "OrderID=" & CStr(iInOrderID)
```

---

[7] The response time listed for the call does not include the initial overhead of parsing the XML document, which can vary, but is a one-time initialization cost of running the application.

[8] For more information, please visit www.develop.com/soap or msdn.microsoft.com/soap.

```
If rRS.EOF = True And rRS.BOF = True Then
    '** report no match
Else
    'report match
End If
```

In this code, you leave all the data in the database. The `Recordset` object is used to cache the result of the `Select` statement, which specifies the table to search and the condition to match: The `OrderID` column must equal the value of the `iInOrderID` parameter.

When run on the test configuration, the response time of the `Select` statement is 0.002 seconds on average, which is 6.5 times faster than the XML `SelectSingleNode` statement. SQL Server can execute the search faster for several reasons. First, the column `OrderID` is indexed in the database, meaning it is optimized for searching. Second, SQL Server has been built for years to optimize Transact-SQL queries. In fact, every SQL statement executed by SQL Server has what is known as an "optimized execution plan," created to achieve (statistically speaking) the best results. XML has none of these benefits.

So you can see that the SQL Server solution is better already. One variable that cannot be accommodated in a generic test is network traffic. Because you have to send a statement across the network to your server and receive the response back across the network, this variable can be very important in determining overall performance. This test was conducted on a local network, with machines close together and not much competing traffic. You should run tests yourself on your target deployment network to see how it affects performance.

The SQL Server method has two other benefits that neither the XML nor the ADO solutions offer. The first is that it doesn't require a possibly expensive one-time initialization to load the dataset. Because the data lives in and remains in the server during the course of its use, you do not have to spend time transferring it to the client machine for the first run. The second benefit is that because the data remains in the server, subsequent searches will search on a live view of the data, finding new additions made by other users since your last search. The other two solutions, relying on cached copies of the data, cannot offer this same feature.

The ADO Disconnected Recordset Way

The final option is to cache the data on the local machine as a disconnected ADO recordset. Functionally, this solution is very similar to the XML document solution: Your component maintains a local, in-memory cache of the dataset on which to perform the search operation. Likewise, this solution also incurs the initial hit of loading the full dataset across the network. Thereafter, however (like the XML solution), your actual search methods do not travel across the network. Your new code will look something like this:

```
rRS.Fields("OrderID").Properties("Optimize") = True
rRS.Sort = "OrderID DESC"
rRS.Find "OrderID=" & CStr(iInOrderID)
```

In this case, you can dynamically specify an optimized index on a given field (the field on which you will search), then sort it (in this case, in descending order). Then you issue the `Find` command. If the match criterion is met, the recordset will now be pointing to the row that met the criterion; otherwise, it will be pointing to the end of the recordset. You can use `rs.AbsolutePosition` to check the current row number, or `rs.EOF` to see if you have fallen off the end.

Run on the test machine, the average response time for the `Find` command is 0.0002 seconds, or an order of magnitude faster than the SQL method, and 65 times faster than the XML method. This is because, when ADO was written, the programming team leveraged a lot of the technologies that had been built into the Microsoft Jet Database Engine. The same sorts of tools are used that SQL uses: index, optimized sorts, and so forth. This allows the ADO `Find` method to access data faster than the unordered, unoptimized XML.

Additionally, this method doesn't have to traipse across the network and contact SQL Server to perform the search, which saves a *lot* of time on the method call. (In fact, most of the time savings of this solution over SQL can be attributed to the lack of network travel.) You have to incur some overhead at start-up, as the original recordset is populated, but you will more than make up for it on the subsequent searches you perform on the data.

Know Which Method to Use for Your Scenario

Remember that these test cases were performed on a relatively small dataset (2,155 records). If you have hundreds of thousands, or even millions, of records in your database, of course the SQL Server option is the most logical. It would be prohibitively expensive to send that many records across the network to your client machine, and you probably wouldn't have enough memory to store it all anyway. If your dataset is huge, use SQL queries (preferably stored procedures) to do the work.

If your data is coming from a non-database source, such as a persisted (non-ADO persisted) XML file or a text stream from another application, it may be prohibitively expensive to hand-roll an ADO recordset and then populate it with the values. In order for ADO to create a recordset automatically from XML for you, remember that XML has to have been written in the ADO recordset schema format. So if your data comes from something other than SQL/ADO, it may make sense to just run with the XML solution.

And, lastly, if your scenario is anything like the test case, in which your data is stored in SQL and the dataset is a reasonabe size, it makes the most sense to use the ADO disconnected recordset approach. Depending on things like network bandwidth capacity and memory availability, as many as 20,000 rows of data can be a reasonable-size dataset to cache locally. If you can design a way to make the initial load unobtrusive for your application (and you are mainly *reading* and *analyzing* data, not writing it), then this solution provides the best response time for your end user.

Take the time to understand the parameters of your problem. Look at factors like expected network traffic, distance between database and middle-tier servers, expected dataset size, and so forth. Don't just rely on the hype surrounding a new technology like XML or the proclamations of industry know-it-alls telling you to "always leave your data in the server." Make the effort to understand how these factors will play into your design, and then choose the approach that is right for your application.

Index

a

Abstraction, 42, 43–44, 46
Access permissions, checking, 170
ACID rules, 142, 154, 155
Activation, COM, 91, 99–110
    `CreateObject` function, 99, 103–105
    `GetObjectContext.CreateInstance` and `Server.CreateObject`, 99, 100, 106–107
    `GetObject` function, 99, 105–106
    `New` operator, 102–103
    performance considerations, 107–110
    types of, 107–108, 109, 118–119
Active Template Library (ATL), 143
ActiveX EXEs, 118–122
Activities in MTS/COM+, 124, 126, 127–128, 131
ADO disconnected recordset, 297
ADO objects, 136–137
`ADO Recordset`, 231–232, 235, 273, 288
    disconnected, 297
Advanced Data Tablegram format (ADTG), 235
Apartment-threaded object, 221
    `Application` variable and, 223–224
    `Session` variable and, 222–223
API calls, 30
`Application` object. *See* ASP `Application` object
Application state management, 184–194
    ASP `Application` object, 191–193
    BAS module data and, 185–188
    SPM and, 188–191
    weighing options for, 193–194
Arguments
    in conditional compilation, 15–17, 19
    in scripts, 58
ASP, 150, 175, 185
    eliminating from distributed application, 206–208
    interaction with COM, 218–227
    intrinsic objects, 219–220
        benefits of, 225–226
        disadvantages of, 226–227
    presentation layer-business logic layer separation and, 236–243
        MTS components and, 238–239
        `WebClasses` and, 240–243
    thread-pooling scheme, 223
    threads in, 186
ASP.dll, 175
ASP `Application` object, 153–154, 220
    apartment-threaded object and, 223–224
    caching using, 191–193
ASP page, object creation from, 137
ASP `Session` object, 194–195, 219
`AspTrackThreadingModel` property, 224
Assignment of class versus type, 38, 39–40
Assumptions, explicit, 8–14
ATL (Active Template Library), 143
Atomicity, issue of, 154
Auto-abort style with transactions, 146–150
Automating mundane tasks, 53–60
    with `nmake`, 53–56
    with Windows Scripting Host (WSH), 56–60

b

Base client, 130
BAS modules, 122, 150
    caching data in, 185–188
    variables, 187–188
Batch files, 53
Batch SQL statement, 261–262
Binary Compatibility setting, 95–96, 97
Binding, client-object, 107
Binding mechanisms, client-object, 100–101
Brittle-code problem, 248–249
Browser, 237
Builds, debug versus release, 15–16

Business logic layer-presentation layer separation, 236–243
   MTS components and, 238–239
   `WebClasses` and, 240–243
`ByRef`, 36, 37, 40
`ByVal`, 36, 37, 40

C

C++, 41
Caching, 151, 156
   of durable state web application, 184–194
      ASP `Application` object, 191–193
      BAS module data and, 185–188
      SPM and, 188–191
      weighing options for, 193–194
   in-memory, 150–151
Callbacks, custom, 83–90
Class(es)
   accessing, 66
   custom interfaces and evolution of, 67–69
   groups of, 48
   real-world entities modeled by, 42–43
   type versus, 35–41
   value types and, 49–52
Class-based events, 83–86
Class-based references, 67
`Class_Initialize`, 43
`Class_Terminate`, 43, 111–114
Cleanup, 111–114
Client(s)
   accidental DLL installation on, 170–171
   base, 130
   compiled, 93–96
   object binding by, 100–101
   scripting, 92–93
   storing session information on, 196–201
      via cookies, 197–198
      in database, 201–202
      in header, 197–198
      in hidden form fields, 200–201
      with `QueryString` variables, 199–200
`Close` methods, 111–112
CLSIDs, 91
Coclass (COM class) definitions, 81
`CoCreateInstance`, 164
`CoCreateInstanceEx`, 164
COM+, 119, 123–172
   activities in, 124, 126, 127–128
   Auto-Abort style with transactions, 146–150

   coding practices for, 169–172
   components configuration issues, 157–158
   context in, 157
   DBMS issues, 150–156
   design of, 124–127
   DLL issues, 159–164
   object creation in, 129–140
   porting MTS to, 164–169
      declarative security checks and, 167
      `GetObjectContext.CreateInstance` and, 164–165
      MSI and, 168–169
      `ObjectConstruct` string and, 166–167
      `RefreshComponents` command and, 167–168
      `SafeRef` and, 165
      secondary object errors and, 165–166
   `SetComplete`, 140–146
   singletons in, 127–129, 132
   synchronization in, 125–126
   threads in, 186
   transactional methods in, 141–142
   transaction infrastructure in, 282–283
   Windows 2000 and, 138–139, 149–150
COM. *See also* DCOM
   activation, 91, 99–110
      `CreateObject` function, 99, 103–105
      `GetObjectContext.CreateInstance` and `Server.CreateObject`, 99, 100, 106–107
      `GetObject` function, 99, 105–106
      `New` operator, 102–103
      performance considerations, 107–110
      types of, 107–108, 109, 118–119
   important concepts in, 91
   interaction with ASP, 218–227
   registration requirements of, 91
COM-based components, 35, 61–122
   ActiveX EXEs and, 118–122
   `Class_Terminate` and, 111–114
   custom callbacks, 83–90
   interfaces and, 61–64
      custom, 64–83
   maintaining compatibility, 90–99
      compiled clients, 93–96
      scripting clients, 92–93
      version-compatible interfaces, 96–99
   modeling in terms of sessions, 114–117

for scripting environments, 209–218
    custom interfaces, 211–218
    default interface, 209–211, 214
    parameter passing to "scriptable" objects, 211
    STA and, 220
COM class (coclass) definitions, 81
Command-line arguments, 15
Compatibility, 62, 63–64
    with COM-based components, 90–99
        compiled clients, 93–96
        scripting clients, 92–93
        version-compatible interfaces, 96–99
    custom interfaces and, 72
    functionality and, 91–92
    version, 94–95, 98
Compilation
    conditional, 14–20
        arguments in, 15–17, 19
        assertions and, 18
        uses of, 15–16
    with makefiles, 53
Compiled clients, 93–96
`Compile On Demand`, 8
Compile-time errors, 3, 18
Compile-time type checking, 2–8
    with `Option Explicit`, 4–5
    `Start with Full Compile` command and, 8
    `variant` data type and, 5–8
Component Object Model. *See* COM; COM+
COM+ Services Library, 128
Concatenation, 36
Concurrency model, MTS, 131–132
Conditional compilation. *See under* Compilation
Configured components, 224
`Connection` class, 111
`Connection` object, 279
Connection strings, 159–161
    declarative, 161–162
`const` statement, 15, 19
Containment, 47–48
Context in COM+, 157
Context proxy, 157–159
Context wrapper, 136–137
Conventions, programming, 1–2
Cookies, 197–198
Coupling, 73
    excessive, 64

`CreateObject`, 92, 99, 103–105, 107, 108, 110, 169
    when to use, 129–140
`CreatePropertyGroup` method, 128
`CreateProperty` method, 128
Cursor(s), 287–293
    dynamic, 289–290
    firehose, 290*n*, 291–293
    forward-only, 289
    keyset, 289
    overhead incurred by, 290–291
    static, 288–289
Custom callbacks, 83–90
Custom interfaces, 64–83
    as abstract class, 65–66
    class evolution and, 67–69
    costs and benefits of, 72–73
    defining, 65, 73–83
    DLLs for, 74–75
    event mechanisms based on, 85–90
    factoring of, 69–70
    implementation of, 66
    polymorphism of, 71–72
    Web-enabled solutions and, 211–218

d

/d argument, 55
Data access, 257–298
    database connections as data members, 277–280
    efficiency basics, 257–265
        provider selection, 262–265
        round-trips, 258–260, 274
        SQL queries, 259, 260–262
    firehose cursors, 290*n*, 291–293
    lock management, 280–287
        deadlocks, 283–287
        serialized transactions and, 281–283
    overencapsulation of, 265–277
        multiple database servers and, 275–277
        object-oriented purism and, 266–270
        stored procedures and, 270–275
    searching, 293–298
        ADO disconnected recordset way, 297
        seek-and-find component, 293–294
        selecting method of, 298
        SQL server way, 295–296
        XML way, 294–295

Database(s), 127
    DLLs and, 162–164
    storing state in, 201–202
Database management, MTS/COM+ and, 150–156. *See also* DBMS
Data consistency
    in BAS module data, 187
    locking and, 189–190
Data-driven design, 163–164
Data durability, 152–153
Data hiding, 44–46
Data sharing
    across computer boundaries, 155–156
    across process boundaries, 155
Data source name (DSN), 160–161
Data types. *See* Type(s)
DBMS
    COM+ and, 150–156
    durable state in, 184–185
DCOM, 203–209
Deactivation of objects, 141–143
Deadlocks, 283–287
    example of, 284
    minimizing, 286–287
`Debug.Assert`, 8–14, 18
Debug builds versus release builds, 15–16
Debugging, `New` operator and, 139–140
Declarative constructor string, 161–162
Declarative security checks in COM+, 167
Declarative transactions, 146
Default interface, 63, 67, 92, 209–211, 214
Destructor methods, 111
DHTML, 234
`DisableCommit`, 166
Disconnected recordsets, 291, 297
Dispenser, 277–278
`Dispose` method, 113
Distributed applications, eliminating ASP from, 206–208
Distributed COM. *See* DCOM
Distributed systems. *See* COM+; MTS
Distributed Transaction Coordinator (DTC), 124
DLLHOST.EXE, 124
DLLs, 74–75
    accidental installation on client, 170–171
    MTS/COM+ and, 159–164
`DOMDocument` object, 230–233
DSN (data source name), 160–161
Durability of data, 152–153
Durable state, 184–185
Dynamic cursor, 289–290
Dynamic HTML (DHTML), 234

e

Efficiency in data access, 257–265
    provider selection, 262–265
    round-trips, 258–260, 274
    SQL queries, 259, 260–262
Encapsulation, 42–43, 265–277
    multiple database servers and, 275–277
    object-oriented purism and, 266–270
    stored procedures and, 270–275
Enumerated type, 23
`Err.Raise`, 170
`Err` object, 22–23
Error codes, 23
Error handling, 26–35
    `On Error`, 28–30
    global, 31–32
    in VBScript, 58–59
Error propagation, 170
Errors
    compile-time, 3, 18
    run-time, 3
    from secondary objects, 165–166
    to signal exceptional conditions, 20–25
Esperanto, 228, 234
Event handling, 83
Events, 83
    class-based, 83–86
Exceptional conditions, errors to signal, 20–25
Exception handling, 21–25
Exclusive locks, 153
`Export` command, 162
Extensible markup language. *See* XML
External assumptions, 9

f

Factoring of custom interfaces, 69–70
File Transfer Protocol (FTP), 174
Firehose cursors, 290*n*, 291–293
Form fields, hidden, 200–201
Forwarding to version-compatible interface, 98
Forward-only cursor, 289
Functionality, compatibility and, 91–92

g

General protection fault (GPF), 3
Generic object references, 92
`GetObject`, 107, 108, 110

`GetObjectContext.CreateInstance`, 99,
    106–107, 164–165, 169
  when to use, 129–140
`GetObject` function, 99, 105–106
Global error handling, 31–32
Graphic user interface (GUI), 83
GUID, 91–92

h

"Has-a" rule, 47
Heap, 36, 50–51
Help file, 24
`helpstring` attributes, 78, 82
Hidden form fields, 200–201
HTML documents, 204
HTML form, 200
HTML templates, 240, 241–242
HTTP (hypertext transport protocol), 203–209
  downside of using, 208–209
  method calls over, 206
  state management with, 205

i

`IContextState` interface, 171
IDL (Interface Description Language), 73–83
  automatic generation of VB-compatible, 80–83
  data type mappings to VB, 79
`If...End If`, 14–20
IIDs, 91
IIS architecture, 174–184. *See also* Web-enabled solutions
  deployment options and, 179–182
  INETINFO.exe, 175–177
  isolation levels of virtual applications and, 177–179, 180–182
  protocols recognized, 174
  scalability issues and, 182–184
`IISIntrinsics` attribute, 191–192
Implementation inheritance, 42
INETINFO.exe, 175–177
Inheritance, 47–48
In-process COM activation, 107, 109, 118–119
`Instancing` property, 65
Interception, 126
  in MTS/COM+, 130
Interception layer, 141
Interface(s), 42, 48
  COM-based components and, 61–64
  custom, 64–83

  as abstract class, 65–66
  class evolution and, 67–69
  costs and benefits of, 72–73
  defining, 65, 73–83
  DLLs for, 74–75
  event mechanisms based on, 85–90
  factoring of, 69–70
  implementation of, 66
  polymorphism of, 71–72
  web-enabled solutions and, 211–218
  default, 63, 67, 92, 209–211, 214
  forwarding to version-compatible, 98
  function of, 62
  marker, 71
  version-compatible, 96–99
Interface-based programming, 64
Interface Description Language (IDL), 73–83
  automatic generation of VB-compatible, 80–83
  data type mappings to VB, 79
Internal assumptions, 9
Internet Protocol (IP), 183
Internet Services Application Programming Interface (ISAPI), 174–175
Intrinsic objects, 219–220
  benefits of, 225–226
  disadvantages of, 226–227
`IObjectConstruct` interface, 166–167, 171
"Is-a" rule, 47
`IsCallerInRole`, 170
Isolation level, 177–179, 180–182, 190
`IsSecurityEnabled`, 170

j

Java, 73
Just-in-time activation (JITA) scheme, 142

k

Keyset cursor, 289

l

Late-binding, 92, 100, 101, 105, 108, 109–110
LibIDs, 91
Line numbers, 24
Load balancer (request broker), 183
`Load` event, 89
Local area network (LAN), 145–146
Local COM activation, 107, 109, 118

LockGetSet method, 128–129
Locking, 280–281
    data consistency and, 189–190
    minimizing, 287
    optimistic, 291
    pessimistic, 290, 291
    in SPM, 189–190
Lock management, 280–287
    deadlocks, 283–287
        example of, 284
        minimizing, 286–287
    serialized transactions and, 281–283
LockMethod, 190
Locks, 153–154
    exclusive, 153
    on resource managers, 141
    shared (read), 153, 281
    types of, 281
LockSetGet, 190
Logging code, 16
Logical property methods, 46–47
Logical thread per client, 131

m

Macros, 55
Main STA thread, 188
Makefiles, 53–54
Marker interface, 71
Marshalling, 51
Memory
    BAS modules and, 186–187
    caching in, 150–151
    for classes versus types, 39
    SetComplete and, 144
    stack versus heap, 50–51
Method-based Web farm, 183–184
Method calls over HTTP, 206
"Method ~ of Object Failed ~," 165–166, 170
Methods, 46
    logical property, 46–47
Microsoft Installer (MSI), 168–169
MIDL, 76, 80
Modeling of objects, 114–117
MSWCRUN.dll, 241
MSXML2.dll, 247
MSXML3.dll, 230
MTA (multi-threaded apartment), 125
MTS, 119, 123–172
    activities in, 124, 126, 127–128, 131
    Auto-Abort style with transactions, 146–150
    coding practices for, 169–172
    components configuration issues, 157–158
    concurrency model, 131–132
    DBMS issues, 150–156
    design of, 124–127
    DLL issues, 159–164
    object creation in, 129–140
    porting to COM+, 164–169
        declarative security checks and, 167
        GetObjectContext.CreateInstance and, 164–165
        MSI and, 168–169
        ObjectConstruct string and, 166–167
        RefreshComponents command and, 167–168
        SafeRef and, 165
        secondary object errors and, 165–166
    SetComplete, 140–146
    singletons in, 127–129, 132
    synchronization in, 125–126
    transactional methods in, 141–142
    transaction infrastructure in, 282–283
    Windows NT4 and, 131–137
MTS components, 238–239
MTS server package, threads in, 186
MTX.EXE, 124
MTXDM.DLL, 278
Multi-threaded apartment (MTA), 125
Multi-threading, 119–121
MultiUse class modules, 73

n

Network News Transfer Protocol (NNTP), 174
New operator, 39, 102–103, 105, 107–108
    COM+ and, 164–165
    debugging and, 139–140
    when to use, 129–140
nmake, 53–56
/n option (nmake), 56

o

Object(s)
    ADO, 136–137
    creation in MTS and COM+, 129–140
    deactivation of, 141–143
    intrinsic, 219–220
        benefits of, 225–226
        disadvantages of, 226–227
    modeling of, 114–117
    passing by reference, 40

root, 136
"Scriptable," 56
secondary, 136, 147, 165–166, 170
Object binding by client, 100–101
`ObjectConstruct` string, 166
`ObjectContext` interface, 171
`ObjectContext` object, 225, 239
`Object` data type, 93
Object-oriented design (OOD), 40, 41–49
    abstraction, 42, 43–44, 46
    containment versus inheritance, 47–48
    data hiding, 44–46
    encapsulation, 42–43, 265–277
        multiple database servers and, 275–277
        object-oriented purism and, 266–270
        stored procedures and, 270–275
    interfaces, 48
    polymorphism, 48–49
Object pooling, 141, 142–143
Object references, generic, 92
ODBC.DLL, 278
Office 2000, 168–169
OLE DB, 263–265
    connection pooling in, 278
`OLEView` utility, 80–83
`On Error`, 28–30
One-to-many design, 217
Online transaction processing (OLTP) system, 141
Open Database Connectivity (ODBC), 160–161, 262–265
    connection pooling in, 278
Optimistic locking, 291
Optimized execution plan, 296
`Option Explicit`, 4–5
`Option Strict` statement, 4
Out object references, 171–172
Out-of-process COM activation, 107, 108, 109, 118
Output parameters, 273
Overencapsulation, 265–277
    multiple database servers and, 275–277
    object-oriented purism and, 266–270
    stored procedures and, 270–275
Overloading, 8

p

Parameter passing, 36
    value versus reference types and, 51–52

Pessimistic locking, 290, 291
Polymorphism, 42, 48–49, 218
    of custom interfaces, 71–72
Postconditions, 12
`POST` method, 200
Preconditions, 12
Predefined types, 36
Prefixes, 2
Presentation layer-business logic layer separation, 236–243
    MTS components and, 238–239
    `WebClasses` and, 240–243
`Private`, 44–45
`Process` method, 128–129
`ProcessNoStateWebClass` method, 241
ProgIDs, 92–93, 133
Programmatic security, 170
Project Compatibility setting, 94–95
Property groups, 128
Protocol, communication, 203
    recognized by IIS, 174
Providers, selecting data access, 262–265
Proxy, context, 157–159
Proxy/stub pair, 108
`PublicNotCreatable` class modules, 73
Public signature, 63–64

q

Queries, SQL, 259, 260–262
`QueryString` variables, 199–200

r

`Raise` method, 22–23
RDS (Remote Data Services), 206
`Read Committed` mode, 282
Read (shared) locks, 153, 281
`Recordset` class, 111
Recordsets, 231–232, 235, 273, 288
    cursor availability in, 288–289
    disconnected, 291, 297
        selecting method of, 298
Reference type, 49–51
`Refresh` components, 167–168
Refreshing techniques, 151–152
RegDB, 126
`Register` method, 86, 88
Registration
    of DLLs, 75
    of TLBs, 76

Registry, 126
Release builds versus debug builds, 15–16
Remote COM activation, 107, 109, 118
Remote Data Services (RDS), 206
Remote Object Proxy Engine (ROPE), 208
Remote Procedure (RPC), 203
Request-based Web farm, 195–196
Request broker (load balancer), 183
Request object, 219
Require Variable Declaration option, 5
Resource managers, locks on, 141
Resources, shared, 124, 287
Response object, 219, 233, 239
Retained in memory project option, 187
Return codes, 20–21
Roles, 167
Rollback facilities, 154
Root object, 136
Round-trips, 286
    data access efficiency and, 258–260, 274
    session-based modeling and, 115–116
Run-time errors, 3
Run-time type information (RTTI), 70

S

SafeRef, 165, 171–172
Save method (ADO Recordset), 235
SCM, 135
    for Windows 2000, 138
"Scriptable" objects, 56
Scripting clients, 92–93
    custom interfaces and, 72
Scripting environments, COM components for, 209–218
    custom interfaces, 211–218
    default interface, 209–211, 214
    parameter passing to "scriptable" objects, 211
Searching databases, 293–298
    ADO disconnected recordset way, 297
    seek-and-find component, 293–294
    selecting method of, 298
    SQL server way, 295–296
    XML way, 294–295
Secondary object, 136
    DisableCommit in, 170
    errors from, 165–166
    transactions involving, 147
Security, programmatic, 170
SecurityCallContext interface, 171

Security checks in COM+, declarative, 167
Seek-and-find component, 293–294
SelectSingleNode, 294, 295
Server.CreateObject, 100, 106–107, 137
Server object, 220
Servers, multiple database, 275–277
Session-based Web farm, 183, 195
Session object, 194–195, 219
Sessions, modeling objects in terms of, 114–117
Session state management, 194–202
    storing session information on client, 196–201
        via cookies, 197–198
        in database, 201–202
        in header, 197–198
        in hidden form fields, 200–201
        with QueryString variables, 199–200
    Web farm configuration and, 195–196
Session (transient) state, 184
Session variable, apartment-threaded object and, 222–223
SetAbort, 136, 141, 165, 170
SetComplete, 140–146
    memory and, 144
    STA thread and, 144–145
Set statement, 39, 109–110
Shared Property Manager (SPM), 128, 150, 153–154
    caching using, 188–191
Shared Property Manager Type Library, 128
Shared (read) locks, 153, 281
Shared resources, 124, 287
Sharing states, 127
Shortcut references, 103
Signature, public, 63–64
Simple Mail Transfer Protocol (SMTP), 174
Simple Object Access Protocol (SOAP), 206–208
"Single point of failure," 183
Single-threaded apartments (STAs), 120, 124–126, 131–132
    COM objects and, 220
    main thread, 188
    SetComplete and, 144–145
    threading model, 220–224
Singletons, 127–129, 132
Single Web server, 195
SOAPMethodName, 207
SPM. *See* Shared Property Manager (SPM)
SQL queries, 259, 260–262

SQL Server, 153, 154–155
    database searching using, 295–296
Stack, 36, 50–51
`Start with Full Compile` command, 8
STAs. *See* Single-threaded apartments (STAs)
State(s)
    sharing, 127
    storing in database, 201–202
    types of, 184–185
Stateful components, 144–146
Stateless programming, 140–141, 145
State management
    application, 184–194
        ASP `Application` object, 191–193
        BAS module data and, 185–188
        SPM and, 188–191
        weighing options for, 193–194
    with HTTP, 205
    session, 194–202
        storing session information on client, 196–201
        Web farm configuration and, 195–196
Static cursor, 288–289
Stored procedures, 262, 270–275
`String` type, 36
Stub objects, 108
Stylesheet, XSLT, 250–253
Synchronization
    ASP `Application` object and, 192
    in MTS/COM+, 125–126
    SPM and, 190
    STA threading and, 220
`Synchronization` setting, 127–128

t

Tabular data stream (TDS), 259
Tasks, automating mundane, 53–60
    with `nmake`, 53–56
    with Windows Scripting Host (WSH), 56–60
Templates
    HTML, 240, 241–242
    in XSLT programs, 249–251
Test harnesses, 15
Thread affinity, 220, 221
Threading model, STA, 220–224
Thread local storage (TLS), 143
    BAS module data in, 185
Thread neutral apartment (TNA), 125
Thread pool, fixed-size, 120–121

Thread-pooling, 124–125
    in ASP, 223
TLB (type library), 76, 170–171
Transactional methods in MTS/COM+, 141–142
Transactions
    "ACID" rules of, 142, 154, 155
    Auto-Abort style with, 146–150
    declarative, 146
    involving secondary objects, 147
    minimizing length of, 286
Transact-SQL language, 270
Transformation, 233
Transformation tree, 245
Transient (session) state, 184
Trapping errors, 26–35
`Try-Catch` mechanism, 31
Type(s)
    class versus, 35–41
    enumerated, 23
    predefined, 36
    reference, 49–51
    user-defined (UDTs), 36–37, 49–52
    value, 49–52
    VB-to-IDL mappings, 79
Type checking, compile-time, 2–8
    with `Option Explicit`, 4–5
    `Start with Full Compile` command and, 8
    `variant` data type and, 5–8
Type library (TLB), 76, 170–171
`TypeOf` function, 70–71

u

Uniform resource locator (URL), 161
Universal data link (UDL), 160–161
`Unload` event, 89
`Unregister` method, 86, 88
User-defined types (UDTs), 36–37, 49–52

v

Value types, 49–52
`Variant` data type, 5–8, 93
    casual or unintentional use of, 5–8
    defined, 6
`vbObjectError` constant, 23
VBScript, 7, 30, 56–60
VB-to-IDL data type mappings, 79
Version compatibility, 94–95, 98
Version-compatible interfaces, 96–99

Version information, 18
Virtual application, isolation levels of, 177–179, 180–182. *See also* Web-enabled solutions
vtable-binding, 94, 100–101, 108, 109

W

Web Application Manager (WAM), 175, 179, 224
`WebClasses`, 240–243
`WebClassManager` object, 240–241
Web-enabled solutions, 173–256. *See also* IIS architecture
    application state management, 184–194
        ASP `Application` object, 191–193
        BAS module data and, 185–188
        SPM and, 188–191
        weighing options for, 193–194
    caching for, 151
    COM-ASP interaction, 218–227
    COM components for scripting environments, 209–218
        custom interfaces, 211–218
        default interface, 209–211, 214
        parameter passing to "scriptable" objects, 211
    DCOM versus HTTP, 203–209
    presentation layer-business logic layer separation, 236–243
        MTS components and, 238–239
        `WebClasses` and, 240–243
    scalability of, 206
    session state management, 194–202
        storing session information on client, 196–201
        Web farm configuration and, 195–196

XML, 227–236, 243
XSLT, 233, 234, 243–256
    drawbacks of, 255
    helpfulness of methodology, 246
    overview of, 244–246
    stylesheet, 250–253
    templates, 249–251
    transformation of dataset with, 249–255
Web farm, 183–184, 195–196
WinAPI, 21
Windows 2000, COM+ and, 138–139, 149–150
Windows NT4, 171–172
    MTS and, 131–137
Windows Scripting Host (WSH), 56–60
`WithEvents` key word, 84
Wrapper classes, 214–218
Write lock, 281

X

XLST, 243–256
XML, 206–208, 227–236, 243
    database searching using, 294–295
XML parser, 152
`XPath` statement, 249–250
`<xsl:apply-templates/>` command, 252
`<xsl:value-of >` command, 251
XSLT, 233, 234, 243–256
    drawbacks of, 255
    helpfulness of methodology, 246
    overview of, 244–246
    stylesheet, 250–253
    templates in, 249–251
    transformation of dataset with, 249–255